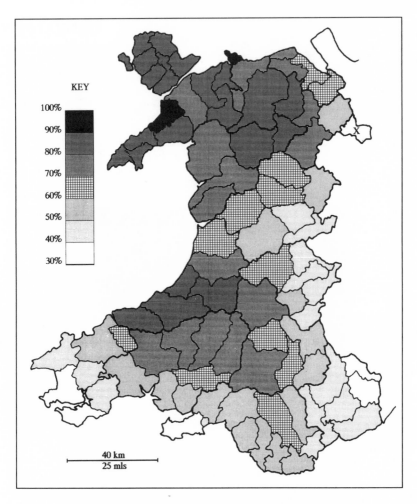

KEY

100%
90%
80%
70%
60%
50%
40%
30%

40 km
25 mls

**Percentage of the population covered by the 10 most
common surnames in each area (1813-37)**

THE SURNAMES OF WALES

for family historians and others

John & Sheila Rowlands

Published in the U.K. by the Federation of Family History
Societies (Publications) Ltd.

Published in the USA by Genealogical Publishing Co., Inc.
1001 N. Calvert Street, Baltimore, MD 21202
Library of Congress Catalogue Card Number 96-76077
International Standard Book Number 0-8063-1516-4
Made in the United States of America

Computer typesetting, layout, and cartography by John and Sheila Rowlands
Cover design by Elgan Davies, Welsh Books Council, Aberystwyth, Wales.

CONTENTS

LIST OF FIGURES

ABBREVIATIONS

AD	Catalogue of Ancient Deeds (PRO)
adj.	adjectival
AN	Anglo-Norman
Bangor Probate	Henson (ed.), *Bangor Probate Records Vol. 1: Pre-1700*
BBStD	Willis-Bund (ed.), *Black Book of St David's*
Brecon Probate	Jones (ed.), *Archdeaconry of Brecon Probate Records Vol 1: Pre-1660*
BT	Bishops' Transcripts (NLW, Diocesan Records)
CG	Continental-Germanic
Cronicl	*Cronicl*, Powys FHS Journal
DAB	*Dictionary of American Biography*
DB	Domesday Book
DNB	*Dictionary of National Biography*
DWB	Jenkins (ed.), *Dictionary of Welsh Biography down to 1940*
Dwnn	Dwnn, *Heraldic Visitations*
EP	*Exchequer Proceedings (Equity) Concerning Wales*, BCS, History and Law Series IV (1939)
Foley	Foley of Ridgeway Collection (NLW)
Fr	French
Glam Marr	Glamorgan Marriage Index (microfiche, Glamorgan FHS, 1994)
Griffith	Griffith, *Pedigrees of Anglesey and Carnarvonshire Families*
GTC	Clark, *Limbus Patrum Morganiae et Glamorganiae*
Guppy	Guppy, *Homes of Family Names in Great Britain*
Hel Achau	*Hel Achau*, Clwyd FHS Journal
HTGlam	Glamorgan Hearth Tax Assessment of 1670
HTPem	Pembrokeshire Hearth Tax 1670 (*WWHR*)
IGI	International Genealogical Index (Latter-Day Saints, Utah: microfiche, 1988; CD-ROM, 1993)
LG	Burke, *Landed Gentry*

loc.	locative (topographical or place-name origin)
LS	Lay Subsidies
MC	*Montgomeryshire Collections*
ME	Middle English
med.	mediaeval
Mer LS	Williams-Jones, *The Merioneth Lay Subsidy Roll 1292-3*
Mgy Muster	'1574 Muster of Men and Horses', for Montgomeryshire, extracted from State Papers Domestic, *MC 22* (1888)
MW	Middle Welsh
NLW	National Library of Wales, Aberystwyth
NLWJ	*National Library of Wales Journal*
Notitiae	St Asaph Notitiae (*MC*)
occ.	occupational
OE	Old English
OED	*Oxford English Dictionary*
OW	Old Welsh
p.	parish (of)
Pem Marr	Pembrokeshire Marriages (collection of the authors)
Pem Muster	1613 Muster (Bronwydd 371-2, NLW)
Picton Castle	Picton Castle Deeds and Documents (NLW)
PR	Parish register
PRO	Public Record Office, London
RadAss	Faraday, 'Assessment for the Fifteenth of 1293 on Radnor and other Marcher Lordships'.
St Asaph Probate	NLW St Asaph Probate 1660-1729
TD	Telephone Directory (modern)
THSC	*Transactions of the Honourable Society of Cymmrodorion*
W	Welsh
WFH	Rowlands (ed.), *Welsh Family History: A Guide to Research*
WG1	Bartrum (1976)
WG1 xxv	Fiche xxv (Index to Surnames) has reference/s to the *surname*
WG2	Bartrum (1983)
WG2 xii	Vol xii (Index to Surnames) has reference/s to the *surname*
WM	*Western Mail*
WS	Morgan & Morgan, *Welsh Surnames*
WT	*Western Telegraph*
WWHR	Green (ed.), *West Wales Historical Records*
*	indicates a postulated form

PREFACE

We have long had an interest in surnames and, because of our own ancestry, in the surnames of Wales in particular. We have been involved in transcribing and indexing documents over a long period and became aware at an early stage of the local characteristics of Welsh surnames, often ignored in general works on surnames. In time we began to realise that the information we had collected was not only of interest to us but could also be of interest and value to many family historians with Welsh ancestry. Out of that realisation has come this book.

Much of the work on which this book is based has been carried out over many years of researching our own ancestors (chiefly in south-west Wales), by helping – through the family history movement and through conducting university courses – others with ancestors in different parts of Wales, as well as through a natural curiosity to see whether the patterns we had seen in our own familiar areas were also in evidence in other parts of Wales. Although this book has been written from the standpoint of family history and with the needs of family historians very much in mind, we hope that it will prove to be of much wider value. We hope too that it will illustrate that the work of family historians can make a positive contribution on a wider historical front.

We would welcome constructive comments on the research represented here. Early or late dated examples (with full references to documents) of *less common* names, patronymic or otherwise, will be gratefully received at the address shown in Appendix C, as will be evidence for the origin of settled surnames which agrees with or conflicts with the opinions expressed in the present edition. We cannot commit ourselves to any but the briefest correspondence, but would naturally acknowledge any such contributions used in any future revision.

Research for this book has been mainly centred on the National Library of Wales, Aberystwyth, but we have also received unstinting help from many individual family historians. At the National Library we have good reason to thank the staff of the Manuscripts Reading Room who have fetched and carried so many documents for us over the years.

Among the individuals to whom we would like to record our thanks for their help are the following who allowed us to use their personal copies of books and articles when access to libraries was difficult: our sister and sister-in-law, Wendy Campbell (*Old Pembroke Families)*; Elwern Jones (Clwyd PR transcripts); Anne Kelly Knowles (*The Olivers of Cardiganshire*); D. Hugh Owen ('The Englishry of Denbigh: an English colony in medieval Wales', *THSC,* 1975); Richard Ratcliffe (Guppy, *Homes of Family Names in Great Britain).* The following people kindly responded to our requests for information about specific families: Chris Pitt Lewis provided the information for the reference to Brigstocke in Chapter 3 and for the Glossary entry for that name; Philip Bufton responded about his own surname; Terry Coslett provided the information in the Glossary entry for Coslett; Emyr Edwards, Department of Manuscripts, National Library of Wales, helped us re Maybery; Michael Gandy, FSG, checked information about Jehu (the subject of a one-name study by the late L.C. Derrick-Jehu) in the Library of the Society of Genealogists, London; Mrs Lilian Lumley sent a useful list of early PR entries for Lumley. Rhoswen Charles and Elwern Jones provided information for case-studies. David Peate and Helen Davies provided valuable information for testing the hypothesis in Chapter 6. Derek Palgrave and Colin Rogers read the final draft and made a number of very helpful suggestions. Any errors or shortcomings that remain are, of course, ours.

Frank Llewellyn of Llewellyn Graphics, Aberystwyth, helped locate the program used for the maps and gave generously of his time when we had computer problems to sort out. Thanks are also due to Elgan Davies and Ruth Evans at the Welsh Books Council (who designed the cover and prepared the coloured frontispiece respectively) and to Bob Boyd of the Federation of Family History Societies for much helpful advice about the presentation and production.

A very special debt of gratitude is owed to our daughter, Catherine Camfield, who not only travelled to London at a very busy time in her life to gather the IGI data we needed, but also devised the computer program which made it possible for us to test thoroughly the hypothesis put forward in Chapter 6, as well as to offer the service described in Appendix C.

The material for this book was put together in 1993-4 and it was not far from completion in April of the latter year when illness and consequent disability struck. This delayed the appearance of the book but has enabled us to augment and modify several aspects. We owe thanks to many who have helped us during a difficult period, but most of all we appreciate the love and support (even to the extent of applying their various skills to reading drafts of this volume) of our daughters and son, Catherine Camfield, Caroline Rusga and Simon Rowlands. This book is dedicated to them.

John and Sheila Rowlands
Aberystwyth, April 1996

CHAPTER 1
INTRODUCTION

No one who has had any significant involvement with family history research can fail to have become involved with some consideration of the subject of surnames. They are, after all, the main indicators which we all use when attempting to identify a family or an individual within the records relating to the population as a whole. In an English context a particular surname could well be a unique identifier of a family within a given community and it would not be uncommon for a present-day researcher to have all sixteen great-great grandparents with different surnames. The same is unlikely in a Welsh context where, other than with recent immigrants, there is a strong likelihood of one or more of the common surnames occurring several times at this level.

The lack of variety in the surnames to be found in Wales has been cause for comment for several centuries. For example, in his Sixteenth Annual Report[1] published in 1856 the Registrar-General, George Graham, commented at considerable length about the surnames which occurred in the records of birth, marriage and death which he was required to keep as a result of the Civil Registration Act which came into effect in 1837. In his comments he made extensive reference to the situation which prevailed in Wales, and stated:

> The contribution of Wales to the number of surnames is very small in proportion to its population. Perhaps nine tenths of our countrymen in the principality could be mustered under less than 100 different surnames; and while in England there is no redundancy of surnames, there is obviously a paucity of distinct appellatives in Wales, where the frequency of such names as **Jones, Williams, Davies, Evans**, and others, almost defeats the primary object of a name, which is to distinguish an individual from the mass. ... The name of **John Jones** is a perpetual incognito in Wales, and being proclaimed at the cross of a market town would indicate no one in particular.[2]

Indeed, he goes as far as to comment on the fact that, of the 328 Registration Officers and their deputies acting in the Districts of Wales, no fewer than 207

(63.1%) were covered by 17 names. There was only one registration officer named Smith.[3]

If the Registrar-General was right and the paucity of surnames within Wales in the middle of the last century was such as to defy attempts to distinguish the individual from the mass, then the prospects of being able to make significant progress in researching one's Welsh ancestors would appear to be very slim indeed. For those with ancestors with the incognito of being a Jones, the cause might appear to be quite hopeless.

However, anyone who has researched many Welsh lines will know that, in reality, this can be far from the case. Difficulties can certainly arise out of the high incidence of a small number of surnames, but usually this merely hinders progress rather than obstructs it. A good understanding of the historical development of surnames in Wales, together with a knowledge of the relative incidence of individual names in different parts as well as a determined attitude, can often overcome those difficulties which do exist. It should be remembered that the individuals concerned had another identifying name, the forename (usually in our period a Christian name, given at baptism), which would frequently conform to a pattern in the family group.

The saving grace for family history research in Wales, which allows genuine progress to be made, lies in the fact that one is seldom seeking to identify an individual within a large population as, certainly up to the early part of the nineteenth century, nowhere did the population begin to approach the levels to be found in many parts of England. Family historians are, on the whole, dealing with small communities in Wales.

Some idea of the differences which exist in the incidence of surnames in the English and Welsh contexts can be inferred from the Registrar-General's Report in which he lists the incidence within his records of the 50 most common surnames in England and Wales (combined). Information from that table is given in Fig. 1-1 and it can be seen that names commonly associated with Wales such as Jones (2nd in that list), Williams (3rd), Davies (5th), Thomas (7th), Evans (8th), Roberts (9th), Hughes (17th), Lewis (19th), Edwards (20th), Harris (26th), James (35th), Morgan (36th), Price (43rd), Phillips (44th) and Griffiths (50th) all feature prominently.

Work we have done on the incidence of surnames right across Wales (described in detail in Chapter 4) has enabled us to derive separate lists for both England and Wales. That for England alone is dramatically different from the listing given in Fig. 1-1 and some of the 'Welsh' surnames referred to above have a much reduced incidence in England and move well down the list as follows:

- Jones occurs at only 0.43% and drops to 4th in the list

- Williams occurs at 0.31% and drops to 14th
- Harris occurs at 0.24% but maintains its position (because many other more prominent names are eliminated from the list)
- Edwards and Roberts both occur at 0.20% and drop to joint 35th
- Davies, Morris and Evans (down to 0.17%, 0.17% and 0.16% respectively) would certainly drop to lower than 39th position and may not feature above 50th position in any new listing.

However, half of those 'Welsh' surnames – Thomas (down to 0.15%), Phillips (0.14%), James (0.14%), Hughes (0.13%), Lewis (0.13%), Price (0.13%), Morgan (0.06%) and Griffiths (0.01%) – would certainly not feature in any purely 'English' list of the 50 most common surnames.

Rank order	Surname	%	Rank order	Surname	%
1.	Smith	1.37	26.	Harris	0.28
2.	Jones	1.32	27.	Clark	0.28
3.	Williams	0.87	28.	Cooper	0.26
4.	Taylor	0.68	29.	Harrison	0.26
5.	Davies	0.62	30.	Davis	0.25
6.	Brown	0.57	31.	Ward	0.25
7.	Thomas	0.51	32.	Baker	0.24
8.	Evans	0.51	33.	Martin	0.24
9.	Roberts	0.43	34.	Morris	0.24
10.	Johnson	0.38	35.	James	0.23
11.	Robinson	0.36	36.	Morgan	0.23
12.	Wilson	0.36	37.	King	0.23
13.	Wright	0.34	38.	Allen	0.22
14.	Wood	0.33	39.	Clarke	0.21
15.	Hall	0.33	40.	Cook	0.21
16.	Walker	0.32	41.	Moore	0.21
17.	Hughes	0.32	42.	Parker	0.21
18.	Green	0.32	43.	Price	0.21
19.	Lewis	0.32	44.	Phillips	0.21
20.	Edwards	0.32	45.	Watson	0.20
21.	Thompson	0.32	46.	Shaw	0.20
22.	White	0.31	47.	Lee	0.19
23.	Jackson	0.30	48.	Bennett	0.19
24.	Turner	0.30	49.	Carter	0.18
25.	Hill	0.28	50.	Griffiths	0.18

Fig. 1-1: Rank order and percentage incidence of the 50 most common names in England and Wales in the mid-nineteenth century.[4]

As the population of Wales was only 6.5% of the population of England and Wales combined, changes on this scale as a result of taking out such a small proportion of the population bear testimony to just how commonplace these surnames (and many others as well) are in Wales. This is illustrated in Fig. 1-2 which gives a comparison of the 10 most common surnames in Wales and England in the early- to mid-nineteenth century.

	WALES[5]			ENGLAND[6]	
	Surname	**%**		**Surname**	**%**
1.	Jones	13.84		Smith	1.37
2.	Williams	8.91		Taylor	0.68
3.	Davies	7.09		Brown	0.57
4.	Thomas	5.70		Jones	0.43
5.	Evans	5.46		Johnson	0.38
6.	Roberts	3.69		Robinson	0.36
7.	Hughes	2.98		Wilson	0.36
8.	Lewis	2.97		Wright	0.34
9.	Morgan	2.63		Wood	0.33
10.	Griffiths	2.58		Hall	0.33
	Total	55.85		Total	5.15

Fig. 1-2: Comparison of the 10 most common names in Wales and England

Against this background, it is the purpose of this book to provide the reader with a detailed insight into the origins and occurrence of the more common surnames within Wales, together with some consideration of those which have established something of a presence at the regional or more local level. We believe that this could be of considerable importance when researching ancestors who may be obscured within a pool of very common surnames. It may also be used to identify the most likely places of origin for those who know no more than that their ancestors 'came from Wales'.

Chapters 2 and 3 give an historical overview of Welsh names, the former dealing particularly with the patronymic naming-system which was native to Wales, but also covering the other categories of name which have contributed to the surnames of Wales in modern times; the latter considers the history of the gradual adoption of surnames in Wales. The examples and case-studies chosen to illustrate these chapters are taken from all parts of Wales and from different periods.

In Chapter 4 we set out the reasons for carrying out a comprehensive survey of surnames in Wales in the period 1813-1837 and discuss the methods used. We also present some of our findings at the all-Wales level. Other surveys which are of relevance to the study of surnames in Wales are also considered. Collecting information *en masse* for this purpose will, we hope, help to throw new light on the history of surnames in Wales. Even so, we believe firmly that family historians working individually can contribute to the understanding of this subject: genealogical research, carefully carried out, may provide clues to the origins of particular names in a way that general surveys cannot always do.

Chapter 5 is a glossary of over 250 of the surnames found in our 1813-37 survey. The selection of names for this was made as follows: all names found in any area at an incidence of 0.7% and above were automatically included; thereafter, names were selected as representative of different categories of names and unusual names in all areas, spread as evenly as possible. Inevitably, an area such as Pembrokeshire, with as many as 17.32 surnames/1000 population, most of them long-standing, has a very large number of different names to choose from, but has only a relatively small proportion of those names illustrated in this section.[7] Conversely, Merionethshire (with 5.93 surnames/1000 population) has a much larger proportion of its names included. In this list, which is arranged alphabetically, we discuss the background and history of the names, particularly from the viewpoint of family history, and describe their distribution and incidence in the period 1813-37. Here we also indicate sources for family history, where the surnames appear in standard works of reference.

In Chapter 6 we consider other findings revealed by the survey such as annual rates of marriage, the dominance of common surnames, the distribution of surnames derived from the *ap* prefix compared to those with the possessive 's' and the incidence of surnames derived from Old Testament names.

Chapter 7 sets out some surname evidence for the presence of people of Welsh origin in populations outside Wales and also describes how a knowledge of the relative incidence in Wales of even the most common surnames can be used to suggest a place of origin for migrant or emigrant ancestors.

There is a complete listing in Appendix A of the Welsh administrative hundreds (as used in this book) and the parishes they contain. Appendix B comprises lists of surnames found in our survey which are based on (a) Old Testament names and (b) *ap* plus forenames. Appendix C sets out how descendants of migrant or emigrant Welsh people can gain access to the predictive method described in Chapter 7 as a first move towards tracing those ancestors about whom all that is known is that 'they came from Wales'.

All this has been written with family historians in mind, drawing on our own experience (and the experience of others) in the field over many years. We are of the opinion that a family history approach can contribute a great deal to the study of surnames in a way which is only now becoming recognised by traditional historians.

CHAPTER 1: NOTES AND REFERENCES

[1] Sixteenth Annual Report of the Registrar General, Abstracts for 1853, published in 1856, (hereafter abbreviated as RG 1853). [Note: This is not a Parliamentary Paper.]

[2] RG 1853, p.xix.

[3] RG 1853, footnote on p.xix which quotes the following surnames held by officers: Jones 46 (14.0%), Williams (7.9%), Davies and Evans each 16 (4.9%), Thomas 15 (4.6%), Roberts 14 (4.3%), Lewis 11 (3.4%), Hughes 10 (3.0%), Edwards and Lloyd each 8 (2.4%), James, Griffith, Morgan and Rees all 6 (1.8%), Owen 5 (1.5%), and finally Morris and Ellis both 4 (1.2%).

[4] RG 1853, based on Table XVI, p.xx.

[5] Derived from the survey described in Chapter 4.

[6] Derived from RG 1853 and above survey.

[7] We plan to compensate for this in a work in progress devoted entirely to the surnames of Pembrokeshire.

CHAPTER 2

WELSH NAMES AND THEIR ORIGINS

The development of surnames in Wales reflects the history of a small country with its own social structure, and the influences – greater or lesser at different times and in different areas – of a larger and dominant neighbour. The native system of naming involved identifying individuals by the name of their father, to which was added the names of preceding generations of (normally) male ancestors. Such was the ingrained acceptance of this straightforward system that it lasted in many parts of Wales until the eighteenth and nineteenth centuries and, in one of those futile imponderables of history, it could be argued that Wales, left to itself, would have kept its patronymic naming-system continuously to the present – at the end of the twentieth century, after all, it is enjoying a modest revival.

Nevertheless, outside and almost exclusively English influences were felt over many centuries, affecting the range of names in use in Wales in several ways, but very often producing some characteristic which is now looked on as being typically Welsh. Because of this, this chapter, the subsequent one and the Glossary of Surnames contain examples of various types of name, ranging from common names of relatively recent formation to uncommon names of purely Welsh origin, and also encompassing names of largely English origin which have been, to some degree or another, domiciled in Wales.

The patronymic naming-system in Wales

We have, first, to consider Welsh surnames in their wider context. If we compare Wales with its nearest neighbour, England, we find significant differences in the range of origins of names. The whole pattern is different. English surnames are often divided into four basic categories (other subdivisions are possible): those derived from a personal name (Bartle, Margerison, Dickens); those derived from a location, which may be either from a place-name (Bristow, Duckworth, Petherbridge) or from a common topographical feature (Down, Meares, Wells);

7

those derived from occupation or status (Carpenter, Fowler, Webster); and those derived from nicknames or descriptions (Merriman, Round, Sparkes).[1]

Such surnames settled mainly between the twelfth and fifteenth centuries in England, largely in response to the needs of growing towns and increasing bureaucracy. There has been considerable variation in the way that individual English surnames have ramified or declined, but today they still reflect the great variety in use six to eight hundred years ago.

Wales at the same period was rarely affected by urban influences and pressures. There were few towns and much of the rural population was unaffected by English social practice. In most of Wales, the ancient naming-system continued: by this system individuals were identified (or 'placed' socially) by their relationships, and chiefly in relation to their father. A similar system had originally led to one thread of English surnames, those described above as of personal origin[2] but, as we shall see, the Welsh system reflected a Celtic social structure and was particularly deeply-rooted and long-lasting. Other European countries also had entrenched patronymic systems.[3]

The Welsh word for son is *mab* (often written as *map*) which is a cognate of the Scottish *mac*. A man called Madog would be known as *Madog mab Owain* (Madog son (of) Owain). In the system of mutation of the Welsh language *mab* becomes *fab*, and the initial soft *f* sound (English 'v') was dropped in normal speech. This would produce Madog ab Owain. The general rule which evolved was to use *ab* before vowels and *ap* before consonants (e.g. Madog ap Rhydderch), but one finds many breaches in actual use in records.[4]

In addition, a Welshman, as a sign of his free status, would know the names of his male ancestors for several generations, perhaps six or seven, each generation divided by *ap*, forming a patronymic string of names. As Michael Powell Siddons has written, 'The kindred was an extremely important unit in Welsh law, and was invoked for the inheritance of land, for the settlement of disputes, the compurgation of witnesses, and the payment and exaction of compensation. It was in fact a legal necessity to know one's pedigree'.[5] An extended example might be cited from the ancestry of Lewis Morris of Môn (1701-1765), whose great-great-great-grandfather is named as David ap William ap David Lloyd ap Thomas ap Dafydd ap Gwilym ap Dafydd Ieuan ap Howel ap Cynfrig ap Iorwerth Fychan ap Iorwerth ap Grono ap Tegerin.[6] Such strings of names were repeated easily: they were both name and pedigree, and the readiness with which Welshmen recited them probably gave rise to the proverb 'As long as a Welshman's pedigree'.[7]

Women were also known by their father's name: *Nest verch Madog* (Nest daughter of Madog). *Verch* becomes *ferch* in modern orthography; it was often shortened to *vch* or *vz* in documents and appears also as *ach* and *ych*.[8]

Because the pedigree aspect of the complex of names was all-important, there was very little reason or incentive to abandon it for a different naming-system. When in due course Welsh families found it necessary to take a single 'surname', they tended to choose from the names in their pedigree. Usually, we shall see, the name chosen would be the last name in common use, frequently the forename of the father; however, examples will be given of the use of the paternal grandfather's name, or one taken from an earlier generation.[9] Dafydd ap Thomas ap Gwilym, taking a surname, might be known as David Thomas, or sometimes as David William. A variant of this occurred when *ap* and *ab*, in common speech, were run into the following name: Hywel ab Owain easily became Howell Bowen; Thomas ap Hugh became Thomas Pugh.

If the pedigree aspect led to the perpetuation of patronymic names, it also tended to discourage the adoption of surnames from places, nicknames or occupations. Yet we shall also see that such names *were* taken, though in smaller numbers.

Sources of patronymic surnames

If Welsh people had taken their surnames generally from the forenames their ancestors used in early mediaeval times, we should hear fewer (or perhaps different) complaints today. From the age of the Welsh princes and leaders, the forenames Dafydd, Gruffydd, Hywel, Llywelyn, Madog, Morgan, Owain and Rhys have all survived to provide significant surnames, though usually in altered form. Less common forenames in use (some of which have not formed modern surnames) are Anarawd, Bleddyn, Cadfael, Cydifor, Cynfyn, Elystan, Idnerth, Iestyn, Nefydd, Peredur, Selyf, Tudwal, Tyfid and Ynyr.[10]

Among common forenames used in the late-thirteenth century were Cynddelw, Cynwric, Ednyfed, Einion, Gronow, Heilyn, Iorwerth, Ithel, Madyn, Rhirid, Tegwared, Tudur and Wasmihangel. Less common were Cedifor, Ednowain, Gwion, Gwrgenau, Hwfa, Ifor, Seisyll, Trahaearn.[11] Some of these names gave rise eventually to surnames but, sadly for researchers, not very often.

The point of these lists of names (selective as they are) is simply to indicate the range of patronymic surnames *which might have been*. The majority of Welsh people, in the period which affected modern surnames, bore names which represented different and later traditions: for Welsh families to have borne truly *Welsh* patronymic family names would presuppose their adoption of surnames when these names were in general usage. As it was, fashions in names changed long before that adoption.

9

Even in the lists of mediaeval names from which we have quoted above, the names Iohannes (John), Thomas and William appear. These and other names popularised by the Normans (Edward, Richard, Robert, Roger, etc) began to be used for children in Wales. David, the patron saint of Wales, was venerated by the Normans and the popularity of his name was thus enhanced. In addition, the range of names in use was already being affected by the great popularity of a limited number of forenames of alien origin. These were the very names which the English adopted so enthusiastically in the mediaeval period, among them John, Thomas, William, Henry and Richard.[12]

Forenames in use in the fifteenth century

By the fifteenth century, the profile of names in use is different from that of earlier centuries. Forenames in use in fifteenth century pedigrees which formed 2% or more of the total of names, averaged across Wales, were (with the commonest forms of resultant modern surname in brackets): Dafydd/David 11% (Davies); Edward 2% (Edwards), Gruffudd 6% (Griffiths), Huw 2% (Hughes, Pugh), Hywel 5% (Howells, Powell), Ieuan 8% (Evans, Bevan), Jenkin 2% (Jenkins), John 12% (Johns, Jones), Lewys 2% (Lewis), Llywelyn 3% (Llewelyn), Morgan 3% (Morgan), Morus 2% (Morris), Owain 2% (Owen, Bowen), Rhys 5% (Rees, Price), Richard 3% (Richards, Pritchard), Robert 3% (Roberts, Probert), Thomas 8% (Thomas), William/Gwilym 6% (Williams).[13]

These forenames attained 1% of all Wales at the same period: Harry/Henry (Harries, Parry), James (James), Madog (Maddocks), Maredudd (Meredith), Philip (Phillips), Rhydderch (Roderick, Prothero), Roger (Rogers), Tudur (Tudor), Watkin (Watkins). All other names were thinly spread (though they were often found more frequently in some regions than in others).

We shall turn later to the question of when Welsh people took surnames but it must be evident from the structure of patronymic names (xx *ab* yy *ab* zz) that the surnames adopted were the product of current fashions in forenames a generation before a surname was taken. A name which was not in common use in an area was less likely to produce a surname in those parts. There is a great deal of scope for research into the use and distribution of forenames in different parts of Wales in the three centuries which followed the period reflected in the lists above.[14]

The few common names mentioned in the previous section (John, Thomas, William, David, etc) and a handful of others dominated the parish registers of the eighteenth century. It hardly mattered that bearers of these names were usually addressed as Siôn, Gwilym, Dafydd, Tomos, etc, for it was the anglicised version which was written down. A parallel may be drawn with pet-names in English: though most family historians can cite examples of individuals known as Betty, Molly or Nancy, or Tom, Dick or Harry, they were normally written down in registers as Elizabeth, Mary or Ann, Thomas, Richard or Henry. It has been suggested that in Wales the mass of the population might have been restricted to a list of conventional names (for instance, avoiding the older and traditional Welsh names)[15] but it seems more probable that – like modern parents – people followed fashion in the names they used for children at key periods for the formation of surnames.

Patronymic surnames from hypocoristic names

Where Welsh forenames survived, some had pet (hypocoristic) versions which evolved eventually into surnames. From Bedo, the popular form of Maredudd, comes Beddoes. Guto (from Gruffydd) has led to Gittins. Dai and Dei (from David) developed into Day and its variants; Daio, Deio, Dio (also from David) produced Dayos. Llelo, from Llywelyn has led to Lello, Lelloes, Flello, while Maddy grew out of Mady (for Madog). It should be emphasised that these less common forms did not leap into surname-status, but were simply part of the patronymic system. Ieuan Bedo ap Cadwgan, David ap Rees Madye, William ap Howell ap Dio and Angharad vz Lello Bedo ap Madock are examples of such names in use.[16] These pet names are inevitably less common because the general tendency in records would be to use a formal version of a name. They became surnames in areas (such as either side of the English/Welsh border) where there were many pressures to adopt settled names at a period before the more common ones we are familiar with today predominated.

Less common patronymic names

The last statement is also true of many, but not all, less common patronymic names. Of the mediaeval names listed earlier, these are some of the consequent surnames: Blethin (from Bleddyn), Bonner (ab Ynyr), Eynon (Einion), Gronnah (Gronow), Hayling (Heilyn), Kendrick (Cynwric), Kenvin (Cynfyn), Nevett (Ednyfed), Tudor (Tudur), Yorath (Iorwerth). More examples are given in Chapter 5, the Glossary of Surnames, and the distribution of such names is indicated there. They are often very localised and, where this is the case, it is sometimes possible to trace modern bearers of the surname back to a single person or family group. However, probably more often, the name is rare in modern Wales but not infrequent in the English border counties.

Women's names

A work such as this is inevitably biased towards male names. As in every comparable country, male surnames predominate in Wales: that is, it was male forenames which were passed on eventually as surnames in the Welsh patronymic system and, over all, settled surnames were passed through the male

11

line. Statistically, it was harder for a metronymic surname (that is, one based on the mother's name) to arise and then survive in Wales than in England where, from mediaeval times, some female names provided family names (e.g. Annis, Catling, Margerison, Sibley, and many more). As surnames settled much later in Wales, even in the period of puritan and nonconformist influence, convention increasingly demanded that a male name was more appropriate. Nevertheless, the biblical name Rachel is found in use as an apparent surname in one area in our survey.[17]

However, a minute number of Welsh surnames have their origin in the given names used for Welsh women. When seeking them we have to ignore all similar names brought in from England (e.g. in the period of our survey Anniss is found in Pembrokeshire and Sibley in Glamorgan, but these cannot be described as Welsh); and we must remember that, for a significant part of the relevant period, traditional Welsh names were being largely replaced by Ann, Catherine, Elizabeth, Margaret, Mary, etc, in a trend comparable with that for the most popular male names.

Gwenlan is derived from Gwenllïan, a traditional girl's name. The forename had considerable popularity in fifteenth century Wales (especially in the south)[18] and in sixteenth to eighteenth century Glamorgan.[19] Nevertheless, Gwenlan is found only rarely, in our survey just once in each of two counties: in Breconshire (Crickhowell hundred) and in Monmouthshire (Skenfrith hundred). Gaenor (a variant of Gwenhwyfar) may have produced the surname Gainor/Gainer (found in Anglesey and Monmouthshire in the same period). Possibly other names of similar origin could be found in the English border counties.

It has already been shown that daughters were described as *verch/vch*. Just as 'p' (*ap*) and 'b' (*ab*) have attached themselves to patronymic names, so too do we find 'ch' adhering to forenames to form surnames, but only occasionally. Critchett appears to have derived from *verch* Richard. Kedward, found in our survey in the Radnor hundred of Radnorshire, exists to the present and is likely to be from *verch* Edward. There are few similar names: Creese, which logically could be from *verch* Rhys, for instance, seems in practice to be a variant of the English surname Crease (OE adj. 'fine, elegant'). There is always the possibility that similar names are abbreviated forms of 'Mac-' and are Scottish, Irish or Manx rather than Welsh.

Women retaining their maiden names

Traditionally women retained their maiden names (that is, the name which identified them as the daughter of their father) throughout life. If, for example, Lowri verch Rhys married Dafydd ap Hywel, she could not take his 'surname', as he did not have one. The following examples of this practice are taken from

Bangor Probate Records: 1648, Tywyn, Ellyw vch Morgan, widow; 1661, Llangïan, Elizabeth vch Thomas, widow of William Griffith, gent.; 1662, Llangoed, Ann vch John ap Hugh, widow of Owen Thomas of Heneglwys, gent.; 1666, Llanfwrog, Alice vch Tyder, widow of Edward John ap Richard; 1680, Llanfachreth, Gwen vch Evan ap William, widow; 1666, Pentraeth, Alice vch John alias Alice Williams, widow. The use of 'alias' implies the husband's name: 1677, Llanynys, Magdalen vch Rees Wynne alias Magdalen Thelwall, widow [of Thomas Thelwall].

Some of the women in these records are described specifically as spinsters, including: 1637, Llanbeblig, Dorothy vch Humffrey; 1661, Aber-erch, Jonett vch Thomas; 1670, Llangïan, Margaret vch Richard Owen. Though it was exceptional for married women to leave wills, where they did the same practice prevailed: 1677, Llangaffo, Agnes vch William David [wife of John ap William ap Hugh].

The retention of the maiden name extended even to English-speaking areas: in 1603 in Manorbier, south Pembrokeshire, Henry Adams named his wife Elizabeth Rhydderch as executrix of his will. Her name may indicate that Henry Adams had married a woman from a Welsh area (which Manorbier was not, being deep in the Englishry of that county) who had carried her local custom to her new home. A hundred years on, in 1703, and also in Manorbier, Mary Gibbon alias Jones, widow, refers in her will to her sisters Jane Cole alias Jones and Margaret Watkins alias Jones. She names too her cousins, the children of Thomas Jones of Ambleston and Dorothy Cod his wife.

Later still, in Llaneugrad, Anglesey, Eleanor Elias appears in the census returns of 1841 and 1851. She was the widow of John Prichard (her children became Jones) and was buried as Ellen Prichard (alias Elias).[20] This is a late example of a practice which should be borne in mind when seeking information about Welsh women ancestors. In some areas it carried on informally into the present century.

Patterns of names in families

A factor in the constant reproduction of a small pool of names was the traditional practice of naming children after grandparents and other close relations, common until the mid-nineteenth century at least in most families, not only in Wales. In many areas of Wales this took the form whereby a couple's first son received his paternal grandfather's forename, the second son took the maternal grandfather's forename; the first daughter received the maternal grandmother's name, the second daughter the paternal grandmother's name; the names of the parents and of uncles and aunts were then honoured.[21] This procedure was not inevitable and one finds examples of recently deceased relations being commemorated out of turn. The general practice of naming after close relations may help sometimes in identifying and distinguishing between families, but it is of dubious benefit where the same few names are repeated in several generations or where special circumstances prevailed.[22] The chief consequence for our subject is that it also helped to reduce the pool of names from which surnames developed.

New forenames in use from the sixteenth century

The religious Reformation in the sixteenth century, with the consequent reading of the Scriptures by lay-people, led to a larger pool of given names in Wales, as in England. The difference between the two countries is that, by this time, England had its settled surnames but Wales did not – therefore, names taken from biblical characters added variety to Welsh surnames from this point. The use of Old Testament given names is often taken by family historians as an indicator of nonconformity. The individual names are for the most part included in the Glossary (Chapter 5), whilst in Chapter 6 we consider their collective pattern across Wales and postulate a relationship to certain forms of nonconformity rather than to nonconformity generally. (See also Appendix B.)

In the search for varied names which evolved from both religious reform and secular new learning, Welsh families chose also from the New Testament, the early Church and classical Greece and Rome, which resulted in names such as the following becoming patronymic surnames in small numbers: Ajax, Augustus, Caesar, Erasmus, Felix, Julian, Theophilus, Timothy and Titus.

Surnames from personal characteristics

Such epithets as 'thin', 'long', 'stout', 'hardy', etc, have led directly to English surnames and examples could be multiplied. There are parallels in Welsh nomenclature, but these are far fewer in number. This category of Welsh surname is, however, the second most numerous and its development goes in tandem with patronymic names.

Adjectival names were used to modify the personal names within the patronymic system we have been dealing with. A man who was one of several Dafydds in a parish might be identified as Dafydd ap Hywel, but also as, say, Dafydd *hir* (tall), or Dafydd *goch* (red-haired). According to circumstances which we can now only imagine, such a man could have emerged with a surname as David Howells, David Powell, David Hire, or David Gough. As the Glossary and other lists make clear, the great majority of family surnames evolved from patronymic names, but adjectival names, though often transitory, existed in large numbers.

In their early forms these are clearly epithets added to names: Ievan Cogh ap John of Builth is a red-haired Ievan (Evan) son of John. Gwillim ap Ievan Tewe

14

of Defynnog was the son of a fat or stout man; and Rees ap David ap Ievan Vain of Llanyre was the grandson of a thin man.[23] Surnames could evolve from either form – that is, from the description of an individual or from that of his near or distant ancestors. It seems more likely that such surnames settled when the 'meaning' or direct relevance of an epithet had been discarded, i.e. after a generation or two had elapsed. Gough, which is one of the commonest of this type of name would, therefore, probably represent the descendants of red-haired men rather than the red-haired men themselves. This is borne out by the survival of surnames with unflattering meanings, such as Brace, Games, Kethin, Tew, etc.[24]

Surnames of adjectival origin are sometimes difficult for non-Welsh descendants to identify because they are found in such a variety of forms. The main reason for this is the system of mutation in the Welsh language, whereby the start of a word alters, depending on the word which precedes it. Therefore, the different forms may not be recognised as versions of the same word by the newcomer to the subject: Gwyn/Wynne, Moyle/Voyle, Tew/Dew.[25]

The authors of *WS* make a distinction between adjectival names which were attached to a person in his own right and those which were used to distinguish between persons. As they point out, it is not easy to tell these apart. They are inclined to think that the first type retained the radical (root) form of the adjective after the masculine name whilst the second type underwent soft mutation – the latter usage would have occurred more often.[26] The majority of surnames of adjectival origin which have come down to the present are in the mutated form. An additional factor is different usage between dialects. It also seems probable that the radical form was 'restored' when the name was in such common use that finer points of grammar and syntax seemed irrelevant. The subject is complex and most readers will simply want to know what variant spellings they can expect to find during their researches. For this reason, the following list of names which derive from adjectives excludes those which do not seem to have survived to the present in Wales:[27]

Anwyl, Anwell, Anwill: *annwyl* 'dear, beloved'
Bach, Batch, Baugh: *bach* 'little' (term of endearment)
Balch, Baulch: *balch* 'proud'
Bengough: *pen/ben* 'head' + *goch* (see Gough)[28]
Bengrisse, Bengry: *pen/ben* + *grych* 'curly'[29]
Brace: *bras* 'fat'
Catharn, Gadarn: *cadarn/gadarn* 'strong'
Cule, Cull: *cul* 'narrow, thin'[30]
Crunn: *cron* 'round'

15

Dee: *du* 'black' (of complexion or hair)
Games: *cam/gam* 'crooked, lame; squinting'
Gethin, Kethin: *cethin/gethin* 'ugly, swarthy'
Glace: *glas/las* 'blue, green'[31]
Gough, Gooch, Goodge: *coch/goch* 'red' (of complexion or hair)
Gwilt, Guilt, Quilt: *gwyllt* 'wild'
Gwyn, Wynne: *gwyn/wyn* 'white/fair' (of complexion or hair)[32]
Haggar: *hagr* 'ugly'
Hier, Hire: *hir* 'long, tall'
Landeg, Landeck: *glandeg/landeg* 'handsome, good-looking'
Lloyd, Floyd, Flood: *llwyd* 'grey, brown' (of hair)
Mabe: *mab/fab* 'son'
Mayn, Vayne: *main, fain* 'thin'
Melling, Mellens: *melyn/felyn* 'yellow' (of hair)[33]
Moyle, Voyle: *moel/foel* 'bald'
Saise, Sayce: *sais* 'English' (usually referring to speech)
Teague: *teg/deg* 'fair'[34]
Tew, Tugh, Dew: *tew/dew* 'stout'
Vaughan, Vane: *bychan/fychan* 'small, younger'
Vawer: *mawr/fawr* 'big'

There are some other possibly adjectival names worth mentioning: Duppa and the variants Tuppa, Toppa, etc, have an obscure origin, but their appearance in the English border areas after Welsh forenames may indicate derivation from *twp* 'foolish, stupid'.[35] Ley (pronounced Lay) is possibly from *lleiaf* 'smallest'.[36]

There is scope for more research into these names but it seems probable that they were encouraged or selected as settled names first and foremost in the anglicised areas, where the difficulties presented by simple patronymics may have seemed more obvious to neighbours who had brought their English surnames into Wales with them.

Nicknames

A further few words must be said of the well-known and long-standing love of nicknames or bynames among the Welsh. In communities of the past where few forenames were in use and where these same few names provided the majority of either fathers' forenames or settled family names, some means of identifying individuals was essential and we have seen how epithets have developed into surnames. Most nicknames, however, remained just that. The important name was the given name and the identifying element was not passed on as a surname.[37]

16

It was and is still commonplace to refer to individuals by their personal name plus a nickname, whether from their residence (Tom Penlan; David Davies, Llandinam), their occupation (Dai Post, Jones the Milk, Morgan Saer) or some physical characteristic (Jemima Fawr,[38] John Coes Bren[39]). The parish register of Tregaron, Cardiganshire, has an amusing entry in 1702, when John, reputed son of 'David Dd ab David alias Treble David' was baptised.[40]

In Cilgerran, Pembrokeshire, in the 1780s, examples can be found of the use of nicknames of this type in the parish register, when children of 'Tom Parsonage' and of 'Tim Tyhen' were being baptised. Probably examples could be found elsewhere in Wales, but this type of entry is the exception and attributable to clerical idiosyncrasies. The fact is that they did not – almost *could* not – give rise to a family of Parsonages or Tyhens.

Nowadays collections of Welsh nicknames – particularly of amusing ones – are published.[41] In fact, the basic problem of distinguishing people with common names still applies today in Wales: a chairman of a Welsh family history society relates a typical situation of the election of officials to any organisation in the area. Amongst the candidates' names is, in all probability, a John Jones. Tension mounts in the audience until someone asks, 'John Jones who?' and the atmosphere changes to relief when the chairman replies 'John Jones Six', thereby excluding all the John Joneses present except the one who resides at 6 High Street.[42] Then again, one of the authors had the embarrassing experience of simply not knowing someone's surname when, on the death of his mother, he needed to contact the local undertaker. Unfortunately, having lived away from the area for some years he could only remember the undertaker by the name he was known by within the community – Evan Stretchem – which was no help at all when using the local telephone directory!

Occupational names

It is not particularly surprising that there are relatively few occupational surnames of Welsh origin. As with other categories, they battled for survival against the dominant patronymic names, and hardly started on fair terms because the largely rural, not to say pastoral, Welsh society would have had a limited number of occupations from which to choose.

In areas with a greater variety of occupations, strong anglicising influences were at work, the development of surnames tended to be closer to that of England and such occupational names as there were would probably be English. The latter type of surname might later spread into other parts of Wales. When we see listed the will in 1697 of Jane Farmer, widow, of Rhuthun, we have to conclude that she was the widow or daughter of a man with an English surname. Similarly, the Spicer family of seventeenth century Caernarfon were far detached from the occupation of their ancestors.[43] Occasionally there is a glimpse of a possible exception: 'Jen'ij goz [Ieuan Goch] alias wever' is found in Montgomeryshire in 1574.[44]

A few truly Welsh occupational names add variety to the scene (though they are very sparsely represented indeed in our survey of 1813-37). Arguably they can be compared with descriptive surnames, the occupation having been added initially to the personal name as an epithet.

Saer, Sare, Sears is a group of variants from *saer* 'carpenter', probably the commonest example of this type of name in Wales, and surviving in 1813-37 in south-east Pembrokeshire and western Carmarthenshire. Sayer is found in the same period in north Cardiganshire and Glamorgan. There is the possibility of confusion with similar English names, including Sawyer, the closer one gets to the English border.

There is really very little evidence that a Welsh family name was regularly derived from *gof* (pronounced 'gove') 'smith', though people are often intrigued by the existence of the Cornish (and Celtic) Angove, with the same meaning. As the pattern of Cornish surnames is so different from that of Welsh names, this is not relevant. Sometimes Gough is cited as a derivation of *gof*, but the sound at the end of *coch/goch* is guttural (as in Scottish *loch*) and tended to be altered to 'ff' (among others), not 'v'.[45] The following examples indicate that there are exceptions: 1582 Llan-faes, Owen David Gove als Owen David; 1580 Devynnock, Thomas y Gove als Thomas Johns – but it is more likely that the *patronymic* names of these individuals became surnames.[46]

Gwas 'servant' has led to the surname Wace, which is not represented in the 1813-37 survey, although it appears in Shropshire lists.[47] William Was appears in Radnorshire in 1293 and he and others like him may have taken the name over the border at an early stage.[48] There are several compounds in earlier records of *gwas/was* + personal names: e.g, Gwasmeir, Gwasmihangel, Gwastewi. However, these were devotional names (in these examples honouring the Virgin Mary, St Michael and St David), given at baptism and thus part of the patronymic system.

Crowther is not found often in Wales, but one of its origins may be from *crythor*, a player of the *crwth*, an early fiddle (see Glossary). Alternatively, it may be simply an English importation. Numerous examples of Goyder (*coedwr* 'woodman') have been found in Glamorgan parishes from the sixteenth to eighteenth centuries, and in Carmarthenshire before that.[49] In the 1670 Hearth Tax for Glamorgan, Goyders are found in the hundreds of Cowbridge (St Athan, Flemingston, Pendoylan) and Dinas Powis (St Brides super Ely). The latest date in which Goyder is found in Glamorgan Marriages is 1776 (Merthyr Mawr) and it is disappointing to record that this unusual name does not occur in the 1813-37 survey, unless it is concealed under Gooder (found in small numbers in Swansea).

The authors of *WS* suggest that *distain*, an obsolete term for a principal court steward, may have become a personal name and may still survive in the rare English surname Distin.[50] We did not find it in our survey. Similarly, Meddick, from *meddyg/feddyg* 'doctor', is not evident in 1813-37 and seems always to have been rare. An example of the mutated form is shown in Katherin vch William *feddig*.[51]

Pannwr/bannwr 'fuller', is found in Brecon Probate in the sixteenth century, but may be simply an epithet at that stage. This word is probably not responsible for Banner as a surname in south-west Wales. The Banner family, in Carmarthen in the late fourteenth century (and possibly connected to people settled in Pembrokeshire) are believed to be of English origin.[52] Similar origins are likely for men with the apparent surname Baner in late thirteenth century Radnorshire.[53]

The Welsh for baker, *pobydd*, is found as an epithet (e.g. 1587 Brecon: Watkin Lewes Bobith) but may not have survived as a surname in Wales. The examples of its use in Shropshire given in *WS* may have led to Bobyth or similar in England. Similarly used is *porthmon* 'drover', which is used in thirteenth to fifteenth century records – modern family historians would leap at the prospect of finding such a name in their family but, on the whole, like most such names, it seems to have been subsumed in the overwhelming patronymic deluge.

Welsh place-names as surnames

The final category – surnames taken from Welsh places – is the least common and its rightful place for consideration is arguably in the next chapter, where the adoption of settled names is discussed. It is an interesting category, not least because such names suggest how varied Welsh surnames could have been if the patronymic system had not survived so long. The list of Welsh surnames from place-names is lengthy if one includes archaic names and names which went into England early, never to return to use in Wales. Here we consider just a few examples of the main types of Welsh locational surname.[54]

Many such names were attached to men – not always Welsh by birth – when they returned to England after holding administrative office in an eponymous place. Similar names were formed when Welshmen went to live and work in English cities: in the mid-thirteenth century John de Cardiff was reeve of Bristol, and John de Kenfig was a burgess in the same city: 'These men had no reason to disavow the surname which their new neighbours presumably gave them.'[55] John Kidwelly was a burgess of Bridgwater, Somerset, by 1395 and had other Welsh neighbours.

19

The Anglo-Norman invasion of Ireland, led from Pembrokeshire, took Welsh place-names into the body of Irish surnames: Angle (Nagle), Carew (Carey), Prendergast, Stackpole, from Pembrokeshire; Barry, Cardiff, Cogan from Glamorgan. Some names went in the opposite direction: Whinnett is found to the present day in south Bedfordshire. It is derived from Gwynedd, a Welsh regional name, and was found by Guppy only in Bedfordshire.[56] John Gwynett was the name of a vicar resident of Luton, Bedfordshire, in the sixteenth century.[57] More generally relevant to the existence of Welsh surnames in Bedfordshire and nearby counties is the fact that Watling Street was a main route for the Welsh drovers over many centuries; Dunstable, Bedfordshire, for instance, has *ap* names in its sixteenth century parish register.

The following are examples of names from local places found in the early Bangor Probate records: Bodurda, Bodvell, Brinkir, Coetmore/Coytmor, Conway, Dolben, Gwnnys/Gunnys, Kyffin, Mostyn, Nanney and Trygan/Trygarn. These names were used by gentry families, many of them taken from their estates, as we shall consider below, but their existence does not alter the general predominance of patronymic names in this region.

In south Wales locational surnames may indicate long-established prosperous families, such as Laugharne, but more often they represent ordinary families who happen to live in anglicised areas where the English practice of taking locational surnames was familiar. Examples of such names are Lougher, Narberth, Philbatch, Picton, Roch, Sutton, Trewent.[58] In Pembrokeshire, where names of this type are fairly common, care must be taken because some places (in origin holdings rather than settlements) appearing on the modern map are named after people who resided there, and not vice versa.[59]

CHAPTER 2: NOTES AND REFERENCES

[1] McKinley (1990) reflects up to date thinking on English surnames; see also the volumes of the English Surnames Series. Hey (1993) sets the subject in a family history context.

[2] McKinley (1990); in northern England such names became settled later than in the south.

[3] Hanks & Hodges (1988) has a good overview of the situation in other countries. In some parts of Europe (e.g. Scandinavia) the patronymic naming-system was abandoned only in the nineteenth century and it continues in Iceland to the present.

[4] *WFH*, Chapter 9, M. Auronwy James, 'Some Basic Welsh for Family Historians', is a useful guide to pronunciation, orthography and mutation in the language.

[5] *WFH*, 209.

[6] Griffith (1914), 348.

[7] Hafina Clwyd, *WFH*, Chapter 1. In Chapter 18 of the same book, Michael P. Siddons gives further background to this practice.

[8] E.g. used frequently in St Asaph Probate: 1694 Jane ych Edward, Caerwys.

[9] See Thorne (1996) for examples of exceptions from the norm.

[10] Bartrum (1983) xxiv.

[11] Mer LS 1292-3.

[12] See Franklin (1986).

[13] The forenames are taken from Bartrum (1981). P.C. Bartrum's article on personal names in Wales in the fifteenth century is based on his compilation of indexes to *Welsh Genealogies 1400-1500* (Bartrum, 1983). Because of the large number of names involved, the territory covered was divided into regions, explained at the start of Chapter 5. Here we are concerned with the overall figures for Wales. Each of the surnames in brackets has a Glossary entry in Chapter 5.

[14] J.B. Davies (1980) is a useful contribution in this field for one region (Glamorgan).

[15] *WS*, 24.

[16] Brecon Probate.

[17] Three marriages in Monmouthshire, Abergavenny hundred.

[18] Bartrum (1981).

[19] Davies (1980).

[20] Benwell (1973).

[21] Further specific research into this and similar practices is needed.

[22] NLW, St David's Probate 1821: Jane, widow of Richard Rees of Llanrhystud, names her four grandsons, Richard Williams, Richard Davies, Richard Isaac and Richard Evans, and her four granddaughters, Jane Jones, Jane Davies, Jane Lewis and Jane Isaac.

[23] Brecon Probate 1576, 1573, 1622.There are many interesting examples of the use of adj. names in the Archdeaconry of Brecon in the sixteenth and seventeenth centuries.

[24] See list of adjectival names below.

[25] The soft mutations, which affect these adj. names, are as follows: initial b changes to *f* (pron, as Eng. *v*); c to *g*; d to *dd* (pron. as Eng. *th* in then); g is dropped; ll changes to *l;* m to *f*; p to *b*; rh to *r;* t to *d*. See also footnote 4 above.

[26] *WS*, 25.

[27] Though others will exist in altered form in England.

[28] Many *pen-* surnames are illustrated in *WS*. These names settled at a relatively early stage in English border counties.

[29] 1426 Philip ap Jac Pengrych (Bronwydd Deeds, NLW); 1670 HTPem Henry Bengrisse, Richard Bengrisse (Rhos hundred, Walton West).

[30] *WS* refers to this name being found in Monmouthshire, Shirenewton; in 1813-37 it is found in small numbers in (hundreds in brackets) Carmarthenshire (Carnwallon), Glamorgan (Cowbridge, Dinas Powis, Caerphilly and Kibbor) and Monmouthshire (Caldicott, which contains Shire Newton).

[31] *Glas* refers to a range of colours, as is not unusual in W colour-names. It is not quite as easy to decide why someone should have this epithet attached to the pers. name as in the case of someone who was probably dark, fair, auburn, etc. Mgy Muster has Thomas glace th'elder, Thomas glace the younger, Edward glace. (Newtown hundred); St Asaph Probate has (e.g.) 1703 John Glace, Betws Cedewain; 1722 John Glase, Guilsfield.

[32] Gwyn was also used, though uncommonly, as a forename.

[33] E.g. Lewis Mellyn of Rhulen (Brecon Probate, 1648).

[34] Though it is possible that some Teagues came from Ireland (derived from a pers. name).

[35] *WS*, 200.

[36] *WS*, 145, says it is numerous in modern Swansea and found there in 16C survey as Leia. However, we found none in that area in 1813-37.

[37] Useful accounts of the customary use of nicknames are given in Jenkins (1971) and Parry-Jones (1947).

[38] We make no apology for quoting in full the marginal note about this impressive woman, recorded in the PR of Fishguard, Pembrokeshire, by Samuel Fenton, Vicar, when he buried her on 16 July 1832: 'Jemima Nicholas, Mainstreet, 82 years. This woman was called *Jemima vawr* i.e. Jemima the great from her heroine *[sic]* acts she having marched against the French who landed hereabouts in 1797 and being of such personal powers as to be able to overcome most men in a fight. I recollect her well. She followed the trade of a shoemaker & made me when a little boy several pairs of shoes'.

[39] *Coes bren* 'wooden leg' – see D.E. Williams (1962) 48.

[40] Tregaron PR, January 1701/2: *Johanes fil: reputat David Dd ab David alias Treble David de parcel Argoed et Ystrad Laborat: et Jana John de eod: parcel baptizat fuit.*

[41] E.g. Chamberlain (1981).

[42] R.R.Williams (1994).

[43] Bangor Probate.

[44] Mgy Muster.

[45] As is clearly expressed in such examples as: 1707, John Goffe, Holywell (St Asaph Probate).

[46] Brecon Probate.

[47] E.g. IGI for Shropshire has almost 90 entries for Wace, Wase, Wass/e, esp. 18C.

[48] RadAss; most occupational names in this list are in Latin.

[49] *WS*, 73, quoting J.B. Davies.

[50] *WS*, 86.

[51] Bangor Probate 1641.

[52] Griffiths (1994), 183.

[53] RadAss.

[54] It does not seem sensible to reproduce an extensive list of surnames from Welsh places here. *WS* has such a list (see comments in *WFH*, 64-5); county by county lists appear in P. Morgan (1990-1; 1995).

[55] Griffiths (1994), 6-8.

[56] However, that it has also existed in Wales is illustrated by its appearance in Pembrokeshire in 1625, when Owen Wynnett witnessed a deed. (Poyston Deeds, NLW).

[57] See *WS*, 29.

[58] All these examples are in current use or are only recently extinct in Wales. There are many more which have died out or which left Wales long ago; for these see P. Morgan (1990-1).

[59] For many examples, see Charles (1992).

CHAPTER 3

THE ADOPTION OF SURNAMES

In understanding how surnames eventually became settled in Wales we have to consider a number of factors, including place and period. Generally, surnames were adopted earlier in the east of Wales, close to the influences of the English border, compared to the west; similarly they were, on the whole taken earlier in the south than the north, especially in those areas influenced by the south-western counties of England. Overlying these generalisations, however, is the fact that the gentry took permanent names before their tenants. This is particularly noticeable in north Wales.

Non-Welsh surnames in Wales

The earliest permanent surnames in Wales were adopted in the areas affected by Anglo-Norman settlement, a typical case being south Pembrokeshire. In that area, Arnold, Cole, Hay, Roblin, Scone, Trewent and Warlow are just a few examples of names found from the thirteenth century to the present day.[1] In 1326, tenants in Lamphey included people called Freyne (Froyne), Philpkyn (Philpin), Prout, Russell and Webb, all with a subsequent long history in south Pembrokeshire.[2]

The conquest of Brycheiniog at a similar time led to the appearance on the Welsh scene of Awbrey, Gunter, Havard and Walbeoff – such names were borne by the conquerors and their widely-spread descendants. The non-Welsh names of the lesser followers of these families were, in this and some other parts of Wales, not always permanent. Often, after a generation or two, the bearers adapted to local life, married Welsh girls, and their offspring took their patronymic name in the native style. Families in northern Pembrokeshire who settled after the military conquest of Cemais bore names like Canton and Hood.[3] When we follow them through the pedigrees (where they are recorded because of their intermarriage with the families of Welsh leaders) we find the senior lines adopting the patronymic system. We may cite the Cantingtons (Canton) of Eglwyswrw 'whose descendants in the main line finally became Griffith and Powell'.[4] Nevertheless, such names have often survived, whether through female lines, illegitimacy or simply the unrecorded younger sons of younger sons.

By the thirteenth century and the Edwardian conquest, further new surnames came into Wales, especially into the newly-established boroughs. For example, in the vicinity of the borough of Denbigh were to be found the families of Duckworth, Wilberley, Sweynemore, Salusbury, Hulton, Pigot, Symondestone and Cliderowe, many of them from Herefordshire or Lancashire.[5] Research into the English of Dyffryn Clwyd in the thirteenth and fourteenth centuries reveals that settlers came from the English estates of the de Grey lords, but also indicates that an element came from the neighbouring parts of England, 'presumably attracted by the opportunity to obtain land in a period of increasing population'.[6] Among the names of English locative origin found in Dyffryn Clwyd at that time and still in use nearby at the time of our survey are Aspull (from Lancashire), and Pulford, Rushton and Thelwall (from Cheshire).[7]

Lists of early burgesses in Flint and Rhuddlan contain personal names which, though not in the Welsh pattern, were probably not firmly settled English surnames, with occupational names (Faber, le Sawier, Carpentar', etc) in Latin or in an early form with 'le', and place-names preceded by 'de'. Some of the latter are useful for indicating what is perhaps the immediate past home of the bearer (de Cestria, de Maclisfeud', de Salop, de Couentr') but they do not seem to relate to later names in the area.

There was steady movement back and fore between England ànd Wales in the late middle ages and the early modern period, showing up especially in the surnames of counties such as Radnorshire and Montgomeryshire. Much of this was the result of natural and inevitable interaction, by trade and intermarriage. However, in addition, evidence has been found in the records of the Court of Great Sessions for the long-suspected English 'plantation' of parts of Montgomeryshire.[8] Murray Chapman, who has worked on these records for many years, believes that a significant in-migration of English people occurred in the lordships of Arwystli and Cyfeiliog from 1576, when Robert Dudley, earl of Leicester, who held these lordships (and those of Chirk, Chirkland and Denbigh in Denbighshire) from the Crown, was permitted by licence to alienate the lands in any way he pleased. A court case relating to an accusation of sheep-stealing (seemingly trumped up by hostile local men) illustrates that John Thornhill, John Bamford, Robert Hatfield, Henry Gregory and his wife Margaret, and Nicholas Bennett, all from communities in Derbyshire, had moved to Llangurig in the lordship of Arwystli in 1576. Witnesses in the case bore such names as Bowring, Cottrell, Downes, Woosencroft, Wilson, Aston, Marple and Cowper. We may reasonably assume that firm evidence of other similar settlements at this period (far later than those in, say, Pembrokeshire and Gower) may emerge in due course to explain the origins of English surnames in this and other parts of Wales.

Although the origins and early background of these 'border' names are characteristically English, in few cases did they remain completely aloof from Welsh influence and, in addition, they were represented at many levels of society. Lewis Brigstocke, (living 1716), probably a descendant of the seventeenth century man who married into the family of Llechdwnni, Carmarthenshire, had among his descendants by 1891 a doctor and a bookseller in Haverfordwest; a wine merchant and a chemist in Carmarthen; and a house painter and a general labourer in St Clears who were bilingual in Welsh and English; others had migrated to Cardiff, back into England, and to the Colonies.[9]

The period of our survey overlaps with the great movement of people into the industrial areas, both from the rural parts of Wales and from other parts of the British Isles. As a result of the latter, many new surnames were coming into certain parts of Wales at this time. However, unless the people who brought them were married in Wales during the period 1813-37, they would not feature in our survey. Earlier industrial activity – such as lead-mining in mid and north-east Wales – had seen skilled workers from other parts of Britain come into Wales. These workers also brought new surnames with them but, as the level of activity was relatively low, this made little impact on the surname scene generally. Nevertheless, surnames such as Bonsall, Hooson, Nuttall and Sheldon still survive in some areas as a result of this earlier activity.

Patronymic to surname

The majority of the Welsh population had patronymic names, however, and it is to how these evolved into surnames that we now turn.

The first to adopt fixed surnames were the wealthier classes, and, in particular those of northern Wales who took the names of their estates, such as Mostyn, Nanney and Pennant[10] It could be said that such families took surnames by decree in 1539 but few ordinary people were affected in practice.[11] The change to settled surnames filtered through society at different levels from the mid-sixteenth century on, but in areas distant from English influence the patronymic system survived much longer.

We see the *ap* system gradually decaying (at different rates in different areas): someone whose name was Laurence ap Llewelyn became Laurence Llewelin; David ap William became David William; the son of Mirick ap Howell ap Phelip was known as Rees Mirick – all these examples are from sixteenth and seventeenth century Glamorgan.[12] There are a remarkable number of *ap* and *ab* names in Llandaff Probate records even in the eighteenth century, both in upland Glamorgan parishes and in western Monmouthshire.

For some time the *ap* was implied and the patronymic system remained, with the name continuing to change generation by generation.[13] Eventually, however, a surname would settle in a family and be passed on from father to son in the English fashion. We use case studies below to illustrate this happening in different ways.

We should not leave the *ap* yet, for it was obviously in daily spoken use and became agglutinated – that is, it attached itself in many cases to the name which followed, so that ap Rosser became Prosser, ap Hugh became Pugh, ap Harri became Parry, and ab Evan became Bevan. Examples of these names appear in the Glossary and we attempt to throw light on their distribution in Chapter 6.

The addition of 's' to form surnames

At a slightly later stage, many newly-acquired surnames of patronymic origin had an 's' attached to them. This was a practice used in England when surnames were forming (and representing the possessive case).[14] It was adopted much later in Wales, probably by clerks originally, but ultimately accepted with general enthusiasm in most areas to form a 'proper' surname. Thus Griffith ap Howell could become Griffith Howell at first, and eventually Griffith Howells. The addition of 's' seemed to form a substitute for *ap*, so it is not surprising that 's' is not usually added to the class of names in which *ap/ab* have become absorbed (Bowen, Prosser, Pugh, etc). However, exceptions are found in the English border counties, with such names as Bevans and Beavans appearing in some quantity.[15]

In many areas of Wales the practice of adding 's' was adopted in the eighteenth century, though in others it was a gradual development as the nineteenth century went on. Researchers should always bear in mind the interchangeability of forms with and without 's' – pedantically looking for one or the other is unwise. Conversely, one should always transcribe the name as found, since the absence or presence of 's' in an area at a certain time may help establish how permanent a particular surname was. Civil registration was probably the factor which decided the final form of such names.[16] It is an interesting sidelight that lists of names ending in 's' are often a good indicator of Welshness.[17]

Settled surnames in combination with the patronymic system

The patronymic naming-system ran in tandem with surnames in areas like north Pembrokeshire: conquest there might have been but Welsh customs eventually prevailed, undoubtedly supported by the Welsh language. (English was the tongue of the south of the county once the military conquest was reinforced by planted settlers from, especially, Somerset and Devon.) This created another category of name, almost a clan-name, though on a small scale and 'kindred-name' is a better description. The existence of this type of name undoubtedly accounts for the long-term survival of 'English' surnames in a Welsh area: 1579, John ap Owen Picton, gent, of Nevern; 1582, John Phillip Yong;[18] 1746, Henry son of William and Anne Thomas Strong baptised.[19] The same development seems to have taken place in the area covered by the Archdeaconry of Brecon, where several men called Havard have patronymic-type names, e.g. 1574, Thomas ap John Lloid Havard; 1586, John Thomas Havard of Brecon. Among people bearing the settled surname Gunter are: 1572, Lewis Rickerd Gunter; 1574, Rees Thomas Gunter. Similar examples exist for Awbrey and Games.[20]

Case Studies

It is very important that historians researching Welsh families should study the communities in which those families lived for an understanding of the trends which affected their surnames. Strict rules are inappropriate and families should not be considered in isolation. It would be beyond the scope of this work to consider all the varied possibilities throughout Wales, but the following case-studies and examples are intended to throw light on the subject by a range of examples.

Caernarfonshire 18-19th century

Richard Thomas married, in 1766 in Bryncroes, Mary Charles, daughter of Charles Mark (Siarl Marc, 1720-1795), Calvinistic Methodist minister and hymn-writer.[21] Richard Thomas was a stonemason, Mary Charles also a hymnist. Their youngest son, John Richard Thomas, emigrated to America in 1795 and founded a family there. Their eldest son, Evan (1769-1832), stayed in Wales and was well known as a bard – he appears in *DWB* as Evan Pritchard. While researching the family's history an American relation also found Evan Pritchard under the following names in a variety of documents: Evan Richard, Evan Richards, Evan Prichard, Evan ap Pritchard, Ieuan Rhisiard, Ieuan ap Rhisiart, Ifan Prisiart, Ifan ap Rhisiart; as well as by the more clearly bardic Ieuan Fardd Bryncroes, Ieuan Lleyn or Llŷn, Evan Lleyn Bard, Efan Lleyn and Bardd Bryncroes.[22] It is clear that, under whatever name his fame has come down the years, Evan was known during his life and shortly afterwards in a variety of different ways and that, in particular, his surname and its spelling was not fixed. Indeed, his fuller patronymic survives: Evan Richard ab Tomos ab Evan ab Tomos Prydderch.[23]

The clearest examples of the formation of surnames through the patronymic system at very late dates are also to be found in the Llŷn area of Caernarfonshire (and also in Anglesey). Thomas Morris, born in Bryncroes in 1812, was the son of Robert and Mary Thomas. The child's paternal grandfather was Thomas Morris, after whom he was presumably named – this was not uncommon.[24] In the

1841 census for Aberdaron, Llŷn, Thomas and Jane Ellis have sons called Ellis Thomas (age 20), John Thomas (17) and Thomas Ellis (14), and daughters called Elizabeth (24), Mary (22), Jane (9) and Catherine (5), all with Thomas as their last name. The point is made that Thomas Ellis the younger was, in full, Thomas ap Thomas ap Ellis and that, rather than refer to his taking his father's 'surname', we should compare the dropping of the middle Thomas with the avoidance of some forms of repetitive name. In this area, 'William Williams, John Jones or Owen Owen ... are often found, whilst names like Morris Morris or Ellis Ellis seem to be avoided.'[25] As late as 1862, the marriage took place in Llangïan, of Ellen Roberts, daughter of Robert Jones, and such an event, though by then unusual, could be replicated in other parts of rural north and west Wales.[26]

Cardiganshire 18th century

A list of Cardiganshire Freeholders in 1760 includes William John Elusdan (his father was John Elystan) of Llanrhystud, whose name appears variously in documents as William Siôn, William John and William Jones, but he signed as Jones and this is how his sons always appear in records. (However, his daughter married as Jane William in 1772.)[27] Elystan does not seem to have become a surname, at least in this area. Llanrhystud was a parish of many small freeholders until the nineteenth century and a similar pattern is found for many of these families. Labouring families in the parish generally assumed a surname about a generation later.

In the neighbouring parish of Llansantffraid, the Revd Thomas Alban appears in the same list of freeholders. He was the heir of one of the chief freeholders of the parish, Alban Thomas (c. 1685-1742), who was described on his tombstone as 'gentleman' and whose infant children, buried alongside him, are named Evan, Mary, Diana and Elizabeth *Thomas*. Three sons (born in the 1730s) lived to maturity (the longest-lived to 1822) and called themselves by the surname Alban, which then became hereditary.[28]

After Alban Thomas died in 1742, his widow re-married (to Morgan Herbert, another Cardiganshire freeholder) as Catherine Evans. Her 'surname' in the marriage entry leads us to investigate the possibility that her parents were Evan Lewis, yeoman of Llansantffraid, and his wife Diana David.[29] The repetition of unusual forenames (such as Diana) is another indicator of relationship.

Fig. 3-1 indicates the gradual change of form from patronymic name to surname in the case of two common names in northern Cardiganshire in the most significant period of surname-formation in this area. It can be seen that the 'surnames' John and David were dominant in the early eighteenth century, but they had become the exception by the early part of the nineteenth century, having been almost totally supplanted by Jones and Davies.

Period	John	Jones	David	Davies
	No.	No.	No.	No.
1710-19	1	2	4	2
1720-29	16	3	16	-
1730-39	41	9	40	-
1740-49	44	8	37	3
1750-59	44	12	64	13
1760-69	68	38	87	38
1770-79	62	64	71	63
1780-89	64	103	63	83
1790-99	35	148	52	127
1800-09	29	211	34	155
1810-13	2	68	5	43
Totals	406	666	473	527

Fig. 3-1: The transition from John to Jones and David to Davies, based on marriages in the Ilar Hundred (Upper and Lower) of Cardiganshire, 1710-1813.

Carmarthenshire/Pembrokeshire 18th century

In Cilrhedyn (Pembrokeshire) in 1760 the marriage took place of Evan Rees of Mydrim, Carmarthenshire, and Elinor John, widow. The groom signed as Evan Prothero. The marriage bond names the couple as Evan Prytherch, yeoman of Mydrim, and Elinor George, widow, of Cilrhedyn.[30] These events illustrate the bride and groom having two forms of name each (with alternative spellings for one of them); undoubtedly one of the bride's names was her maiden name.

Denbighshire 17-18th century

The will of Rowland Charles of Gartheryr, proved in 1693, names his two sons as Henry Charles and Charles Rowland. Henry Charles was a student at this time at Queens College, Cambridge, graduating BA in 1687-8 and MA in 1695; he was later curate of Marchwiel and then Vicar of Llangollen (1706-37). His brother Charles succeeded their father as tenant of Gartheryr and other properties of the Chirkland and Wynnstay estates in the Tanat valley – he is always referred to in rentals as Charles Rowland.[31] In this example we see how the father's 'surname' was passed on when one son moved to England and the university; we can deduce that the family had ambition and probably status, yet the patronymic form was still very normal and acceptable at home.

Glamorgan 16th-18th centuries

The following examples from Glamorgan documents illustrate how patronymic forms could become surnames with 's': 1556, John and Walter Jones, sons of William ap John; 1562, David Evans, son of Evan ap David; 1609, David Williams, son of William ap David. Other documents show the interchangeability of forms with and without 's': 1625, William Jenkin, signs William Jenkins; 1738, Humphrey Matthews, signs Humphrey Mathew; 1757, Roger Howell, signs Roger Howells; 1761, James William – his wife signs Ann Williames.[32]

Merionethshire 18th-19th centuries

The parish register of Llandrillo in Edeirnion records the baptism in 1720 of 'Fulko fil. John Foulk de Penant'. This child grew up as Foulk Jones and he and his wife Gwen baptised a son Watkin in the same parish in 1754. When the latter married Elizabeth Ellis at Bryneglwys in 1785 it was as Watkin Foulkes and the family retained the surname of Foulkes thereafter.[33] Though the name Foulk existed in the family much earlier, it did not become a surname until the late eighteenth century.

Thomas ap Robert of Derwen (died 1738) married Gwen Cadwalader, the daughter of Cadwalader ap Hugh of Llandderfel (died 1716) – the latter's full patronymic name was Cadwalader ap Hugh ap Ieuan ap Rhys Goch. The son of Thomas and Gwen was known as Cadwalader Thomas (1719-93), and *his* son as Thomas Cadwalader (1746-1836). The next descendant, born 1791, was known as Thomas ap Thomas Cadwalader, but was buried in 1843 at Betws Gwerful Goch as Thomas Cadwalader. The latter's son (born 1835) married in 1866 as Edward Thomas, naming his father as Thomas Thomas (blacksmith, deceased). The descendants of Edward Thomas carry the surname Thomas to the present.[34]

Hugh Humphrey (1729-1823) of Maentwrog was married twice. By his first wife he had children known by the following names: Robert Hugh (1752-1813); Edmund Humphrey (1755-1821); Margaret Hugh (1758-c.1822). By his second wife he had: Humphrey Pugh (1762-c.1840); Elizabeth Hugh or Hughes (1765-?); Ellis Humphrey or Humphreys (1767-1862); Richard Humphreys (1770-1840).[35] This example illustrates how children could take both the father's and grandfather's forenames; how *ap* might be attached to such names; and how added 's' became increasingly acceptable with passing time.

There is evidence of the continued use of the mother's maiden name in nineteenth century Meirionnydd. A frequent pattern for baptisms in parish registers is: 1810, Margaret daughter of John Hugh, yeoman, and Jane Williams his wife; 1811, Margaret daughter of William Richard, yeoman, and Catherine Owen his wife.[36]

Monmouthshire 17th century

In the will of Harry David Powell of 1604, reference is made to 'Elizabeth Harry, my daughter; John Harry, my son; Samuel Powell, my son; Cecil Harry, my daughter'. The same John Harry is referred to in a pedigree as John ap Howell, so that he and his brother Samuel used their great-grandfather's name.[37]

30

Pembrokeshire 18th century

The populous (in local terms) parish of St David's had distinctive surnames in the eighteenth century, among them Amblott, Grinish, Oakley, Pardoe, Stork, Tegan, etc, as well as the commoner Welsh names. The marriage registers show few clear patronymic names: in 1737 (i) John Evan Morris married Margaret Symmon and (ii) Thomas Hugh Emont married Margaret Moses.[38] To show the different ways in which the clergy might deal with the next stage of parish register entries we have these baptisms: 1738, David son of John Evan and Margaret Morrice; 1745, Thomas son of John and Margaret Evan Morrice; 1738, Dorathy daughter of Thomas and Margaret Hugh Emont; 1740, Jane daughter of Thomas and Margaret Hugh alias Emont. In 1747 Thomas Hugh alias Emont of St David's was buried at the age of 66. A later sighting of this family occurs in 1764, when Elizabeth Hugh (according to the clerk's entry) married Edmond Hulme, signing as Elizabeth Hugh Edmund – the final name has, of course, nothing to do with the groom's forename.

In 1749 Joseph Phillip married Anne Ed: Richard, the sole female patronymic entry noted. No further references to the bride could be expected – she was presumably a sister to Henry Edward Richard of Pencarnan, St David's, who was buried aged 22 in 1742. Also of this family is likely to be John Edward, who married Elizabeth Perkin in 1735, since a child Mary was baptised in 1741, daughter of John and Elizabeth Edward alias Richard.

A similar instance is concealed in the family recorded in this register as David alias Max: in 1727, John the son of Thomas and Mawd David alias Max was baptised; by 1731 we have Elizabeth daughter of Thomas and Maudlin Max. An older generation in this family appears thus in burials: in 1742 Lettice David alias Max was buried aged 86, followed in the same year by Henry David alias Max, aged 84. In the Hearth Tax for 1670, Maximilian Davids is among those certified as paupers in St David's and possibly it was his offspring's generation which first became known as David alias Max.

These are rare entries in this parish from the earliest surviving register, but we may suppose that in an earlier generation still the overt patronymic would be more numerous. The use of alias is an indicator that both the alternative names were possible longer term surnames within these families. Their scarcity indicates that during the first half of the eighteenth century the patronymic naming system was fading fast in this part of north Pembrokeshire.

The story of Betsy Cadwaladr

An illustration of a reason for assuming one surname rather than another is shown in the story of Elizabeth Davis (1789-1860), one of Florence Nightingale's nurses.[39] Betsy, as she was known, was the daughter of Dafydd Cadwaladr, a Methodist preacher, and his wife Judith Erasmus, and spent her childhood in Bala. Her paternal grandfather, Cadwaladr Dafydd of Cerrigydrudion, Denbighshire, had five sons, each of them, according to Betsy, with a different surname. As a young woman, Betsy made her way to England to seek work: 'I was always known in Merioneth as Betsy Pen Rhiw. On coming first to Liverpool, I called myself by my proper name, Elizabeth Cadwaladyr; but on finding that the English people could not pronounce that surname, I afterwards adopted my father's Christian name instead, and signed myself Elizabeth Davis; my elder brothers and sisters having done the like, in changing Cadwaladyr for Davis.'[40]

Misapprehensions about surname origins

It has been commented before that Welsh people, having assumed permanent surnames, quickly forgot that they had ever been without them.[41] Much false family history has been built on this basis and parish histories, useful as they may otherwise be, often appear ignorant in this respect.

Legends about surname-origins go back a long way. The Salusbury family were once thought to have been descended from the royal house of Bavaria and to have taken their surname from Salzburg;[42] the Stradlings were supposed to have been Danes or, later, Normans.[43] In recent years, misapprehensions about even common Welsh surnames have been perpetuated, the straightforward Bowen (ab Owen) being described as from 'the Norman de Bohan'.[44] Supposed Norse, Flemish or Huguenot origins abound without regard to historical context or date. Charles is thought by more than one modern family to have French origins; often a French soldier is cited, although no-one seems able to supply details of the military occasion and there is ample evidence of its simple patronymic origin. More than one of the unrelated Alban families – taking their name from an uncommon patronymic name which can be traced back to known individuals, active in local affairs and certainly Welsh-speaking – claim that two brothers arrived in a particular west Wales parish from Scotland (*Yr Alban* in Welsh). Two brothers manifest themselves again in Montgomeryshire, but German counts this time, to explain Woosencroft.[45] Perhaps people thought up such stories when they could not find their surname in earlier registers. In the late nineteenth and early twentieth centuries, newspapers and even articles in learned journals perpetuated such myths, seeking 'exciting' origins.

Family historians, it should go without saying, should seek only the truth and can make a considerable contribution to the history of Welsh surnames by tracing individual families through standard genealogical methods and even, in the case of the rarer names, using the techniques of one-name studies to solve problems of origins.[46]

Indexes of Welsh names

Names of individuals appear in lists and, for the family historian, such lists are highly valued when they are indexed. Here we should consider briefly the problems of indexing Welsh names, caused by the complexities of the patronymic naming-system and by the difficulties at many periods of defining a surname in Wales.[47] If a man is named Richard ap Rees or John Griffith Goch or Ieuan Gwilym ap Cadwgan, what is his 'surname' for indexing purposes?

One strategy adopted by indexers is to have parallel patronymic and surname indexes; that is, indexes of first names and of last names. If the list consists of people with simple two-element names (e.g. David Thomas, Howell Griffith, Hugh Lewis, etc), then indexes based on first and last names are not unreasonable, though in fact such a list would tend to suggest that surnames were settled in the area which formed its subject and, for reasons of space and cost, a single last name/surname index would probably be chosen.[48] However, clearly this would not help with the more complex names of Richard, John and Ieuan mentioned above. Where such names occur in a list, indexers may choose to produce two indexes:

(i) A patronymic index arranged alphabetically by first name, which includes all names containing *ap* or *verch* and all names containing more than two elements – this would encompass the examples in the first paragraph of this section, in the following order:

> Ieuan Gwilym ap Cadwgan
> John Griffith Goch
> Richard ap Rees.

Ap and *verch* are not usually counted, so that John ap Griffith and John Griffith Goch would appear close together in the index.

(ii) A surname index of all two-element names – this would include the examples in the second paragraph as:

> Griffith, Howell
> Lewis, Hugh
> Thomas, David

It is true that some individuals with two-element names did not have settled surnames but this system of indexing, followed consistently, allows readers to know where they stand.

As an increasing number of indexes of genealogical value (e.g. probate, marriage bonds) are now computerised, it is becoming possible of course to search for names under variant forms, using any known element.

33

Modern names

The nineteenth century saw the final adoption of surnames by Welsh families. Most people had assumed them by the second decade and reinforcement of the practice came with the use of printed registers for baptism and burial, from 1813, with a column headed 'Surname'.[49] By 1837, births, marriages and deaths were to be registered, and this effectively enforced the use of surnames and some degree of consistency in their use. There were exceptions, as the case studies above show, but the second half of the century saw few Welshmen departing from the two-element standard forename/surname of the David Thomas, John Evans, William Roberts type.

When such people left Wales for overseas, frequently travelling with or settling among groups with similar names, the need to have some distinguishing feature was clear. In the United States of America, many assumed a middle initial according to American custom – this might be, in a last gesture towards the patronymic system, based on a man's father's forename, or it might be taken from his mother's surname. It is often the custom for family historians with Welsh ancestry to quote complex names, for example, 'John Thomas Evans, left Cardiganshire in 1839 for America'. For the most part, these turn out to be names which have grown since departure from Wales. Such a person would probably have left Wales as John Evans. It is possible that he referred to himself as John (son of) Thomas Evans, but the more frequent case is that descendants, again using the American pattern, tended to insert the mother's surname.

Complex names did develop in Wales in the later nineteenth and in the twentieth centuries as the problems caused by common names became clear to the better-educated and more ambitious. Men entering the professions (and therefore about to appear in published lists) were encouraged to take an extra name rather than be one of several John Joneses in their year. The mother's surname was frequently adopted, or that of another family member. Mostly, such names were common themselves, so that Evans-Davies, Morris-Jones, Parry-Williams, etc, evolved. Other names were formed by assuming a place-name associated with the family or by using a bardic name, though these were generally not hyphenated or permanent (in the sense of being passed on through successive generations).

In the second half of the twentieth century, with renewed national awareness and growing interest in the past, there has been a trend towards reviving patronymic names (though sometimes this involves using *ap* plus personal name as a *fixed* surname, occasionally even for women). Many present-day bearers of the standard surnames in our survey have chosen to give them a more distinctly Welsh appearance: Hughes becomes Huws, Vaughan becomes Fychan, and so on. Similar feelings have led to some Welsh families removing the 's' (arguably a sign of anglicisation) from their name. The result is that modern names may look more 'authentic' but may not always represent continuity with earlier generations.

CHAPTER 3: NOTES AND REFERENCES

[1] Charles (1960).

[2] *BBStD.*

[3] Charles (1973); *WFH,* 65-6.

[4] F. Jones (1960); *WGI,* etc.

[5] D.H. Owen (1975).

[6] Barrell & Brown (1995).

[7] Barrell & Brown (1995). In 1813-37, Aspull is found in Denbighshire (Rhuthun hundred), Pulford in Denbighshire (Maelor Bromfield) and Flintshire (Mold), Rushton in Denbighshire (Chirk), Thelwall in Denbighshire (Maelor Bromfield and Rhuthun).

[8] *WFH,* Chapter 7, 66-7 and notes 28-30.

[9] We are grateful to Chris Pitt Lewis for this information. For the history and further distribution of this surname, see Glossary.

[10] See Glossary entries for the first two and *WS* for this type of name.

[11] Pennant (1810) quotes the occasion when the president of the Council of the Marches, Rowland Lee instructed the jury of the court of Great Sessions to drop all their *aps* and instead 'assume their last name, or that of their residence'.

[12] D.E. Williams (1962), which is essential reading for Glamorgan surnames.

[13] D.E. Williams (1962) describes it usefully as a ghost form.

[14] The suffix '-son' was used alternatively to 's' in the formation of English surnames (largely in northern England) and is noticeably absent from Wales. Colin Rogers has made the point that this reflects the proximity of Wales to southern and midland England. It can only be a matter of conjecture whether, in a different geographical relationship, '-son' would have achieved the same popularity as 's'.

[15] Oddities such as 'ap Bevan' appear occasionally even in Wales, e.g, Glamorgan, Miskin hundred in 1813-37.

[16] The authors' Rowlands family, from an eighteenth century patronymic in mid-Cardiganshire, was spelt Rowland in most records up to the mid-nineteenth century. Since then, only Rowlands is 'correct'– in *this* family.

[17] E.g, when Wales played England at Rugby on 3 February 1996, eleven of the Welsh XV had surnames ending in 's' – Davies (3), Thomas (2), Jones (2), Lewis (2) Evans and Humphreys – while the two substitutes were Williams and Jenkins! None of the English team, nor the one substitute, had a surname ending this way.

[18] Both NLW, Bronwydd II.

[19] NLW, St David's PR.

[20] Brecon Probate.

[21] *DWB.*

35

[22] It should be borne in mind that all the attributed forenames are equivalent: Ieuan is a Welsh form of John and evolved into Ifan, Efan and Evan.

[23] Elizabeth E. Brown, of Littleton, Colorado, USA, provided this information while attending a Family History in Wales Course at UWA in 1992.

[24] Benwell (1973) 116.

[25] Benwell (1973) 116. Useful examples are given in this work and others by the authors.

[26] *WFH*, 61.

[27] *WWHR*, iii; Llanrhystud PR, parochial documents, wills, Rhiwbwys chapel history.

[28] They were active in church, chapel and parish life, signing many documents; it is a matter of good fortune for their genealogically-minded descendants that they elected to use their father's unusual first name rather than Thomas.

[29] NLW: St David's Probate 1718/19; Tre-faes Deeds; Llangwyryfon PR.

[30] Cilrhedyn PR; St David's Marriage Bonds, NLW (published in *WWHR* v, 60).

[31] Details of this family were kindly supplied by Miss Rhoswen Charles of Bushey, Herts.

[32] D.E. Williams (1962) 59-60.

[33] Ex inf. Miss Rhoswen Charles.

[34] Details of this family were kindly supplied by Mrs D. Elwern Jones of Rhyl.

[35] From information supplied by Miss R. Williams, 1991.

[36] NLW, Llanfair-juxta-Harlech PR. Illegitimate children were described as such.

[37] Bradney (1904), quoted in D.E. Williams (1962) 56. Cecil was in frequent use for girls in this area.

[38] Emont/Emment are local variants of Edmund (see Glossary).

[39] J. Williams (1987). *DWB, sub* DAVI(E)S (or CADWALADR), ELIZABETH.

[40] J. Williams (1987) 18.

[41] *WFH*, 62-3.

[42] D.H. Owen (1975) 72, quotes this and the evidence against.

[43] See Griffiths (1994), 'The Rise of the Stradlings of St Donat's'.

[44] Godwin & Toulson (1977).

[45] *Cronicl* 7, 1983/4.

[46] The Guild of One-Name Studies, Box G, 14 Charterhouse Buildings, Goswell Road, London EC1M 7BA, England, sets standards for this approach and publishes a *Register* regularly. Some surnames of Welsh origin are already registered with the Guild.

[47] This is a simplified account. Matters related to indexing Welsh names are discussed very fully in (e.g.) Henson (1980) and N.C. Jones (1989).

[48] The International Genealogical Index is an example of parallel surname and given name indexes, produced on a vast scale. It does not address the problems of complex patronymics, resulting in a great loss of genealogical information.

[49] The compilers of the IGI (Wales and Monmouthshire) assumed, on the basis of this, not only that 1813 was the date from which Welsh people could be said to have surnames but also that they did not have them before – hence the dual Given Name and Surname Indexes for these sections of the IGI. The truth is far more subtle and varied. See *WFH*, Chapter 10, for details of problems with the IGI for Wales and suggestions for solving them.

CHAPTER 4

A SURVEY OF SURNAMES IN WALES

As far as we know no-one has carried out a comprehensive survey of surnames throughout Wales, for the period since settled surnames became the norm, which takes account of all surnames, their rates of occurrence, and the variations which exist between different areas. Some work on surnames in Wales has been done on specific local areas, but this often appears in print only as an adjunct to other work.[1] There is, of course, also the pioneering work of Guppy for *The Homes of Family Names,* as well as the excellent book, *Welsh Surnames,* by T.J. Morgan and Prys Morgan *(WS).*

Although work on local areas can give snapshots of the pattern of surnames for the areas in question, it cannot be used to suggest a pattern for Wales as a whole. Guppy on the other hand, although he deals with the whole of Wales, has only three subdivisions: North Wales, South Wales and Monmouthshire. This offers little by way of refinement and this shortcoming can mask important local concentrations of some surnames, a point which is considered more fully later in this chapter. While the content of *WS* also deals with the whole of Wales it is primarily related to names which are predominantly of Welsh origin, so that names such as Jones, Davies, Thomas, Williams, Evans, which have dominated the surname scene in Wales for the last two centuries, are only referred to indirectly.

It is, perhaps, not surprising that no comprehensive survey has been carried out. To many it would seem to be setting out to illustrate the obvious; to illustrate, for example, that the whole of Wales is largely populated by people named Jones or one of the other very common names. However, family historians who have worked on records for different parts of Wales which contain a representative selection of surnames (such as parish registers) will know that this common preconception can be very much a misconception. They will know, for example, that different areas have their own distinctive patterns of surnames which are only contributed to, and not determined by, those common surnames. Those who have worked on areas in both north and south Wales will know that, whereas the surname Jones is extremely common in parts of north Wales, it has a relatively low incidence in Pembrokeshire and certain parts of Glamorgan. Then again, while the surname Davies is prominent in many parts of south Wales (particularly Cardiganshire), it has a relatively low incidence in parts of north Wales. This regional emphasis is even more marked in the case of the slightly less common surnames, where Jenkins, James and Rees are names of south Wales which are seldom found in the north, while the reverse is the case with Ellis and Roberts. Other less common surnames (but very common by English standards) are specific to quite small localities, as is the case with Foulkes (Denbighshire), Gittins (Montgomeryshire), Edmunds (Monmouthshire), Hopkins (Glamorgan), Eynon (Pembrokeshire), etc.

It appeared to us, therefore, that a comprehensive survey of surnames across Wales would not only be of considerable general interest, but could also offer a great deal to those living outside Wales who are experiencing difficulties in identifying the place of origin of their ancestors within Wales. The way the information from such a survey can be used to help narrow down the area in which a search might prove to be most fruitful is considered in detail in Chapters 6 and 7.

Deciding on the survey

Having decided to carry out a comprehensive survey, it was necessary to identify a body of records which would yield the sort of information required in sufficient volume to represent a reasonable sample of the population as a whole. As a result it was decided to study all surnames which were recorded in the marriage registers of all parishes in Wales (or in their absence the bishops' transcripts) for the period 1813 to 1837. There were a number of reasons for deciding on this, namely:

- it was a manageable period, yet long enough to cover the majority of a single generation
- each record would provide two surnames
- to contract a legally recognised marriage during this period it was necessary to be married in the parish church, the only exception to this being marriages of Quakers or Jews. As a result, Church of England marriage registers can be considered to be a reasonably complete record of all marriages within the population, irrespective of the religious persuasion of the individuals involved

- the introduction of new-style baptismal and burial registers in 1813 had resulted in all registers being better kept and their survival rate thereafter is dramatically improved in most areas compared with earlier periods
- we had already worked on marriage registers for this period for a significant area of south-west Wales (mainly Cardiganshire, Pembrokeshire and parts of Carmarthenshire) and we had a substantial body of information readily available to us
- others (both individuals and organised groups) were known to be working on marriage registers for this period for other areas and it was hoped that we might be able to obtain surname information from them.

By far the most important reason for deciding on this period, however, was the fact that it was sufficiently late for settled surnames to be the norm in almost every part of Wales. The results of some preliminary work by us on the transition from the patronymic naming-system to settled surnames within the heartland of Wales (where the patronymic system can be expected to have survived longest) has been given in Fig. 3-1. This shows that the transition had largely been completed by the early years of the nineteenth century. Further, the style for recording baptisms and burials (which also changed in 1813) was based on the recording of surnames and this would undoubtedly have influenced the way in which names were recorded in marriage registers as well.

Collecting the data

Our hope that we might have access to transcription work which had been done by others was only partly realised. The Gwynedd Family History Society had transcribed and indexed the marriage registers (1813-37) for the counties of Anglesey, Caernarfonshire and Merionethshire and the indexes (on microfiche) were available for purchase.[2] In addition, as a result of the sterling work of one person, many of the parishes of Monmouthshire (the second most populous county in Wales) had also been covered.[3]

From this point, we were unable to have access to other bodies of information, although our requirements were essentially statistical and academic, and not commercial. As a result, we extracted the remaining information (Cardiganshire and Pembrokeshire already having been completed by us) from those parish registers which were at the National Library of Wales, Aberystwyth. Where the registers were on deposit elsewhere or have not survived, we used the bishops' transcripts. In the case of the detached part of Flintshire it was not possible to obtain any information as both the parish registers and the bishops' transcripts are on deposit in various locations outside Wales. This is the only area of Wales not covered by our survey.

39

The scale of the study

Work by others in an English context had indicated that marriages usually occurred at a rate of between 5 and 10 per 1000 population per annum.[4] Taking the average population of Wales (the detached part of Flintshire excluded) over the period 1813-37 suggested that our survey would yield between 200,000 and 400,000 surnames (from between 100,000 and 200,000 marriages). Because of this we reluctantly accepted that we would have to confine ourselves to collecting surnames alone in all our new survey work if it were to be completed within a reasonable amount of time. We only departed from this where we wanted to carry out local tests on characteristics such as the rate of out-of-parish and out-of-hundred marriage partners. Even so it took nearly two years to collect the outstanding data.

When the collection of data had been completed we found it had yielded a total of 135,880 marriages and 271,591 surnames. The fact that the latter figure is less than twice the former has come about because in a few instances no surname had been recorded for one of the partners.

Sample size

Because the population in different parts of Wales was varying in a complex way during this period – as a result of births and deaths, as well as migration and significant in-migration – it is difficult to determine what size of sample these records represent. However, it is probably between 30% and 40%, which is large enough to ensure that the surnames recorded in an area are likely to be representative of the pool of surnames actually present in that area. Also the period (24½ years) should have captured the majority of a single generation (normally taken to be about 25-30 years). Clearly, incidental names which may have only a fleeting association with Wales, or those which were only moving in during this period, may not have been captured.

Analysing the data

The use of parish registers or bishops' transcripts meant that all the surname information was collected by parish and it was necessary to aggregate this in some way in order to avoid the idiosyncrasies (of spelling or inadequate recording) which could occur at the parish level. At the same time, however, it was necessary to avoid too great an aggregation (as had been the case with Guppy's work) which could mask genuine local variations.

The unit we chose as being particularly suitable for this aggregation was the old administrative hundred, of which there were 89 covering the whole of Wales (see Fig. 4-1 and Appendix A). Apart from *seeming* to be about the right size, hundreds have the merit that they are the basis for much of the population

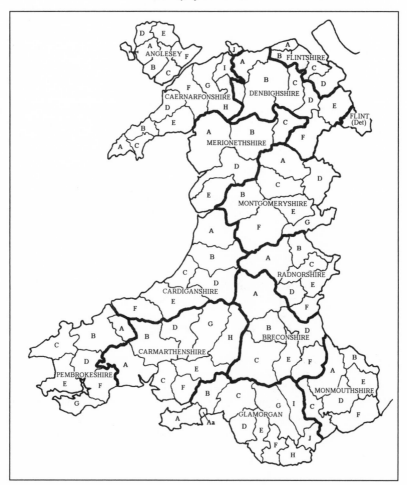

Fig. 4-1: The Administrative Hundreds of Wales (see also Appendix A)

information in the early nineteenth century censuses and, unlike registration districts (which we might have chosen), they largely respect county boundaries.

However, it was necessary to ensure by some more objective measure that such areas did not merely *seem* right, but *were* right. It was necessary to ensure, for example, that the stock of surnames within such an area would be typical of the indigenous names within its boundaries and would not be significantly distorted by an outside influence, and a simple test was carried out for this.

Three sample hundreds were taken and analysed to identify the proportion of out-of-parish partners who were (a) from within the same hundred, and (b) from a different hundred. If a significant percentage (say 30%) of marriage partners in a given area came from outside the hundred in which the marriage took place, we felt that the pattern of names within that area would begin to become as representative of other areas as the one under consideration. The areas chosen for this test were the Upper Division of Wentloog (Monmouthshire), the Lower Division of Ilar (Cardiganshire) and Isgwyrfai (Caernarfonshire). They were chosen partly for their geographical spread across Wales, but also because they had very different types of population.

In the period 1813-37 Wentloog Upper was located between the developing towns of Cardiff and Newport (St Woolos), which were in separate, but adjacent, hundreds. It was also immediately south of the rapidly expanding industrial parishes in Wentloog Lower which, for this particular exercise, was taken to be a separate hundred. As such it was an area which could be expected to have been subject to considerable external influence.

Ilar Lower on the other hand was a predominantly rural area on the west coast of Cardiganshire with no strong centres of population. The hundreds which surround it were all similar in character.

Unlike the other two, Isgwyrfai has two strong centres of population within its boundaries – Bangor and Caernarfon. Bangor is not only a cathedral city but is also the main crossing point (of the Menai Straits) for Anglesey, and has long been a focus for activity over a wide area. Much the same may be said about the castle stronghold and seafaring centre of Caernarfon (Llanbeblig). Both towns had significant populations within a Welsh context in the early part of the nineteenth century when, for example, the 1841 Census gives the population of the city of Bangor as 7232, while that for the borough of Caernarfon was 8001.

Bearing in mind their very different contexts, it is interesting that all three hundreds show virtually identical characteristics in relation to out-of-parish and out-of-hundred partners. This is shown in Fig. 4-2, from which it can be seen that approximately 90% of those marrying in each hundred came from within their boundaries.

Hundred	Total No. of Marriage Partners	Persons Out-of-parish but in-hundred	Out-of-parish and out-of-hundred
Wentloog Lower	718	75 (10.45%)	86 (11.90%)
Ilar Lower	2434	318 (13.06%)	248 (10.19%)
Isgwyrfai	6322	712 (11.26%)	627 (9.92%)

Fig. 4-2: Out-of-parish and out-of-hundred marriages for selected hundreds

As a result of this test, we feel confident that taking the hundred as the basic area gives a pattern of surnames which is representative of that area.

Results from the survey

The main purpose of our survey was to identify all the names which occurred in each hundred, together with their incidence. From this, variations in the spread and concentration of different names could be identified. In turn this can be used – for all but the most common of surnames – to suggest possible areas in which to search for that elusive ancestor. However, it will be shown in Chapter 6 that a knowledge of the incidence of even the most common of surnames can be used to similar advantage in certain circumstances.

The survey showed that, in the period 1813-37, a small number of surnames could be found throughout Wales, a somewhat larger number were only occasionally absent, while a similar number had a strong regional presence which readily identified them with a particular part of Wales. Thereafter, a few surnames had a strong local presence, but the vast majority of individual surnames occurred only infrequently (often only a single occurrence within a hundred) and could not be considered as 'having a presence', even at this relatively local level.

In order to identify a list of surnames which it would be useful to comment on regarding their presence in an area it was necessary to decide on a level of occurrence below which a name might reasonably be considered as largely incidental to an area. The level set for this – more by instinct than any attempt at calculation – was seven occurrences of a surname per 1000 occurrences of all surnames; or, put another way, a rate of 0.7%. Above this level it is useful to rank surnames broadly in line with the description outlined above. Those ranks are (the percentages quoted relate to the whole of Wales):

I   Surnames found throughout Wales, with an overall incidence (i.e. across Wales) greater than 2.5%. There are 10 surnames within this category – Davies (7.09%), Evans (5.46%), Griffiths (2.58%), Hughes (2.98%), Jones (13.84%), Lewis (2.97%), Morgan (2.63%), Roberts (3.69%), Thomas (5.70%) and Williams (8.91%).

II   Surnames which are only occasionally absent, with an overall incidence of between 0.7% and 2.5%. There are 11 surnames within this category – Edwards (1.97%), James (1.51%), Lloyd (1.19%), Morris (1.26%), Owen (2.08%), Parry (1.08%), Phillips (1.18%), Powell (0.73%), Price (1.35%), Rees (1.83%) and Richards (1.26%).

III   Surnames with a strong regional presence (that is they are absent from many areas) and with an overall incidence greater than 0.3%. There are 15 surnames in this category – Bevan (0.30%), Bowen (0.45%), David (0.99%), Ellis (0.44%), Harris (0.87%), Hopkins (0.32%), Howells (0.62%), Humphreys (0.45%), Jenkins (1.48%), John (0.86%), Llewelyn (0.37%), Pritchard (0.68%), Pugh (0.39%), Rowlands (0.56%) and Watkins (0.57%).

IV   Surnames with a strong regional or local presence (locally greater than 0.7%) but with low overall incidence. There are 23 names in this category – Allen (0.08%), Arthur (0.06%), Ashton (0.02%), Austin (0.02%), Bennett (0.08%), Beynon (0.17%), Breese (0.05%), Brown (0.14%), Daniel (0.25%), Edmunds (0.18%), Foulkes (0.16%), Francis (0.27%), George (0.28%), Harry (0.15%), Havard (0.07%), Herbert (0.09%), Matthews (0.24%), Prosser (0.20%), Prothero (0.12%), Rogers (0.29%), Smith (0.21%), Stephens (0.23%) and Vaughan (0.27%).

Below this threshold certain surnames may usefully be ranked in two further categories, namely:

V   Surnames having a purely local presence and usually in a significant concentration (greater than 0.7%) in only a single hundred. There are 57 names in this category.

VI   Other names of predominantly local interest but never found in significant concentrations (i.e. always less than 0.7%). There are 137 names in this category.

All the surnames ranked in this way (a total of 253 names) have been included in the Glossary given in Chapter 5.

Beyond these rankings lies a large number of unranked surnames (there are more than 2000 in Glamorgan alone), many of which occur only a handful of times throughout the whole of Wales.

Results relating to some specific surnames

Consideration of the survey results relating to a selection of names from the six rankings described above will help to illustrate the basis on which the comments which are contained in the Glossary have been made. The surnames selected have been chosen to illustrate the variations in the levels of occurrence and range of distribution which we have found to occur.

JONES: (See Fig. 4-3) As one might expect – both by reputation and by casual observance – this surname is by far the most common one in Wales, and in the early part of the nineteenth century (1813-37) was held by 13.84% of the population. However, this overall percentage, whilst high even by Welsh standards, masks the fact that in parts of north Wales the incidence can be in excess of 30% yet in parts of south Wales it can be as low as 1% .

It can be seen from Fig. 4-3 that, apart from north Wales, this surname is also strong in mid Cardiganshire, while the lowest concentrations are to be found in Pembrokeshire, Gower and the Vale of Glamorgan. Along the English border the percentage occurrence is quite high, ranging progressively upwards from Monmouthshire (Skenfrith, 6.75%) to Denbighshire (Chirk, 20.99%). These figures would lead one to expect the name to have a significant presence in the border counties within England, and so it proves. Guppy, for example, identified occurrences of the surname within these counties as follows: Gloucestershire, 1.05%; Herefordshire, 3.50%; Shropshire 5.00%; and Cheshire, 0.81%. These percentages may be compared with the incidence he found for the surname Smith in those same counties, namely: 2.70%, 1.60%, 0.50% and 0.56% respectively.

WILLIAMS: (See Fig. 4-4) This surname also has its greatest concentrations in north Wales and on the Llŷn peninsula of Caernarfonshire in particular. The surname also has a significant presence in south-east Wales centred on south Breconshire. The average incidence of the surname over the whole of Wales is 8.91%, within the range of 3% to 22%.

The surnames Hughes (2.98%) and Owen (2.08%) exhibit broadly the same distribution pattern but their areas of concentration are confined to north Wales.

DAVIES: (See Fig. 4-5) This name has an average incidence across Wales of 7.09%. The heartland of the name is mid Cardiganshire but it takes in much of the remainder of Cardiganshire as well as large areas of Breconshire and north Carmarthenshire. Outside this heartland the areas of least incidence are the anglicised areas of south Wales and, in direct contrast, the intensely Welsh areas of north Wales.

THOMAS: (See Fig. 4-6) This is very much a surname of south Wales where it has a general incidence in the range 5% to 13%. The only exception to this is Monmouthshire where the incidence is generally well below 5%. The average incidence across Wales is 5.70%.

EDWARDS: (Fig. 4-7) This surname is typical of a number of surnames which are found throughout Wales with few, if any, areas of concentration. It has an average incidence across Wales of 1.97%.

Other names exhibiting a similar distribution are Griffiths (2.58%), Morris (1.26%) and Richards (1.26%).

ROBERTS: (Fig. 4-8) This figure clearly illustrates how much a name of north Wales it is. Concentrations of 10-15% throughout much of Caernarfonshire, Denbighshire and Merionethshire are in marked contrast to levels below 0.7% in much of south Wales. The average incidence across Wales is 3.69%.

Other surnames with similar distributions are: Humphreys (0.45%) and Ellis (0.44%).

REES: (See Fig. 4-9) This surname is found throughout south Wales and has its greatest concentration on the Carmarthenshire/Glamorgan boundary. It becomes increasingly less common as one moves northwards and eastwards until it becomes absent from many parts of north Wales. It has an average incidence across Wales of 1.83%. The following surnames all have broadly similar distributions: Howells (0.62%, no concentration), James (average 1.51%, main concentration on the Cardiganshire/Pembrokeshire border), Jenkins (1.48%, Glamorgan and Cardiganshire), Phillips (1.18%, no concentration) and Watkins (0.57%, no concentration).

PRICE: (See Fig. 4-10) The distribution of this surname is typical of the many *ap* names – such as Powell, Probert, Prosser, Prothero/Prydderch, etc – which are prominent on the border between mid Wales and the English areas of Herefordshire and south Shropshire. The surname Price is, however, found in significantly greater concentrations than is the case with these other names. The overall incidence is 1.35% and it has its greatest incidence on the Breconshire/ Radnorshire border.

DAVID: (See Fig. 4-11) The survival of the given name David, as a surname without transition into the more familiar form Davies, is largely confined to Carmarthenshire, south Cardiganshire, north Pembrokeshire and the Vale of Glamorgan. It has an overall incidence of 0.99%. The surname John (0.86%) also survives without transition into Jones in almost exactly the same area.

HOPKINS (See Fig. 4-12) A surname with a significant incidence only in Glamorgan and the Usk area of Monmouthshire. Elsewhere it occurs only spasmodically and in generally low concentrations. It has an average incidence of 0.32%. The occurrence of the name is typical of those surnames which have a presence which is greater than local, but which is more local than regional.

Other surnames showing this type of distribution/concentration are Mathias (Pembrokeshire), Pierce (Denbighshire), Foulkes (Denbighshire/Flintshire), Hamer (Montgomeryshire/Radnorshire), Probert (Radnorshire/Breconshire) and Prosser (Breconshire/Radnorshire/Monmouthshire).

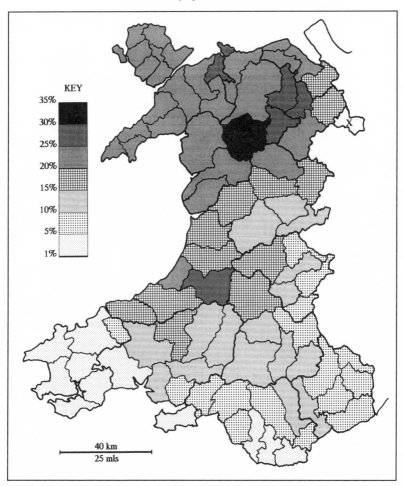

Fig. 4-3: Distribution and incidence of the Surname JONES
Maximum incidence – Merionethshire, Penllyn, 30.71%
Minimum incidence – Pembrokeshire, Dewisland 1.06%

47

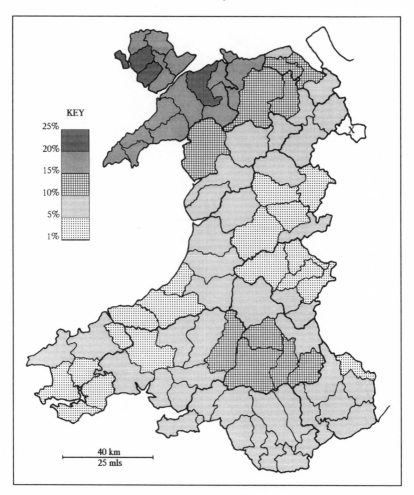

Fig. 4-4: Distribution and incidence of the Surname WILLIAMS
Maximum incidence – Caernarfonshire, Uchaf 22.50%
Minimum incidence – Radnorshire, Cefnllys 2.82%

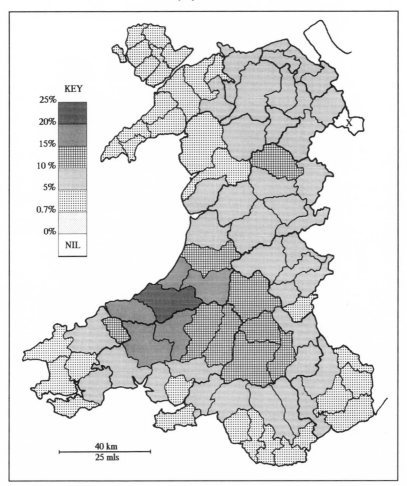

Fig. 4-5: Distribution and incidence of the surname DAVIES
Maximum incidence – Cardiganshire, Moyddin 22.48%
Minimum incidence – Anglesey, Talybolion 0.70%

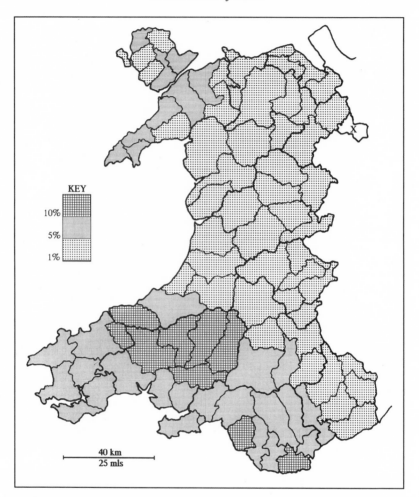

Fig. 4-6: Distribution and incidence of the surname THOMAS
Maximum incidence – Carmarthenshire, Cathinog 12.56%
Minimum incidence – Denbighshire, Maelor Bromfield 1.00%

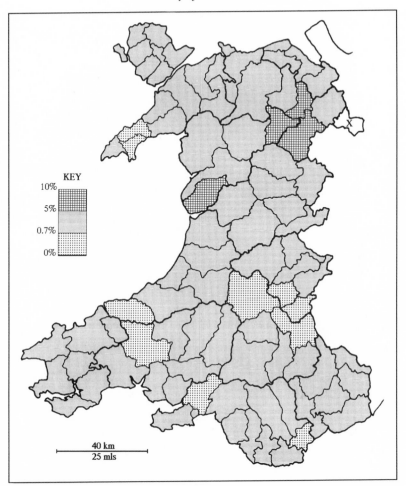

Fig. 4-7: Distribution and incidence of the surname EDWARDS
Maximum incidence – Denbighshire, Chirk 6.44%
Minimum incidence – Radnorshire, Colwyn 3.00%

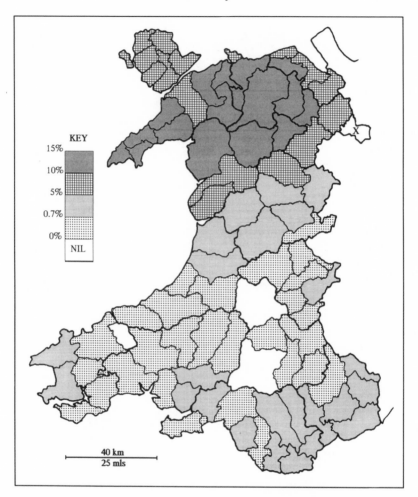

**Fig. 4-8: Distribution and incidence of the surname ROBERTS
Maximum incidence – Denbighshire, Isaled 14.87%**

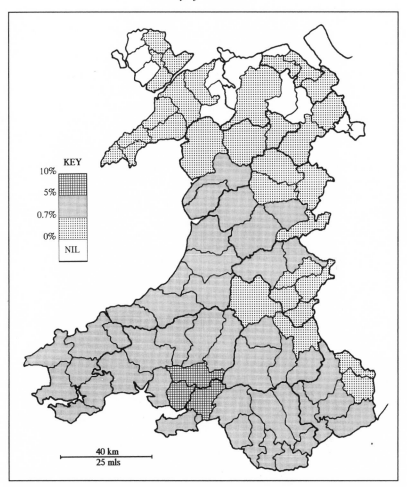

Fig. 4-9: Distribution and incidence of the surname REES
Maximum incidence – Glamorgan, Llangyfelach 6.18%

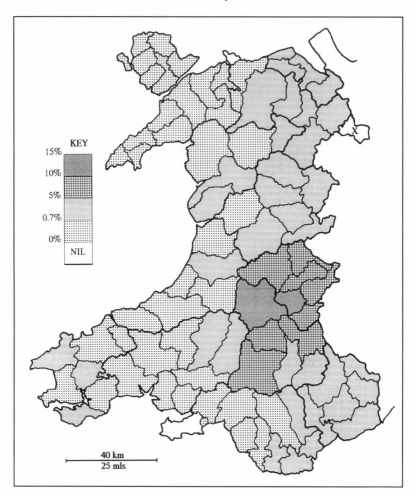

Fig. 4-10: Distribution and incidence of the surname PRICE
Maximum incidence – Radnorshire, Colwyn 12.19%

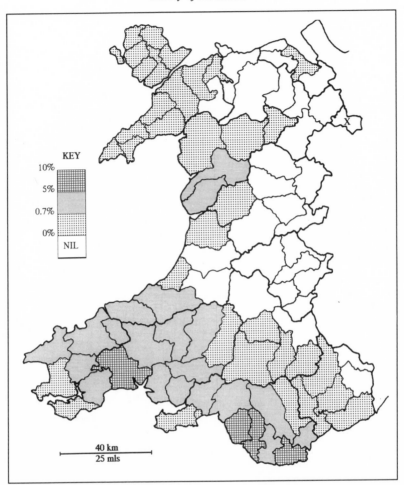

Fig. 4-11: Distribution and incidence of the surname DAVID
Maximum incidence – Glamorgan, Newcastle 7.98%

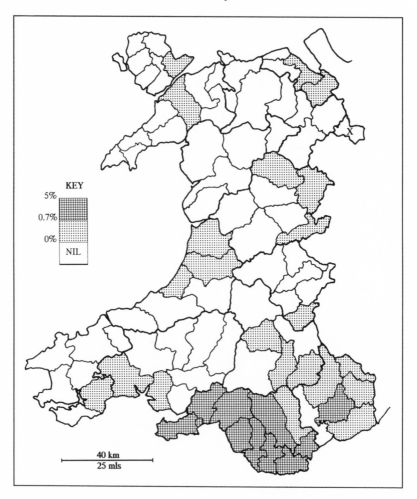

Fig. 4-12: Distribution and incidence of the surname HOPKINS
Maximum incidence – Glamorgan, Ogmore 3.27%

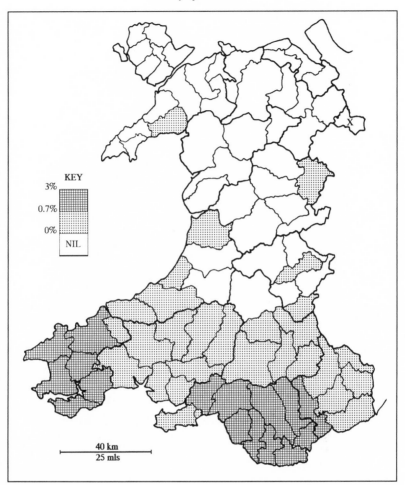

Fig. 4-13: Distribution and incidence of the surname LLEWELYN
Maximum incidence – Glamorgan, Dinas Powis 2.88%

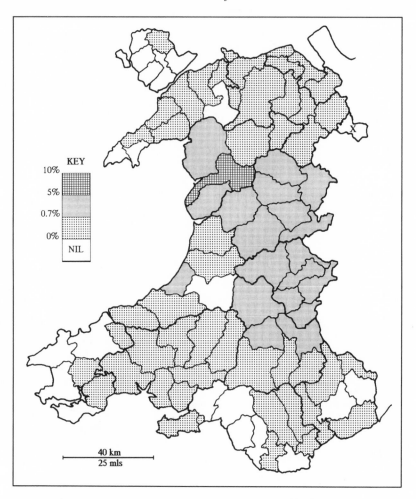

Fig. 4-14: Distribution and incidence of the surname PUGH
Maximum incidence – Merionethshire, Talpont 5.43%

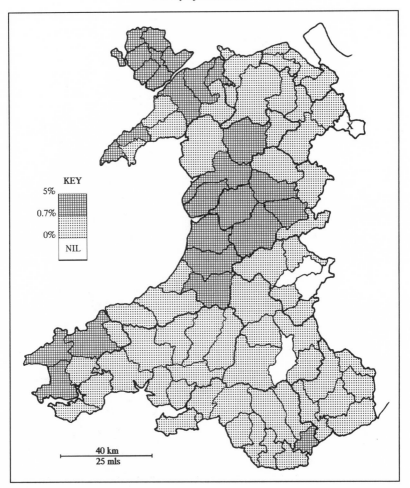

Fig. 4-15: Distribution and incidence of the surname ROWLANDS
Maximum incidence – Montgomeryshire, Cyfeiliog 3.25%

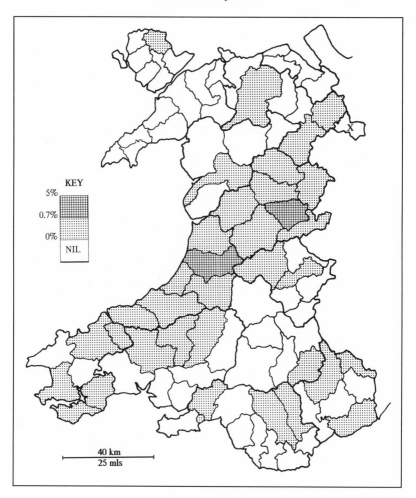

Fig. 4-16: Distribution and incidence of the surname OLIVER
Maximum incidence – Cardiganshire, Ilar Upper 0.79%

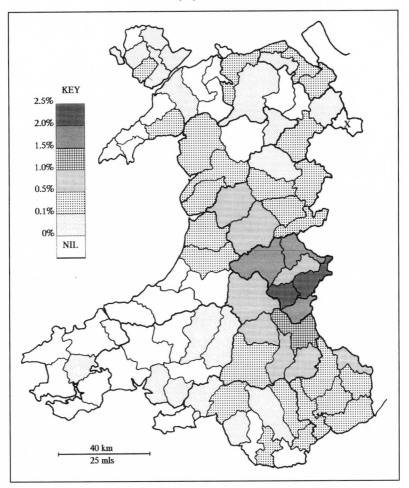

Fig. 4-17: Distribution and incidence of the surname MEREDITH
Maximum incidence – Radnorshire, Radnor 2.38%

61

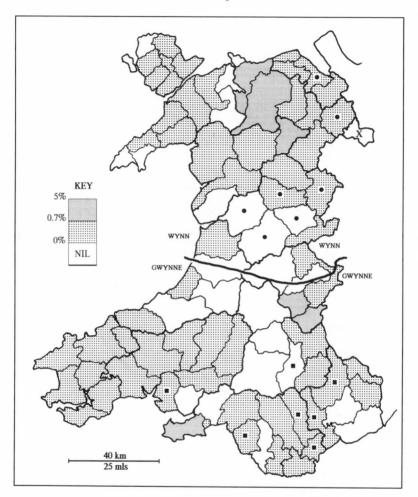

Fig. 4-18: Distribution and incidence of the surname GWYNNE/WYNN
Maximum incidence (GWYNNE) – Radnorshire, Painscastle 0.91%
Maximum incidence (WYNN) – Denbighshire, Isdulas 1.87%

■ Incidence of the surname Gwynne in the north (<0.19%)
● Incidence of the surname Wynn(e) in the south (<0.11%)

LLEWELYN: (See Fig. 4-13) A surname which is largely confined to the southernmost part of south Wales and in particular Pembrokeshire and Glamorgan. It has an average incidence of 0.37%.

PUGH: (See Fig. 4-14) This surname is prominent within the central area of Wales but is absent from peripheral areas such as Anglesey, western Caernarfonshire, Pembrokeshire and the coastal hundreds of Glamorgan. It has an overall incidence of 0.39%.

The distribution is also exhibited by the surnames Rogers (0.29%) and Vaughan (0.27%).

ROWLANDS: (See Fig. 4-15) Found throughout Wales it has its main concentrations on Anglesey, in mid-Wales and in Pembrokeshire. It has an average incidence of 0.56% and its general distribution is typical of that shown by Matthews (0.24%), Pritchard (0.68%) and Parry (1.08%).

OLIVER: (See Fig. 4-16) The distribution of the surname Oliver exhibits a clearly identifiable pattern for which we have no ready explanation. That it should be found consistently along a diagonal line across Wales, stretching from Pembrokeshire in the south-west to the southernmost part of Denbighshire in the north-east, does not reflect any obvious social, cultural or religious axis. It does not, for example, reflect a tendency towards surviving forms of nonconformity which have their roots in early Puritanism (such as the Baptists and Independents), whose adherents might have been influenced by Oliver Cromwell at the time when settled surnames were beginning to be taken. Certainly for much of the area in which the surname exists, Methodism – with its roots in the Established Church and for whose adherents the convictions and actions of such as Oliver Cromwell would have been total anathema – was the predominant denomination by the early nineteenth century.

MEREDITH: (See Fig. 4-17) The distribution of the surname Meredith, like the surname Oliver, has a clearly defined pattern for which we have no ready explanation. As can be seen from Fig. 4-17, it is found along an axis stretching from north-west Merionethshire to south-east Monmouthshire. However, unlike the surname Oliver which occurs with a fairly even incidence along its axis, the surname Meredith has a significant area of concentration in south Radnorshire (greater than 2%), with the level of incidence decaying as one moves outwards (in both directions) along the axis. This would tend to suggest an axis of migration and, while movement towards the developing industrial areas of Monmouthshire would explain the southern part of the axis, there are no immediately obvious geographical or economic characteristics to explain any movement in a north-western direction. Indeed, it is the symmetry of the overall axis about the point of concentration which is most puzzling, albeit that it is a characteristic shared with other surnames such as Jarman (centred on north Radnorshire) and Mills (south Montgomeryshire).

GWYNNE/WYNN(E): (See Fig. 4-18) These two versions of the name commonly given to those who were fair of hair or complexion would normally be taken together if it were not for their almost totally separate regional occurrence. It can be seen that, whereas the surname Gwynne (0.07%) is found fairly consistently across south Wales, it is rarely found to the north of a line through the mid-Wales hundreds of Ilar (Cardiganshire), Rhaeadr and Cefnllys (both Radnorshire). Wynne (0.11%) on the other hand exhibits the opposite characteristic in relation to that same line.

The work of P.C. Bartrum

Peter Clement Bartrum's extensive work on early Welsh genealogies was often consulted in the course of our research. Here we must refer specifically to his work on personal names found in fifteenth century Welsh pedigrees (Bartrum, 1981), in which the author found that there were 'very distinct preferences for certain personal names' in the different regions of Wales. The names belong to a particular class, those who appear in pedigrees, the *uchelwyr* or land-owning gentry. With this limitation in mind, we still consider that the tables of names and their distribution provide a rare clue to the names in use by a substantial section of the Welsh population, for such people were 'not necessarily wealthy' – the result of the division of their inherited lands and the relative poorness of the countryside.

Modern Welsh surnames have evolved from many of the names current during that period, though we cannot, of course, assume any direct connection: for example, modern families called Howells, Thomas or Williams could not normally expect to be able to prove their descent from a fifteenth century man called Hywel, Thomas or William. Nevertheless, this most useful statistical work provides, we believe, evidence which may explain – in many but not all cases – regional variations in surname-distribution. We should emphasise that the work covers far more names than those quoted herein. We have used these figures only in appropriate Glossary entries (Chapter 5). Many men's names listed in Bartrum have not apparently given rise to a surname or, at least, if so they have not crossed our path. In addition, the women's names in the fifteenth century list are barely treated in this book.

Bartrum's work is based on mediaeval divisions of Wales as follows: Caernarvonshire & Anglesey; Merioneth (except Mawddwy); Rhos & Rhufoniog; Tegeingl & Dyffryn Clwyd; Powys Fadog; Powys Wenwynwyn (including Mawddwy); Deheubarth (Ceredigion, Dyfed & Ystrad Tywi); Rhwng Gwy a Hafren; Brycheiniog; Gwent & Morgannwg (see Fig. 4-19).[5] Figures are

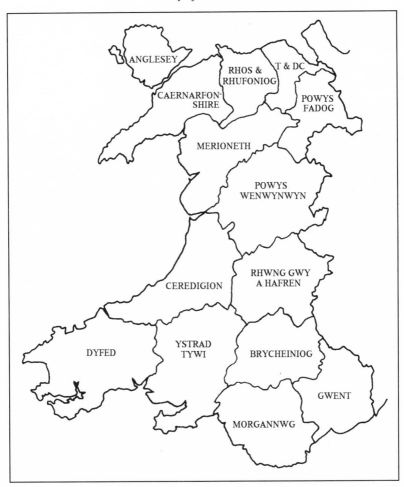

Fig. 4-19: The areas of mediaeval Wales

T & DC denotes Tegeingl and Dyffryn Clwyd
The three areas of Dyfed, Ceredigion and Ystrad Tywi together are often
referred to as Deheubarth

given in percentages generally, but fractions of less than ½% are shown as 'T' if greater than ¼%, or 't' if less than ¼% – we have shown these as >0.25% or <0.25%, to facilitate comparison with other percentages given in this book.

The work of Henry Brougham Guppy

Towards the end of the nineteenth century, Henry Brougham Guppy, a naval surgeon (who also had some skill as a geographer), had been studying topics as widely different in nature as measuring the flow of water in the Yang'tse, the origins of coral islands, and the distribution of names in Great Britain. In 1890 he published *The Homes of Family Names*. It is a measure of the comprehensiveness of his work that, more than a century later, it remains today an important point of reference for more local studies.

Faced with the daunting possibility of having to survey the names of all the population at that time (26 million), Guppy decided that, in order to identify the homes of family names, he would be justified in confining his survey to the names of farmers alone as he considered that they formed the most stay-at-home class in the country, often being tied to an area by inheritance or tenure over many generations. This aspect of Guppy's work has, however, always been the subject of much criticism. Nevertheless, farmers did exist in sufficient numbers (between 1000 and 10,000 per county) to give a reasonable picture of the incidence of the longer-standing names within each county. For his survey he analysed the names of farmers given in Kelly's Post Office Directories and confined himself to recording those names which had an incidence of 7 (or more) per 10,000 of the population within each county or, put another way, an incidence equal to or greater than 0.07%.

On the face of it, Guppy's reasoning seems quite sound and the abiding popularity of his work as a point of reference more than a century later supports this view. However, those with any knowledge of surnames within an English context will know that analysis at county level will mask important characteristics at the more local level. The larger the county, the greater the likelihood that this will occur, and one can only wonder what characteristics lie hidden as a result by, for example, Guppy's decision to combine the North and East Ridings of Yorkshire into a single unit. Furthermore, his treatment of much of Wales can only give rise to even greater fears.

The particular weakness of Guppy's work for the study of surnames in Wales lies in the geographical subdivisions he has used. Monmouthshire he dealt with as if it were an English county, but the rest of Wales has been subdivided into only two areas: North Wales (consisting of Anglesey, Caernarfonshire, Merionethshire, Denbighshire, Flintshire and Montgomeryshire) and South Wales (Breconshire, Cardiganshire, Carmarthenshire, Glamorgan, Pembrokeshire and

Radnorshire). The consequences of this lack of refinement – a characteristic we specifically sought to avoid in our own survey – can be seen quite clearly by considering the distribution within Wales of the interesting surname Meredith. By comparing the distribution which can be derived from our own survey and that given by Guppy we get two quite different pictures.

Guppy records the surname Meredith as being present in the English counties bordering on Wales with an incidence as follows: Gloucestershire, 0.18% (given by Guppy as 18 per 10,000); Herefordshire, 0.61%; and Shropshire, 0.30%. In Wales he found the following: Monmouthshire, 0.26%; North Wales, 0.15%; and South Wales, 0.17%. It would be quite reasonable to infer from these figures that Meredith was an uncommon surname of the English border counties which appears to have made some penetration into Wales.

However, the work we have done gives a wholly different picture. It can be seen quite clearly that Meredith is very much a surname of Radnorshire (the least populous county in Wales), Breconshire and south Montgomeryshire, but it also has a significant presence in a swathe running diagonally across Wales from north-west Merionethshire to south-east Monmouthshire. Locally within Radnorshire (Radnor, 2.38%; Colwyn, 2.16%) it has an incidence which is nearly four times that found by Guppy in Herefordshire. Then again, the incidence of the name locally within Monmouthshire (Skenfrith, 0.55%) is more than twice that recorded by Guppy for the county as a whole. Indeed it is a measure of how significant the surname Meredith is locally that, in the areas of Radnorshire quoted above, it has an incidence which is well in excess of that for the surname Smith generally throughout England (see Fig. 1-1).

Nevertheless, despite these reservations we have found Guppy's work of considerable value and interest in relation to our own work, both as an overall check (in the case of the border counties of Cheshire, Shropshire, Herefordshire and Gloucestershire), but also as an extremely useful indicator of possible lines of migration into and out of Wales. Counties such as Somerset, Cornwall, Devon as well as the southern part of Lancashire have long had a strong association and interaction with Wales. As a result we have frequently quoted figures derived from Guppy's work in the glossary of the surnames of Wales given in the next chapter.

Recent work on the distribution of English surnames

Work on English surnames in the past two decades has helped to establish the essentially regional nature of many English surnames, particularly those based on place-names and on occupations.[6] Such work has been taken a stage further in *The Surname Detective* by Colin D. Rogers, published in late 1995, which includes distribution-maps based on telephone directories for the modern period, seventeenth-century sources and mediaeval sources. The author carried out research into one hundred surnames of varied origin and type as background for his work. Of these names, only four appear in our glossary: Rogers, Smith, Tucker and Weaver. The work is subtitled 'Investigating surname distribution in England, 1086–present day' and deliberately excludes consideration of the rest of Britain. Nevertheless, there are some pointers for research into Welsh surnames, not least because the distribution-maps based on telephone directories include Wales. Unfortunately the use of this method can give rather misleading results (from either a Welsh or an English standpoint) where, for example, the area covered by a directory includes substantial areas in both England and Wales – as is the case with the directory for Chester and North East Wales and also that for Shrewsbury, Hereford and Mid Wales. However, this problem could be overcome by using the new generation of directories (just coming in) which are not so wide-ranging in their coverage. Certainly, we consider that light could be shed by this method on the origins of names believed to have migrated into parts of Wales from the English border counties.

CHAPTER 4: NOTES AND REFERENCES

[1] For example: in Harper & Sunderland (1986), no fewer than seven of the 23 chapters draw on surname studies for the identification of Welshness.

[2] We would like to express our thanks here to the many unknown (and unsung) members of the Gwynedd Family History Society who contributed to making this work available to family historians and others.

[3] We are deeply grateful to David Woolven of Newport for allowing us free access to the indexes of his work on the parish registers of Monmouthshire.

[4] L. Bradley (1978), 64.

[5] See also M. Richards (1969), the standard source of information about all Welsh administrative units, which have inevitably changed over the centuries.

[6] McKinley (1990) summarises this.

CHAPTER 5

GLOSSARY OF SURNAMES

KEY TO THE GLOSSARY

The Glossary follows a standard pattern. First, a short historical and linguistic paragraph about each name. An indication of the existence of earlier work on families is given in many cases. The references are to be found in the list of Abbreviations, and in the References and Select Bibliography. For the most part, the historic counties (pre-1974) are referred to.

Frequently included in the historical paragraph is a reference to the work of P.C. Bartrum on personal names found in fifteenth century Welsh pedigrees (Bartrum, 1981). For an explanation see Chapter 4. The Welsh mediaeval divisions used in Bartrum's work are quoted. Figures are given as percentages.

For many entries, a summary of sources (not intended to be comprehensive) is given in brackets after this paragraph. Where the existence of pedigrees is indicated, the reference should not be taken to refer to *all* families bearing the name.

Following this is a paragraph with the main conclusions from the 1813-37 survey; the rankings are explained in Fig. 5-1.

Notes from Guppy are included where appropriate: i.e. where names are counted in Wales, Guppy's figures (expressed as percentages here, to enable comparisons to be made) are shown in the following list; figures are also given for the English counties along the Welsh border, where they are included; for other English counties we have been more selective, indicating the figures where they seem to us to be relevant. Many names in this Glossary are totally unrepresented in Guppy's work. The order chosen here is: North Wales, South Wales, Monmouthshire; the four border counties of Cheshire, Gloucestershire, Herefordshire, Shropshire; other English counties. For details of Guppy's method, see Chapter 4.

Cross-references between entries are indicated by the use of block capitals.

Rank	Incidence (across Wales)	National	Presence Regional	Local
I	>2.5%	Yes	—	—
II	0.7%-2.5%	Yes	—	—
III	>0.3%	—	Yes	—
IV	Low	—	Yes	Yes
V	Low	—	—	Yes
VI	Very Low	—	—	Yes

Fig. 5-1: The Ranking of Surnames (see also Chapter 4)

ACE This is an English patronymic surname, from the CG personal name *Azo,* OFr *Ace,* (from compound forms beginning *Adal-*) which is found in DB and was still in use in the period when English surnames were forming, but not at the later period of the formation of Welsh surnames. Early examples of its use in Wales are to be found in Radnorshire in 1293 (RadAss). The IGI has Ace in several English counties, including 16C London and 17C north Devon, but the majority of Ace entries, including some 16C, are for Glamorgan – there it may have Devon origins. In HTGlam, Asse is found in Oxwich, Reynoldston and, possibly, Penrice, all in Gower.

1813-37 (V): This name is only found in west Glamorgan. It is particularly strong in Gower (1.64%) but only occasionally found in nearby hundreds.

ADAMS This personal name is biblical in origin, its popularity in England enhanced by med. drama. As a surname, Guppy found it widespread in English counties and it is possible that some examples of the surname in Wales have come from England. But the given name was used also in med. Wales, though it was scarce in 15C (Bartrum, 1981). Its Welsh version, Adda, was rather more popular. Both versions gave rise to Welsh patronymic surnames in due course: Atha/Athoe and Batha/Bathoe (from *ab* + Adda) are to be found in several parts of Wales and in English counties bordering Wales. Adams becomes Baddam/s and even Badham. Athoe appears in south Pembrokeshire, an example of how a spelling closer to the Welsh may be found in anglicised areas, where surnames settled earlier. (Note that Athy has a separate Irish origin.)

(*WG2* xii, re Adams of Paterchurch, Pembrokeshire; Adams of Castleton and Llandaf, Glamorgan; Nicholas.)

1813-37 (VI): A name chiefly found in the counties along the English border and in Pembrokeshire (Rhos 0.64%; Castlemartin 0.63%) where it has greatest prominence. If the variant Atha is included, the incidence rises to 0.76% in Castlemartin.

Guppy: North Wales, 0.15%; Monmouthshire, 0.33%; Gloucestershire, 0.20%; Shropshire, 0.38%. Also: Bather, Batho: Shropshire, 0.20%.

AJAX A classical forename, curiously adopted in one part of Cardiganshire, entering the patronymic pool possibly via a single prolific family.

1813-37 (VI): This name is confined to one area of Cardiganshire (Pennarth, 0.10%) and then only locally in the parish of Llanddewi Brefi.

ALBAN The name of the first British Christian martyr was used occasionally from Tudor times. It seems probable that it entered the patronymic system indirectly as a result of the presence in Pembrokeshire of Alban Stepney or Stepneth of Prendergast, receiver-general of the diocese of St. David's from 1561. The name was taken up among his circle – for example, Alban son of George Owen of Henllys was his nephew and godson. The name spread sparsely through mid and north Pembrokeshire (though not, of course, influencing surnames in those parts of the county where they were already settled), south Cardiganshire and then further afield into Carmarthenshire and Glamorgan. Existing Welsh families with this surname can be traced back to a very small number of individuals bearing Alban as their first name.

1813-37 (VI): Found spasmodically in south Wales, it has a significant incidence in mid Cardiganshire (Ilar Lower, 0.51%).

ALLEN is an English patronymic surname, from Alan, which is actually a British forename re-imported from Brittany at the time of the Norman invasion. It was the 38th most common surname in England and Wales in 1853. Richard Alen (sic) was of Haverford in 1505 (Picton Castle) and the Allens were well-established in Pembrokeshire in Tudor times, when John Allen of Newton, p. Llanstadwell (*fl.*1555) first appears as ancestor of Allen of Rickeston, Gelliswick and Cresselly (*LG*). He was not alone, for Thomas Allen of Milton, p. Carew, is listed in 1543 LS. The various branches proliferated throughout the middle and south of the county. In 1670 HTPem, the name is found widely in south Pembrokeshire, but is most numerous in many parishes in Rhos hundred. Some Allens in Flintshire may have emanated from Derbyshire and are thought to descend from two couples marrying in Ysceifiog and Halkyn in early 18C (Ellis, 1994).

(Nicholas.)

1813-37 (IV): Found in many parts of Wales but seldom in significant numbers or to any clear pattern. It is, however, decidedly more common in Pembrokeshire (Narberth 0.71%; Rhos 0.67%) than elsewhere.

Guppy: Cheshire, 0.20%; Gloucestershire, 0.30%; Herefordshire, 0.10%; Shropshire, 0.14%; plus numerous English counties.

ANDREW The name of the first disciple was not a common forename in med. Wales. In 15C it is found in very small traces in south-east Wales and in Powys Fadog (Bartrum, 1981). *WS* found evidence of it in Shropshire PRs, as Bandrew, Bandra, etc.

(*WG2* xii, re Glamorgan.)

1813-37 (VI): Found in several parts of Wales, it is at its strongest in Montgomeryshire (Newtown, 0.64%).

Guppy: Cornwall, 0.43%; Devon, 0.22%.

ANTHONY This is a patronymic taken ultimately from the Roman name *Antonius*, later the name of the 3C saint considered to have founded monasticism. In 15C it is found at <0.25% in Powys and Deheubarth (Bartrum, 1981), and has led to a fairly uncommon family name, usually including the (silent) 'h' which has been added to the 'correct' Antony.

1813-37 (VI): Found mainly in south Wales and also in Merionethshire but never in significant numbers. It has a maximum incidence in Carmarthenshire (Iscennin, 0.42%).

Guppy: South Wales, 0.50%. Guppy writes, 'It has its home ... at Kidwelly'.

ANWYL W adj. name from *annwyl* 'dear, beloved', a common epithet. The authors of *WS* believe that it must have had the additional sense of 'favourite child' in north Wales to make it a 'fixed epithet', thus developing into a surname in this region. The name may appear under various spellings in earlier registers, e.g. Anwell, Anwill, as well as Annoil (reflecting the W diphthong *wy*).

(Dwnn, Griffith, Nicholas.)

1813-37 (VI): A name which is confined almost exclusively to north Wales where it is found to no discernible pattern or in any significant concentration (Flintshire, Rhuddlan 0.18%; Merionethshire, Estimaner 0.15%; Montgomeryshire, Cyfeiliog 0.15%).

ARTHUR would appear to be a straightforward patronymic surname. However, it is worth noting that Arthur was a rare first name in Wales for many centuries after the British hero is thought to have lived (*c.*6C – see *DWB*). Bartrum (1965) suggests an element of superstition about the use of the name during that period. It was used by Henry VII for his eldest son, perhaps reviving Welsh interest for it must have been used again in time to form the patronymic surname: for instance, in 1574 Arthur ap Morys appears in the Mgy Muster in Newtown hundred. Some families of this name may have originated in England, perhaps especially from Somerset (Doddrell) or Cornwall (White).

(*WG2* xii.)

1813-37 (IV): Found in many parts of Wales but seldom in significant numbers and never to any clear pattern. A local concentration in Glamorgan (Ogmore 0.70%) is more than twice its occurrence elsewhere.

Guppy: Monmouthshire, 0.22%; Cornwall, 0.19%.

ASHTON There are places of this name in many English counties, including Cheshire, Lancashire and Gloucestershire. One Derbyshire family, with lead-mining connections, is the subject of Madge (1995). The surname is found in Trefeglwys in early 17C (E.R. Morris, 1982) and proliferated throughout Montgomeryshire. Charles Ashton and John Ashton (19C) have entries in *DWB*.

1813-37 (IV): Chiefly found in Montgomeryshire and north Radnorshire, it is only found incidentally in other parts of Wales. Its only concentration is in the Llanidloes hundred (0.83%).

Guppy: Derbyshire, 0.23%; Lancashire, 0.16%.

ASTLEY An English loc. name – there are places called Astley in Lancashire, Shropshire, Warwickshire, Worcestershire and the West Riding of Yorkshire. Three men called Asteley are listed in 1574 Mgy Muster (Llanidloes and Ystrad Marchell hundreds).

(*WG2* xii.)

1813-37 (VI): Virtually confined to Montgomeryshire but in no great concentration (Llanidloes, 0.38%; Newtown, 0.35%).

AUGUSTUS As a forename (from Latin *augustus* 'great, magnificent', attributes of the Roman emperors), this name must have had an exotic ring in rural Wales – it had a brief vogue in 18C England as a result of its use by royalty. It entered the patronymic system late, and in a very small way. *DWB* has an entry for William Augustus, pre-scientific weather forecaster, living at Cil-y-cwm (Carmarthenshire) late 18C, though a single bearer in 18C Llandygwydd, Cardiganshire – Augustus Aaron – may be the forebear of the very small number of people with the surname in south-west Wales (TD; *WM*, New Year Honours List 1995).

1813-37 (VI): A rare surname confined to Cardiganshire and Carmarthenshire. It has a maximum incidence in the former county (Troedyraur, 0.08%).

AUSTIN This is a common English surname, formed from the ME version of Augustine. (It is worth noting the common practice of shortening long forenames in the period of English surname-formation: cf. Benet from Benedict.) There are examples of the use of Austin as a forename in 15C Powys and south-east Wales (Bartrum, 1981). This continued later: for example, Austen ap David appears in Mgy Muster in 1574 (Montgomery hundred). E.R. Morris (1982) refers to Augustine ap Rees (1600), son of Rees ap Lewis of Carno; his son was John ap Austin.

1813-37 (IV): This name is confined to the coastal belt of south Wales (from Carmarthen to Chepstow) and the eastern half of Montgomeryshire. There is a significant concentration in Gower (0.77%).

Guppy: The closest areas to Wales are Derbyshire, 0.06%; Staffordshire, 0.10%.

AWBREY This surname is found in Breconshire shortly after the Conquest, from the Norman family de Alberico or Awbrey which arrived with Bernard de Neufmarché (or Newmarch). The Awbreys of Abercynrig and of Ynyscedwin in the county are well-recorded, becoming 'a substantially Welsh family' (Nicholas). As with so many surnames of similar origin, it proliferated locally and spread into nearby counties. Aubrey is a common variant, while one family became Obray in 19C Pembrokeshire.

(*WG1* xxv, *WG2* xii, Dwnn i; Nicholas.)

1813-37 (VI): A name which is largely confined to south Wales but totally absent from Cardiganshire and Monmouthshire as well as large parts of Carmarthenshire and Pembrokeshire. It has its greatest concentration in Glamorgan (Dinas Powis, 0.47%)

BAMFORD is the name of places in Derbyshire and Lancashire. The former is probably responsible for the appearance of this name, for John Bamford from Derbyshire settled in Llangurig, Montgomeryshire, in 1576. (*WFH*, 67.) Bumford seems to be the most common spelling, and there are also Bampford, Bamforth, Boundford and Bumpford. In 1681 Matthew Bumfort and George Bumfort are listed in Llanllugan (Notitiae). E.R. Morris (1982) describes the name as found in Llanwyddelan and Tregynon [and] still extant in Trefeglwys and Llanfair Caereinion.

1813-37 (V): A name which is largely confined to Montgomeryshire (Newtown 0.93%; Kerry 0.81%) and only found incidentally elsewhere. The spelling is confined to Bamford, Bumford, Boumford and Bounford during this period.

Guppy: Bamford: Lancashire, 0.12%.

BASKERVILLE This surname has a long history on the border between England and Wales, having arrived in England at the time of the Norman Conquest (from Boscherville, Eure). The Baskervilles of Aberedw, Radnorshire, connected with the Herefordshire family of the same name, are well-documented, though the sprinkling of examples in our survey may well have come in later from (e.g.) Herefordshire parishes rather than have a direct link with this family. In common with several names of this type, it has often been anglicised by replacing, e.g. 'ville' with a more familiar word, producing Basketfield, etc.

(Dwnn i, Nicholas, *WG1* xxv, *WG2* xii.)

1813-37 (VI): Found in very small numbers in Glamorgan (Newcastle 0.03%) and Monmouthshire.

Guppy: Cheshire, 0.14%; Staffordshire, 0.12%.

BATEMAN A derivative of Bartholomew through a pet form Bate or Batte; the suffix '-man' indicates 'servant of'; Bateman was used early as a given name (Reaney, 1980) – this refers to England but would apply equally to Pembrokeshire, where there are numerous med. references to aldermen, mercers, etc, of this name in Haverfordwest (H. Owen, 1911-18, index). The name was quite numerous in the county in early modern times and still remains there. (*WG2* xii, Nicholas.)

1813-37 (VI): Strongest in Pembrokeshire (Castlemartin, 0.38%), there are also clusters in Monmouthshire, Denbighshire and Flint.

BAUGH Baugh derives from the W adj. *bach* 'small, little', a tiny word which carries many connotations, e.g. of affection or contempt. The rules of mutation vary in north and south Wales. As a surname, it is rare in Wales itself but is found along the English side of the border; *WS* has several examples where the same person is Bach and Baugh. Robert Baugh, 18C map-maker, a Montgomeryshire man, has an entry in *DWB*. Batch and Beach are other established variants; in all cases they tend to indicate a Welsh person who has taken a surname over the border in England.

1813-37 (VI): Found in small numbers in Denbighshire (Bromfield, 0.05%) Montgomeryshire (Newtown, 0.02%) and in Glamorgan (Swansea 0.08%; Gower 0.05%).

Guppy: Has Bach (see Corrections page) corrected from Back: Shropshire, 0.14%.

BEBB Long associated with Llanbrynmair, Montgomeryshire, where the name is found in 1596, this name has become widespread in mid Wales where there are numerous Bebbs listed in the modern TD (38 residential, 16 business, 1995). It seems likely that it came from the Midlands, possibly from Derbyshire, where there are 17C Bebbs. If so, the surname appears to be a variant of Babb/s and Bibb/s, also numerous there, possibly related to the OE personal name *Bebbe*, which is also found in the place-name Bebbington. The surname Bebb is found widespread in Shropshire from at least 16C (IGI). Bebbs emigrated from Montgomeryshire to the USA and William Bebb (1802-73), Governor of Ohio from 1846 to 1848, was a descendant of one of these families.

1813-37 (V): This name is almost wholly confined to Montgomeryshire where the chief concentrations are in Caereinion (0.79%) and Cyfeiliog (0.69%).

Guppy: North Wales, 0.40%.

BEEDLE Reaney (1961) has many widespread early examples of this name in England – it is probably occ. from ME *bedele*, 'beadle, town crier', or from various places called Bedwell (Essex, Hertfordshire) or Bidwell (Bedfordshire, Northamptonshire, Devon, Somerset).

1813-37 (VI): Local to Montgomeryshire and chiefly concentrated in the Llanidloes hundred (0.68%).

Guppy: (Beedell) Devon, 0.11%.

BELTH This rare surname and its variant Belt are from the Welsh place-name Buallt, now commonly rendered as Builth (cantref or town). Buelth is found early in north Pembrokeshire (LS 1292, Cilgerran), suggesting an origin among the *advenae*. In 17C, Bealth is found in Dungleddy hundred (1613 Muster; 1656 Llawhaden PR; 1670 HTPem). A very small number of Belth/Belt families over the centuries ensured their survival in Pembrokeshire to the present day.

1813-37 (VI): Found only in Pembrokeshire but with very low incidence (Castlemartin, 0.06%).

BENBOW This English surname is from 'bendbow', a nickname for an archer (Reaney, 1995). It is found in London in mid 14C and was fairly numerous in the English midlands, from where it could easily move into Wales. It is found in all parts of Montgomeryshire and, according to one author, all these families have a common ancestor, William Bendbowe, born *c.*1510, of Prees, Shropshire (Benbow, 1983). *WS* quotes a significant example of the use of the name after *ap* – in other words, it was also being used as a forename in Wales (H. Ellis, 1838, 75). The surname is frequently spelled Benbough in records.

1813-37 (VI): Mainly centred in Montgomeryshire (Newtown, 0.39%).

Guppy: Shropshire, 0.12%.

BENGOUGH represents one of a group of adj. names formed from a compound of *pen* 'head' + another adj., in this case *goch* (mutated form of *coch,* 'red'). The name is found in Shropshire and other border counties. A variant found in our survey is Bangough.

1813-37 (VI): Found in small numbers only in south-east Wales (Monmouthshire, Trelleck 0.05%) and north Carmarthenshire (Caio 0.03%).

BENJAMIN This biblical name began to be used in Wales after the Reformation, thereby becoming an occasional patronymic surname, with a Jewish appearance. It was the name of one of the founders of the twelve tribes of Israel (Genesis) and was traditionally given to a son of old age, and so to a youngest or last son. (See also Fig. 6-1.)

1813-37 (VI): Fairly widely spread throughout Wales but never in significant numbers. It has its maximum concentration in Glamorgan (Neath, 0.25%).

BENNETT Benet was the common ME version of the forename Benedict, the name of the 6C saint who founded the eponymous monastic order. As such, it produced a common (46th in 1853) English surname. Nicholas Bennett of

Derbyshire settled in Llangurig, Montgomeryshire, in 1576, and he and others like him may have founded families (*WFH*, 67). As with so many common names, there is more than one possible origin, for Bennet/t was used independently as a forename in Wales, being found in small traces in northern Wales in 15C, and as such entered the Welsh patronymic naming-system (Bartrum, 1981). Of the Gower family, with its long-established surname, GTC (477) writes that the Bennet of Kilfiggin pedigree has at its head 'Sir Benedict or Bennet of Penclawdd in Gower, lord of Kilfiggin, a very apocryphal personage, the reputed father of William Bennet of Gower, 1302-50'.
(*WG2* xii.).

1813-37 (IV): Found throughout Wales largely in those areas which have been most subject to outside influence – Pembrokeshire, west Glamorgan, and along the English border. It has a significant occurrence in Montgomeryshire (Llanidloes 0.80%).

Guppy: South Wales, 0.22%; Cheshire, 0.24%; Gloucestershire, 0.60%; Herefordshire, 0.54%; widespread in other English counties.

BEVAN Formed from ab Evan (see EVANS). Bevans is an illogical development, for the natural outcome of Evan is Evans *or* Bevan. Nevertheless, Bevans is found widely in the English border counties. (See also Fig. 6-3.)
(Nicholas, *WG1* xxv.)

1813-37 (III): A name which is almost totally absent from north Wales and the northern part of mid Wales. It is found in largest numbers in Breconshire/south Radnorshire (generally in the range 1% to 1.7%) with a distinct concentration in west Glamorgan (Gower 4.6%).

Guppy: South Wales, 0.55%; Monmouthshire, 0.66%; Cheshire, 0.09% (commonly as Bevin); Herefordshire, 0.38%; Shropshire, 0.20%. Beavan was found in Herefordshire, 0.42%; Wiltshire, 0.35%.

BEYNON From ab Eynon (see EYNON). Variants include Beinon, Bennion, and also Baynham and Beynam. Bunyan is more problematic: though some instances *may* represent ab Onion (variant of Eynon), it is usually the Bedfordshire surname, already hereditary in 13C (Reaney, 1995). (See also Fig. 6-3.)
(*WG2* xii.)

1813-37 (IV): This name is found generally throughout the whole of south Wales where it co-exists quite happily with Eynon. It has concentrations in west Glamorgan (Gower 3.22%), west Carmarthenshire (Derllys 0.95%), Radnorshire (Painscastle 0.83%) and Pembrokeshire (Dewisland 0.75%).

Guppy: South Wales, 0.27%.

BIDDER This is described (*WS*) as an English occ. surname, from one who was responsible for bidding people to attend, e.g. a wedding-feast. However, this sense of 'bidder' has only late (16C-19C) examples in *OED*. If the surname has an English meaning, then the obsolete usage as in 'bidders and beggars' (Langland, *Piers Plowman*), i.e. those who made a trade of begging, may be relevant, or simply one who commands or orders. The Welsh wedding-custom of bidding is described in T.M. Owen (1959) and in *WFH*, 280. The surname is frequent in the anglicised area of Gower, which *may* support a mixture of English and Welsh origin. However, it does not altogether explain other occasional sightings of the name. Mer LS (1292) has Ieuan ap Budur. The following north Pembrokeshire PR entries may also derive from a patronymic name – 1689 Cilrhedyn: Elizabetha Buddyr buried; 1703 Manordeifi: Thomas Bydder married; 1772 Clydey: George Byddir witness. Byther, which suggests a W pron. of *dd*, is found in Denbighshire (Bromfield hundred) in 1813-37. For Bidders from Gower, GTC 481 has a pedigree of Bidder of Highway, Pennard, the progenitor being Harry Bidder or Byddyr.

1813-37 (V): A name local to west Glamorgan (Gower 0.82%).

BLACKWELL An English loc. name, found in seven counties (Cottle, 1978), but the most significant in the present context is Derbyshire, since a number of Welsh families of the name have been traced back to that county (Ellis, 1994). At least one Blackwell family was in Flintshire in the mid-seventeenth century, when Henry and Ann Blackwell were living in the parish of Ysceifiog. As with other surnames which migrated from Derbyshire, the connection is in lead-mining.

1813-37 (VI): Found incidentally in several parts of Wales. There is a significant concentration in Flintshire (Coleshill 0.66%) and a minor presence in Cardiganshire (Genau'r Glyn 0.15%). Both these areas have had a strong lead-mining tradition.

Guppy: Buckinghamshire, 0.20%; Derbyshire, 0.09%; Gloucestershire, 0.20%.

BLAYNEY One of the rare W loc. names, from *blaenau* 'uplands'; singular *blaen* refers to a river-source and *WS* has early examples of its use as a personal name. Dwnn shows the succession of the family of Gregynog, Montgomeryshire, which took this name: Gruffydd ap Llewelyn Evan Blaeny ap Griffith → Gruffydd ap Evan Blaeney → Evan Lloyd ap Gruffydd → Thomas Evan Lloyd → David Lloyd Blaeney of Tregynon and Edward Blaeney of Maesmawr; from this point the name was passed on consistently. Of the Radnorshire Blaeneys, Thomas (1985) writes: 'This Blayney family was a quite distinct and separate one from the historic and well-documented family of Montgomeryshire and Castle Blayney, Ireland. On the other hand it seems to have been the only other Welsh family ever to have adopted the common topographical term *Blaenau* ... as a patronymic [*sic*] or permanent surname, Blaene, rather than a nickname. In both

cases the name was anglicised in the 16th century as "Blayney" and in both cases the first recorded use of the name was *c.*1400'.
(*WG1* xxv, *WG2* xii, Dwnn i, Nicholas.)
1813-37 (VI): Mainly found in Montgomeryshire. (Newtown, 0.39%).

BONNER is the most usual modern form of ab Ynyr. The W forename *Ynyr*, with the same root as Latin *Honorius*, was found widely in 13C records, but in small traces only in north-west Wales in 15C (Bartrum, 1981). Many of the earlier men who were 'ab Ynyr' must have moved across the border, resulting in numerous Shropshire examples of Bunner, Bunna, Binner, Bunnell and Binnell, quoted extensively in *WS*. However, examples are also found in W records: 1725 John Bynner, Llangynog (St Asaph Probate). The first vowel sound of 'Bynyr', as a 'correct' surname could be spelt, should rhyme with 'son', 'mother', etc, and the letter 'o' has been used similarly in Bonner. Gradually the spelling-pronunciation took over, leading to the present rhyming with 'honour'.
1813-37 (V): Mainly confined to north Cardiganshire where it is local to the Ilar Upper hundred (0.79%).
Guppy: Herefordshire, 0.14%; Surrey, 0.20% – the latter may have an English meaning (Cottle).

BONSALL One of a number of surnames brought into Wales by lead miners from Derbyshire. Thomas Bonsall (later Sir Thomas), of Bakewell in Derbyshire, came to Cardiganshire via the lead mines of Shropshire in the latter part of the 18C. There is a parish of Bonsall a few miles south of Bakewell.
1813-37 (VI): Mainly to be found in small concentrations in north Cardiganshire (Genau'r Glyn 0.21%) and adjacent hundreds. It occurs only incidentally in Pembrokeshire and Monmouthshire.
Guppy: Derbyshire 0.07%; Staffordshire, 0.12%.

BOULTER An English surname, a variant spelling of Bolt and Bolter: an occ. name, from someone who sifts meal (OFr *buletor*) or alternatively from someone who makes bolts.
1813-37 (V): Found only in Radnorshire, it is local to the Cefnllys hundred (1.06%).
Guppy: Worcestershire, 0.14%.

BOUND An English surname, a variant of Bond, from 'bondsman'. Sometimes as Bound it is derived from the Old Danish forename *Bundi*, still in use even after the Norman Conquest (DB). Reaney (1961) has an example of Henry le Bounde 1297 (Hertfordshire). Guppy lists Bounds as peculiar to Herefordshire and the name is numerous there in the modern TD. It is found in Llangurig and Llandinam (Montgomeryshire) in 17C and perhaps earlier in adjacent

Radnorshire parishes (E.R. Morris, 1982). William Bownd, *fl.* 1658, Arminian Baptist with an entry in *DWB,* lived in Llandinam.

1813-37 (V): Mainly to be found in Radnorshire where it is prominent in two hundreds (Cefnllys 0.94%; Rhaeadr 0.87%). It is also found in small numbers in parts of Monmouthshire and Breconshire.

Guppy: (Bounds) Herefordshire, 0.14%.

BOWDLER Of the famous 'censor of Shakespeare' Tyler says, 'The Bowdlers were an old Shropshire family – the Bowdlers of Hope Bowdler, in a village near Church Stretton'. (Thomas Bowdler was born in Bath in 1754 and moved to Swansea in 1811.) A loc. origin from Shropshire would explain the presence of this name in mid Wales.

(*WG1* xxv, *WG2* xii; Dwnn i.)

1813-37 (VI): Strongest in Montgomeryshire (Newtown, 0.48%), it is also found in a few other hundreds bordering on Shropshire.

Guppy: Shropshire, 0.14%.

BOWEN Formed from ab Owen (see OWEN). (See also Fig. 6-3.)

(*WG1* xxv, *WG2* xii, Nicholas, *WWHR* xi.)

1813-37 (III): This surname is widely spread throughout much of Wales but is totally absent from Anglesey, Caernarfonshire, much of Merionethshire and the western half of Denbighshire. It is strongest in Pembrokeshire (Cilgerran 2.24%), along the coast of west Glamorgan (Swansea 1.54%), Carmarthenshire (Carnwallon 2.52%) and also in north Breconshire (Builth 1.46%).

Guppy: South Wales, 0.82%; Herefordshire 0.17%, Shropshire, 0.50%; Worcestershire, 0.14%. (Bown, associated by Guppy with Bowen, has a different origin, being a variant of Bohun, Boon – see Reaney, 1995.)

BRACE W adj. name from *bras* 'fat'. Like several other adj. surnames it has tended to survive in the border areas. 1670 HTPem has three heads of household called Brace in Narberth hundred (Amroth and Lampeter Velfrey).

1813-37 (VI): Found mainly in Pembrokeshire (Narberth, 0.42%) and occasionally in south-east Wales (Radnorshire, Painscastle 0.23%).

BREESE Whether spelled Breese or Breeze (pronounced as the latter), it is not usually reckoned that this is a Welsh name, in spite of its superficial resemblance to derivatives of Rhys/Rees The reason for this is chiefly linguistic: Rhys/Rees should take *ap*, not *ab*, and the final consonantal sound would be sibilant (as in Preece/Price). 'Reeze' is hard to envisage. In addition, if Breese were *ab Rees*, we could expect it to be less local in its distribution. There is a perfectly good English surname, Breese, found in 12C Notts and 13C Norfolk and Yorkshire, formed from OE *breosa* (gadfly) and it seem likely that this found its way into Wales. E.R. Morris (1982) gives early Montgomeryshire examples, centred on

Llanbrynmair (the name is not spelled with 'z' at this period). 1574 Mgy Muster has John Bryse, Machynlleth hundred, John Bryste, Cawrse (Ystrad Marchell) hundred. There are wills of 1586 and 1624 (St Asaph Probate). *DWB* has four Brees/Breese/Breeze entries.

(Griffith, Nicholas.)

1813-37 (IV): A name largely confined to Montgomeryshire with a minor presence in adjacent counties but virtually non-existent elsewhere. It is found most frequently in the Machynlleth (1.61%) and Newtown (0.88%) hundreds.

Guppy: North Wales, 0.50%; Norfolk, 0.15%; Suffolk, 0.07%.

BRIGSTOCKE An English loc. name, from Brigstock, Northamptonshire; variants include Brigstock, Brickstock and Bridgestock. A rare name, with its core area in the east Midlands and the Fens – south Wales is one of the very few other places where it is at all frequent before mid-19C. John Brigstocke, whose immediate ancestors were freeholders at Croydon, Surrey, came to Carmarthenshire in 1626 when he married the daughter of Morris Bowen of Llechdwnni near Kidwelly, and later acquired his father-in-law's substantial property there; his descendants inherited estates in Cardiganshire and remained major landowners in both counties until 20C (F. Jones, 1984). Lewis Brigstocke, who first appears in St Clears, Carmarthenshire, in 1716, is presumably a junior descendant of John, but the connection cannot be proved. A third Brigstock family, perhaps unconnected with these and representing a separate migration from England, was settled in the Monmouthshire valleys by 1761; by 1891 this line had moved into Glamorgan, like the descendants of Lewis. The surname disappeared from the South Wales TD between 1992 and 1993, and may now be extinct there.

1813-37 (VI): Confined to south-west Wales, especially Carmarthenshire (Derllys, 0.16%), and also parts of Monmouthshire.

BROOKS An English loc. surname, meaning someone who lived at the brook. Brooks, together with Brook and Brooke/s, form a very common group of English names.

(*WG1* xxv, *WG2* xii.)

1813-37 (V): Confined to the hundreds along the English border, it is only found sporadically and generally in low numbers. The only concentration of the name is in Flintshire (Prestatyn 0.93%).

Guppy: Cheshire, 0.11%; Herefordshire, 0.17%; Shropshire, 0.12%.

BROWN This is essentially an English surname, the sixth commonest name in England and Wales in 1853. It derives from OE adjective *brun*, referring to hair or skin colour; or from the OE personal name *Brun*, which was not uncommon in England 11–14C. It could have come into Wales from any direction at many different times. In Pembrokeshire it was settled early, appearing in records (as Bron, Broun, Brown, Brun) from the late 13C on. (*WG2* xii.)

1813-37 (IV): Found throughout Wales with the exception of Merionethshire and Cardiganshire. It has a fairly solid presence in Montgomeryshire (Kerry 0.97%, Llanidloes 0.94%) and Radnorshire (Knighton 0.81%). It is also found in significant numbers in one part of Monmouthshire (Raglan 0.71%).

Guppy: South Wales, 0.22%; Monmouthshire, 0.28%; Cheshire, 0.54%; Gloucestershire, 0.30%; Herefordshire, 0.31%; Shropshire, 0.80%; also numerous English counties.

BUFTON An English loc. name, from OE elements meaning 'upon the hill' – Hanks & Hodges (1988) has it as from Bovingdon, Hertfordshire; there are places called Bufton in Cornwall and Leicestershire. It seems probable that the name spread into Wales from Herefordshire, where it is found in some PRs from mid 16C (e.g. Bromyard, near the Worcestershire border). David Bufton the elder, of Llanddewi Ystradenny (Radnorshire), is listed in Brecon Probate in 1633. The surname is particularly numerous in Herefordshire in the modern TD.

1813-37 (V): Confined to Radnorshire and north Breconshire, it is found in significant numbers in the former: (Knighton 1.86%; Cefnllys 1.06%; Radnor 0.93% and Colwyn 0.77%).

BULKELEY 'One of the most powerful families in north Wales' (*DWB*), the Bulkeley family, which had roots in north-east Cheshire, was established in Anglesey before 1450, around which date they were also in Conwy. At the height of their ascendancy they held lands extensively in Anglesey and Caernarfonshire, were involved in politics and were created Irish and (briefly) United Kingdom peers. Many junior branches of the family emerged during this long connection with the area.

(*DWB,* Griffith, *WG2* xii, Dwnn i, Nicholas.)

1813-37 (VI): A surname which is almost totally confined to Anglesey, where it occurs in modest numbers in the Menai hundred (0.36%).

BUTTON As an English surname, this is described as occ., one who makes or sells buttons, or a nickname for one with a wart or other excrescence. In Glamorgan the name is related to one family and its branches, for which GTC has pedigrees (369-371) and in a note describes the 'local' version of its origin. Among others, Sir Thomas Button (d.1634), admiral and explorer, (*DWB*), was son of Miles Button, sheriff of Glamorgan in 1565. Button Gwinnett, one of the signatories of the American Declaration of Independence, was associated with this family (*DAB*).

(*WG1* xxv, *WG2* xii.)

82

1813-37 (VI): Virtually confined to Glamorgan where it has a significant incidence (Gower, 0.68%).

Guppy: Suffolk, 0.26%.

CADDOCK *Cadog* is a W forename, no doubt given in honour of St Cadog (more properly known as St Cadfael) who lived in the mid 5C. It does not appear to have been popular in med. Wales, and may have been taken at an early date into the English border counties, there to become a surname. Caddock formed in the same way as Maddock from Madog; another variant is Caddick.

1813-37 (VI): Wholly confined to central Monmouthshire (Usk, 0.07%).

CADOGAN Cadogan is a W patronymic surname, from the ancient forename *Cadwgan* (which has elements in common with Gwrgan/Wogan – see WOGAN). As a forename it appears in small numbers in 15C pedigrees: in small traces (<0.25%) in Powys Wenwynwyn, Deheubarth and Gwent & Morgannwg, and 1% in Rhwng Gwy a Hafren (Bartrum, 1981). As a surname it is subject to several variant forms, including Carduggan, Cardigan, Gudwgan, even 'KDuggan' (Cosheston PR, Pembrokeshire) and, most notably misleading, Duggan. Though some of the latter may be directly Irish, that many are Welsh may be deduced from their numbers in the border counties (*WS*), and illustrated from Pembrokeshire PRs: 1736, Rhoscrowther, William Carduggan otherwise Duggan, of Pwllcrochan, married; 1737, St Twinnells, Humphrey Dogan married – he is Duggan in later entries. Dogan, the result of the W pronunciation of Cadwgan (with emphasis on the penultimate syllable) is found much earlier still: 1592 Thomas Dogan of Camrose, juror (Charles, 1967, 39).

(*WG2* xii.)

1813-37 (VI): Found only spasmodically across south Wales. It is at its greatest concentration in Glamorgan (Miskin, 0.24%) but is also to be found in limited numbers in Monmouthshire (Usk 0.07%) and Pembrokeshire (Dungleddy 0.07%).

CADWALADER An ancient W forename *Cadwaladr* from elements *cad,* 'leader' and *gadwaldr,* 'battle'. In 15C it is in small numbers in a number of regions, the greatest being 1% in Powys Wenwynwyn (Bartrum, 1981). Cadwaladr was still in use in the surname-formation period and, because of its length, open to much mis-spelling, Coedwallider (1718, PR Llawhaden, Pembrokeshire) perhaps being an extreme example. In some areas, the first syllable drops, leading to Walliter, etc, easily absorbed with Walter.

(*WG1* xxv, *WG2* xii.)

1813-37 (VI): Found mainly in north Wales as far south as Radnorshire. It can be found in modest numbers on the border between Merionethshire (Ardudwy 0.38%; Penllyn 0.32%) and Caernarfonshire (Nant Conwy 0.33%), and also in

Radnorshire (Rhaeadr and Cefnllys both 0.24%). It occurs only sporadically elsewhere in south Wales.

Guppy: Shropshire, 0.17%.

CANTON The earliest roots of this long-settled Pembrokeshire surname are found in Cemais, where it arrived with Anglo-Norman followers of the Martin family. Among the 12C *advenae* was Sir William de Cantington of Eglwyswrw (d.1230), also called Hen Wiliam Caentwn, important enough to marry a daughter of the Lord Rhys (Rhys ap Gruffudd). The name also appears in documents as Canteton, and spellings varied over the next few generations, including Caunton and settling in due course as Canton. Cantington is an English loc. name, and its use in Pembrokeshire should not be confused with Canton in Glamorgan (also briefly in use as a surname), nor with Scolton in Pembrokeshire as has been suggested (P. Morgan, 1990-1, 1995) – Scolton is found as *Scaneton* in an early reference, described by Charles (1992) as probably an error of transcription. The senior lines of this family (which typically of similar ones in the area became quite Welsh) adopted the patronymic system and are to be found represented by 18C in (e.g.) Lloyd of Grove. Junior branches perpetuated the surname, which survived in small numbers to 17C. Sightings over the centuries show the Cantons moving slowly southwards through the county, descendants of the 1670 Coedcanlas (HTPem: Martletwy, Narberth hundred) family by good fortune producing prolific sons at last – their progeny led to a 20C preponderance in the Castlemartin hundred, as far from their first Pembrokeshire home as could be. (*WG1* xxv.)

1813-37 (VI): This surname is only found in the four southernmost hundreds of Pembrokeshire. It occurs most frequently in the Narberth hundred (0.31%).

CHARLES A patronymic surname which does not come from a native Welsh forename. Charles, from Latin *Carolus*, Fr. *Charles* (cognate with OE *ceorl*, 'man') was introduced to England by the Normans but did not become common there until the accession of the Stuart kings. Even so, it is found in 15C Wales, in a small trace (<0.25%) in six areas, from Powys southwards – any such adopted English name might form a characteristic Welsh surname from this base (Bartrum, 1981). The following examples illustrate its patronymic nature: Syr Meredith Charles, Vicar of Mathry, Pembrokeshire, and Brecon, gave his father's name as Charles son of Sion ap Thomas ap Sion o Dre Aberhonddi – on his grandmother's side he was descended from Sir David Gam (Dwnn). Manordeifi 1809: David Charles Owen marries; he signs as David Charles and was often a witness under this name.

1813-37 (V): This is a surname which is found in many parts of Wales but never in significant numbers. It occurs mainly in south Wales where it is at a maximum in Carmarthenshire (Carnwallon 0.63%), but it also features quite strongly in Monmouthshire (Raglan, 0.57%). In north Wales it is mainly found in the area around Bala (Penllyn 0.23%).

CHRISTMAS The feast-name was used first as a given name, undoubtedly for a child (always, it seems, a boy) born on or near Christmas Day. From this origin it became a patronymic surname, early in England, late in Wales. Examples of its use as a forename include Christmas Samuel (1674-1764), Independent minister, born in Llanegwad, Carmarthenshire; Christmas Evans, Welsh preacher, born 25 December 1766 in Llandysul, Cardiganshire (both *DWB*); and less famously Christmas, illegitimate son of Matthew Hugh, baptised on 25 December 1744 in Llanddewi Velfrey, Pembrokeshire.

1813-37 (VI): Found only in south Wales, but with only a low level of incidence. It has its maximum incidence in Carmarthenshire (Caio, 0.12%).

Guppy: References to the name apply only to England.

CLAYTON This name also appears as Cleaton (often pronounced locally Cleeton, but the older pronunciation would have been Clayton, cf. 'great') and Cletton. There are several places called Clayton in Lancashire, as well as in other English counties. 1574 Mgy Muster has Thomas Cleaton in Caus hundred (Ystrad Marchell). E.R. Morris (1982) says it occurs in Llandinam PRs in the 1590s and is found in most of the Arwystli parishes [i.e. Llanidloes hundred]; Reynold was a favourite first name.

(*WG1* xxv, *WG2* xii.)

1813-37 (V): Occurs in a narrow belt across mid Wales from the English border to Cardigan Bay. It is mainly concentrated in Montgomeryshire (Llanidloes 0.83%; Kerry 0.77%).

Guppy: Cheshire, 0.26%; Derbyshire, 0.21%; Lancashire, 0.11%. (Cleeton) Shropshire, 0.12%.

CLEMENT Described as a popular forename in 12C England – it was the name of a disciple of St Paul and used by several popes. Clement was an English surname in 12C, 13C. It appears as a fixed name in some families in Wales but was available to the patronymic pool as well, for Clement is represented in 15C with a small trace in areas of north, south and central Wales (Bartrum, 1981). Later examples include Ieuan ap Llewelyn ap Clement, p. Clydey 1539; Gr' ap Clement, Cilrhedyn 1542-3 (H. Owen, 1911-18, ii).

(*WG1* xxv, *WG2* xii.)

1813-37 (V): Very much a name of west Glamorgan (Gower 0.87%) and east Carmarthenshire (Carnwallon 0.49%), but occasionally found elsewhere in small numbers.

Guppy: South Wales, 0.17%.

CLOCKER This name came into Cardiganshire prior to 1800 with a lead-mining family from Cornwall (*Cornwall FHS Journal*, Dec 1995). Quite separately, the surname Clougher (pron. similarly) appears in south Pembrokeshire in a family of stationers of Irish origin – Clougher is a place in the north of Ireland.

1813-37 (VI): Found only in north Cardiganshire and south Pembrokeshire and then only in very small numbers (Ilar Upper 0.05% and Dungleddy 0.04% respectively).

COLE An English surname, derived from more than one origin (though those which involve Norse words are unlikely to be relevant here). One possibility is as a byname from OE *col*, 'coal' (i.e. swarthy); another is from Col, a diminutive of Nicholas. The surname is especially common in the English West Country, and it may have arrived in the border areas at any time. Perhaps the heartland in Wales was Pembrokeshire, where it has been for many centuries: Fenton says that the Coles came into Cemais with the Martins and that the family branched out under three names, viz., Cole, Younge and Mathias (Fenton 293, 298). Adam Cole was reeve of Haverfordwest 13C, and the name is seen in many med. county documents. The place-names Colston (p. Little Newcastle) and Coleston (p. Walwyns Castle) are evidence of other early individuals (Charles, 1992). In 1670 HTPem, Cole (sometimes Coale) is found throughout the southern hundreds of the county.

(*WG1* xxv, *WG2* xii.)

1813-37 (V): This name is to be found in three quite separate areas namely, north-east Wales, south-east Wales and south-west Wales. The only areas of concentration are in Pembrokeshire (Narberth 0.87%; Castlemartin 0.79%).

Guppy: Gloucestershire, 0.27%; Herefordshire, 0.20%; Devon, 0.70% (Coles, 0.26%); Somerset, 0.20% (Coles, 0.40%).

CONNAH This is the W patronymic name *Cwna*, variously spelled Connah, Cunnah; in its diminutive form *Cwnws* it appears in the adjacent areas of Rhos & Rhufoniog and in Tegeingl & Dyffryn Clwyd in north Wales in small traces (both <25%) in 15C (Bartrum, 1981). The same personal name is found in place-names: e.g. Connah's Quay, Flintshire.

1813-37 (VI): Almost wholly confined to Flintshire (Mold, 0.27%) and a small part of east Denbighshire (Iâl, 0.09%).

COSLETT This name's arrival in Wales can be dated to *c*.1568, when a man named Corslett was brought over from Westphalia to work for the Mineral and Battery Company, whose owners Schutz and Humphrey had a licence from the Queen to make iron wire. Corslett was a smith skilled in making osmond iron, a soft iron need for wire making, and he worked at the forge at Monkswood, near Usk, Monmouthshire, from where the iron was sent to Tintern. His descendant

George Corslett was born *c.*1569 and is named (spelt Coslett) in a list of deponents as a finer of osmond iron in an action between Hanbury and the Exchequer in 1596. Parish records show many Cosletts working at the Machen and Trevethin forges from late 17C to early 19C. They are concentrated in the area bounded by Cardiff, Caerphilly, Trevethin and Newport up to the mid 19C and have a strong connection with the metal industries, though some were in coal mining, agriculture, innkeeping and general trade. The IGI before 1850 shows virtually no examples anywhere else in the UK, with the exception of London. The spellings Coslett and Cosslett are common, while Corslett can still be found in 19C records. Patronyms are entirely absent, but one or two 19C cases of 'Coslett Coslett' occur (*DWB*). Even today this surname is to be found mainly in Gwent and Glamorgan (see TD).

1813-37 (VI): Largely confined to east Glamorgan (Kibbor, 0.30%) and Monmouthshire (Wentloog, 0.22%) but with minor occurrence on the Glamorgan/Carmarthenshire border.

CRADDOCK The spelling reflects the common pron. of the W forename *Caradog* – this name of great antiquity is the same as Latin *Caractacus* from British *Caratacus*. A single example (in south-west Wales) is recorded in 15C pedigrees (Bartrum, 1981). *WS* finds it now fairly numerous as a surname in the English border counties.

(*WG1* xxv, *WG2* xii, Nicholas.)

1813-37 (VI): Confined to Glamorgan (Kibbor, 0.07%).

Guppy: Berkshire, 0.20%; Kent, 0.18%; Oxfordshire, 0.15%.

CROWTHER This surname is not necessarily always W in origin. As a Welsh name it is one of the rare occ. surnames, from *crythor*, a player of the *crwth*, an early fiddle. But essentially the same word is found in ME, *crouthe, croude*, with the same meaning and e.g. Reaney (1980) gives only an English origin, Cottle has it as Lancashire–West Yorkshire, though giving the Welsh etymology. Mer LS (1292) has Edenevet Crouthour, David Crouthur, Griffid Crouthur – none sounds English, though the following Pembrokeshire example does: 1317 John le Crother and Isabel his wife (Charles, 1960). In 1574 Mgy Muster, are listed George and Thomas Crowther (Montgomery hundred).

(*WG2* xii, Dwnn i, re Crowder.)

1813-37 (VI): Almost wholly confined to Radnorshire, it is at its maximum in Cefnllys, 0.47%.

Guppy: Lancashire, 0.08%; Yorkshire West Riding, 0.26%.

CRUNN A W adj. name from *cron*, 'round', added to a man's personal name as an epithet. The name can be detected in an early stage of surname-formation in St David's Probate: 1602 David Thomas Cronne, Letterston, and 1604 Thomas

Harry Crunne of Treflodan. The latter is in p. Whitchurch where it appears in 1613 (Pem Muster) in Whitchurch, Dewsland, under John Thomas Cronne. By 1670 (HTPem) John Crunne is an inhabitant of Dale, and, in 18C, a number of Crunns are found in central and north Pembrokeshire.

1813-37 (VI): Totally confined to Pembrokeshire but never found in significant numbers; maximum Rhos, 0.07%.

CUNNICK This is the main pronunciation-spelling found in our survey – though Cwnic is also present – but the name often appears in other documents, such as PRs, as Connick. It seems probable that it is patronymic from the Welsh forename *Cynog*, the name of a 6C saint (*DWB*), falling into the pattern of similar surnames found on the boundaries of English- and Welsh-speaking areas (e.g. DEVONALD, FOLLAND).

1813-37 (VI): Chiefly confined to the Pembrokeshire/Carmarthenshire border. It is at its maximum in the former county (Dungleddy, 0.32%).

DANIEL The forename of the Old Testament prophet has a Welsh parallel in the form of Deiniol, the name of a 6C saint to whom churches are dedicated in several parts of Wales (which has enhanced Daniel's popularity as a modern forename). However, neither version appears in 15C (Bartrum, 1981). It is likely that, like many other Old Testament names, Daniel was adopted in the post-Reformation period as a forename, leading to its development as a patronymic surname.

1813-37 (IV): Although the surname is found throughout Wales (with the exception of much of Montgomeryshire and Radnorshire) it is seldom found in significant numbers. The highest incidence is in north Carmarthenshire (Cathinog 1.3%) but elsewhere the incidence is usually well below 1%.

Guppy: South Wales, 0.10% (Daniel), 0.10% (Daniels) – both versions are also found in English counties.

DAVID (See also Fig. 4-11.) The name of the great Israelite king whose story is recorded in the Book of Samuel was adopted early in the Christian era in Wales. It became extremely popular, and remained so throughout the centuries, as a result of being the name of the Welsh patron saint. Its Latin version is *Davidus*, resulting in two variants: *Dewydd*, leading to *Dewi*, was the name by which the saint was usually known and was rarely used as a forename in med. times; *Dafydd* was widely used and most of the small Davids baptised in parish registers answered to Dafydd in daily life, at least in non-anglicised areas. In the 15C pedigrees, Dafydd/David formed 11% of the forenames in pedigrees for all Wales, being widely spread and with as many as 15% in Powys Wenwynwyn (Bartrum, 1981).

1813-37 (III): As a patronymic surname, David continued unchanged in some areas of Wales, but the usual form as a surname became DAVIES. Although it is found in Anglesey, Caernarfonshire and Merionethshire, the incidence is very low (<0.5%). It is, however, quite common in parts of south Wales and in particular in west Carmarthenshire (Derllys 5.8%) and the vale of Glamorgan (Newcastle 7.5%; Ogmore 6.2%). There are isolated occurrences of the surname Dafydd in some parts of Anglesey and Caernarfonshire.

Guppy: South Wales, 0.87%; Monmouthshire, 0.28%.

Diminutives of David David and Dafydd are shortened colloquially to Dai or Dei, leading occasionally to the surname Day, though it has an English origin too (Cottle). Deio, another related diminutive, led to Dyas and Dyos, numerous in Shropshire. Dakin from Dai, plus the adopted suffix '-kin', is found in small traces in several parts of north Wales in 15C (Bartrum, 1981), and led to a surname, spelt e.g. Daykyn, which is found widely in Shropshire PRs and in other records of the English border counties. 1574 Mgy Muster has George Deakyn (Llanfyllin hundred) – here it already looks like an English name. It seems probable too that the name's small but significant presence in Radnorshire is the result of in-migration in early modern times, rather than indicating a surname formed locally. Variants include Dackins, found in Llangurig and Trefeglwys, Montgomeryshire, 17C (E.R. Morris, 1982), and Dykins (William, poet and writer, b.1831 Holywell, Flintshire, in *DWB*). A Dackin family emigrated to the USA in 19C (*Cronicl, 5*).

DAVIES (See also Fig. 4-5.) The most common modern surname derived from the forename David (see DAVID). The spelling Davis most frequently suggests English origin, but there are Welsh exceptions; emigrants from Wales sometimes adopted this spelling, especially in the USA.

(*WG1* xxv, *WG2* xii, Dwnn ii, Nicholas.)

1813-37 (I): This surname is found in significant numbers throughout Wales and it is only on the northern tip of Anglesey that the incidence falls below 1% (Talybolion 0.7%). The main concentration of the name is centred on south Cardiganshire (Moyddin 22.5%) and extends over the majority of that county as well as north Carmarthenshire, north Pembrokeshire and west Breconshire, where the incidence is in the 15% to 20% range. There is also one area of high incidence in north Montgomeryshire (Llanfyllin 11.2%). The lower than average incidence of the name in parts of south Wales reflects the high incidence of the surname David in those areas.

Guppy: North Wales, 5.00%; South Wales, 6.00%; neither region figures under Davis, but Monmouthshire has this variant, 0.12%. Needless to say, both versions are quite numerous in English counties.

DAWKINS This name is another derivative of the forename David, similar to but with a separate development from Dakin. Daw (also leading to the surname Dawe/s and Dawson) was a popular English diminutive of David. Daw + kin was therefore a double diminutive, used in anglicised areas (such as Pembrokeshire) when surnames were forming, leading to Dawkin/s. Thomas Daukyn, tenant in Castlemartin in 1480-1, must come into this category as so many in this lordship did (H. Owen, 1911-18). Evidence for a separate development in med. north Pembrokeshire includes the family of Dawkin ap Griffith and his grandson Meyler ap Llewelyn ap Daukin who held the same land in p. Mathry in the first half of 14C. (*BBStD*, AD). In 1670 HTPem Dawkins is found in Dungleddy and Castlemartin hundreds.

(*WG1* xxv, *WG2* xii, Dwnn i, Nicholas.)

1813-37 (V): Totally confined to the south Wales coastal belt from Wentloog (Monmouthshire) to Rhos (Pembrokeshire). Generally found in small numbers with the exception of south Pembrokeshire (Castlemartin 0.76%).

Guppy: Leicestershire and Rutland, 0.17%.

DEERE From ME personal name *Dere* (from OE *Deora*), a short form of various compound names with the first element meaning 'dear'. Writing in 1872, GTC says: 'No pedigree of this family is found among Glamorgan collections, the name has long been known in the county, and is not yet extinct.' He gives references to the name from deeds and documents, including one John Deyr or Deer of St Mary Church, living in the reigns of Henry VII and Henry VIII, whose daughter married Jenkin Mathew; and William Deere of St Mary Church who married Margaret David ap Howel David, and had a daughter Jenet who married Thomas Bassett (Golden Grove Book).

(*WG2* xii.)

1813-37 (V): A name almost totally confined to Glamorgan. It is never in large numbers except in the Cowbridge hundred (1%).

DEVONALD (See Fig. 5-2.) A W patronymic name from *Dyfnallt*, which tended to survive as a surname on the fringe of an English-speaking area, typically in mid and north Pembrokeshire. Here, though under English influence to take surnames earlier, the Welsh-speaking community kept a greater variety of indigenous forenames. Variants include Davenold, Devenallt.

(*WG1* xxv, *WG2* xii.)

1813-37 (VI) A surname which is local to south-west Wales where it is at its strongest in Pembrokeshire (Dungleddy, 0.60%).

DODD The origin of the English surname lies in the med. forename *Dodde, Dudde*, OE *Dodda, Dudda*, still widely used until 14C. The Dod family of Edge, Cheshire, had the name from the time of Cadwgan Dod, who settled there in the

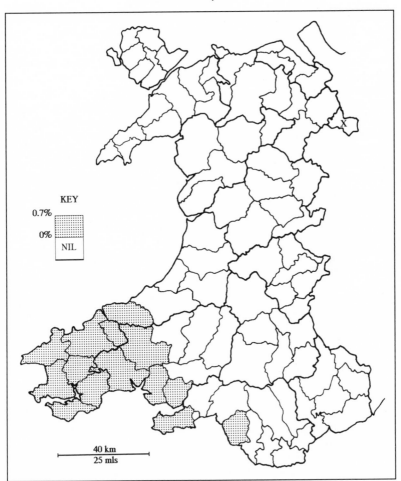

Fig. 5-2: Distribution and incidence of the surname DEVONALD
Maximum incidence – Pembrokeshire, Dungleddy 0.60%

reign of Henry II. 'A direct line has been traced back to 14C' (Hanks & Hodges, 1988). This family married into Gwasanau and Llannerch, Denbighshire. (Nicholas.)

1813-37 (VI): Mainly found in north-east and south-east Wales. It is at its strongest in Denbighshire (Bromfield, 0.54%).

Guppy: Cheshire, 0.32%; Shropshire, 0.14%.

EDMUNDS The English forename Edmund is formed from the OE elements *ead* 'rich' and *mund* 'protector' and was the name of kings and saints – this combination kept the name alive in England after the Norman Conquest (cf. Edward). It appears in 15C in small numbers in several parts of Wales, reaching 1% in Caernarvonshire & Anglesey and in Gwent & Morgannwg, sufficient base for the emergence of a patronymic surname (Bartrum, 1981). A variant is Edmond/s, from OFr, but this signifies nothing more than personal inclination about spelling. In Pembrokeshire, the name tended to become Emment, quite numerous in some parishes by 18C.

(*WG2* xii.)

1813-37 (IV): Although found generally throughout Wales, it appears in significant numbers only in Monmouthshire (Usk 1.27%; Wentloog 1.14%) and the vale of Glamorgan (up to 0.64%).

Guppy: South Wales, 0.27%; Monmouthshire, 0.83% (Guppy comments that Edmunds is the common form in these areas); Gloucestershire, 0.14%.

EDWARDS (See also Fig. 4-7.) The origin of Edward is OE (compound of *ead*, 'rich' and *weard*, 'ward' or 'guardian'). It remained popular after the Norman Conquest because it was the name of kings and royal saints – Edward the Elder, Edward the Martyr and Edward the Confessor (the last-named being especially venerated and the predominant reason for the name's popularity in England). As a result, Edward became the name of several Plantagenet kings and their descendants. In spite of the Edwardian conquest of Wales, the name seems to have been acceptable to Welsh people – by 15C it comprised 8% of names in pedigrees in Powys Fadog, and 2% through all Wales (Bartrum, 1981). The W forename *Iorwerth* was held to be an equivalent of Edward and this enhanced the assimilation of the latter and, no doubt, its popularity against heavy odds. The two names are actually unrelated in meaning (see YORATH). Bedward from ab Edward, is fairly uncommon in Wales – there is an example (1695/6 Llaneilian, Anglesey) in Bangor Probate.

(*WG2* xii, Dwnn ii; Edwardes of Sealyham, Pembrokeshire, *WWHR* viii.)

1813-37 (II): A surname which is found in every area of Wales. It is not, however, in the first rank of common surnames and it is only on the Merionethshire/Denbighshire border (Edeyrnion 6.37%, Chirk 6.44%) and in south Merionethshire (Estimaner 5.39%) that there is anything approaching a real concentration. Bedwards occurs in small numbers along the English border (Montgomeryshire: Newtown, Kerry, Pool and Radnorshire: Colwyn), while there are three occurrences of Kedwards in the Radnor hundred.

Guppy: North Wales, 1.50%; South Wales, 1.40%; Monmouthshire, 1.40%; Cheshire, 0.34%; Gloucestershire, 0.15%; Herefordshire, 1.36%; Shropshire, 2.10%; widespread in other English counties in modest numbers.

ELIAS A biblical name, from the Greek version of Elijah, the Old Testament prophet. As so often with Scriptural names, Elias came onto the Welsh scene after the Reformation, so forms a later patronymic surname. It was frequently thought to be the same name as ELLIS, though their origins are quite separate. (See also Fig. 6-1.)

(Griffith.)

1813-37 (VI): Found in many parts of Wales but seldom in significant concentrations. It is at its strongest in Cardiganshire (Troedyraur, 0.45%) and Glamorgan (Neath, 0.44%).

ELLIS Derived from the W forename *Elisedd*, found frequently in early texts. In speech the final *dd* was dropped, giving Elise (three syllables), Elisa and Elisha (both reflecting dialect pronunciation). Elisa/Elissa survived in records fairly late and even appears as Eliza in some: 1670 Jane vch Ellissey (St Asaph Probate); [1673] Eliza John ap William, yeoman; 1674 Hugh Elissa, labourer; [1688] Lewis Ellissey (Bangor Probate). Elias and Eliseus, biblical names, came on the scene after the Reformation, the former being late and wide-spread enough to form a small surname of its own (see ELIAS). Both these names may have augmented the numbers of Ellis as a surname. (At an earlier period, it should be noted, Elis/Ellis was used in England as a form of OT Elias, and an uncommon English surname formed as a result; variants include Ellice and Helis.) From ab Ellis comes Bellis, prevalent in nearby English counties, and this is one source of the name Bayliss.

(*WG2* xii, Dwnn ii, Griffith, Nicholas.)

1813-37 (III): Ellis is found in significant concentrations across much of north Wales, particularly throughout Merionethshire (Ardudwy 2.10%) but also in north Montgomeryshire (Llanfyllin 3.14%), Flintshire (Rhuddlan 2.96%) and Caernarfonshire (Cymydmaen 1.52%). Elsewhere it is found only spasmodically and with a very low incidence (usually <0.2%).

Guppy: North Wales, 0.25%; Cheshire, 0.11%; Gloucestershire, 0.14%; Shropshire, 0.22%; also eastern and southern English counties, probably reflecting English med. origin.

EMANUEL The biblical name Emmanuel (Hebrew 'God is with us') was a popular forename in many European countries (e.g. Spanish Manuel), but not in England (though Emanuel and Manuel are in Cornwall in 15-16C (Withycombe, 1977). Neither was it found in med. Wales, but it began to be used in post-Reformation times both as Emanuel and as Manuel. These names often referred to the same person, e.g. Emanuel/Manuel Edward in Cilgerran PR, Pembrokeshire, from 1703; Manuel is also a 'surname' in this area from the same period. It comes into the significant category of patronymic surnames which now look both Jewish and Welsh. (See also Fig. 6-1.)

1813-37 (VI): Found in many parts of Wales but seldom in significant concentrations. It is at its strongest in Montgomeryshire (Llanidloes, 0.34%).

EPHRAIM Hanks & Hodges (1990) comment that this Old Testament name, of the founder of one of the twelve tribes of Israel (Genesis), was not particularly popular with the Puritans and came into use more in 18C and 19C. Though considered typical of Merionethshire (but not frequent), there is a locally-born family in Hayscastle, Pembrokeshire, in 1851 (Census). (See also Fig. 6-1.)

1813-37 (VI): Only found in Merionethshire (Ardudwy, 0.06%).

ESAU A biblical forename (of the brother of Jacob, Genesis 25-28, etc) which, considering its meaning of 'hairy', was perhaps destined not to be a popular name, and it became an uncommon patronymic surname. It is quite typical of this type of name that it was soon acclimatised and pronounced as a Welsh name: in late 18C/early 19C south Cardiganshire it was often written as Esay. (See also Fig. 6-1.)

1813-37 (VI): Mainly found on the Cardiganshire/Carmarthenshire/Pembrokeshire border. It has its maximum incidence in Carmarthenshire (Elvet, 0.13%).

EVANS This is one of the major W patronymic surnames, ultimately derived from John (see JOHN) through W *Ieuan* (from Latin *Johannes*). Ieuan was subject to sound changes (which must have been compounded by the written forms equating 'u' and 'v') which produced Iefan, Ifan and Evan. These were late forms: in 15C pedigrees, Evan does not appear, though Ieuan forms 8% of forenames in all Wales (Bartrum, 1981).The patronymic surname Evan/Evans was the outcome of these names, and Jeavans, Jevons, Jeavince, etc, are part of the same group – as indeed are Evance and Heavens. In modern times, the spelling Ifans has been adopted by some families. BEVAN is from ab Evan. It is interesting to note that Evans is found in PRs from 16C in Cornwall (White). (*WG2* xii, Nicholas.)

1813-37 (I): The pattern of occurrence of this surname closely parallels that for the surname DAVIES (q.v.). The main concentration is again centred on south

Cardiganshire (Ilar Lower 17.8%; Moyddin 15.1%) but it does not extend as far to the east as Breconshire. There is a further concentration in north Montgomeryshire (Llanfyllin 10.9%; Caereinion 10.8%). There is a minor concentration of the name in the rapidly developing areas of Glamorgan (Miskin 5.3%; Caerphilly 5.4%) which may be further evidence of the migration which was known to have taken place from west Wales to this area at this time.

Guppy: North Wales, 5.00%; South Wales, 5.20%; Monmouthshire, 2.20%; Cheshire, 0.30%; Gloucestershire, 0.46%; Herefordshire, 0.82%; Shropshire, 2.10%.

EYNON (See Fig. 5-3.) A patronymic name from W *Einion*, which in south Wales speech becomes Einon, a surname-spelling which still exists in small numbers. The Welsh common noun *einion* means 'anvil'. *WS* describes Einion as one of the commonest forenames in Wales, but by 15C it does not exceed 1% in any area and, averaged over all Wales, was <0.25% (Bartrum, 1981). BEYNON (ab Eynon) has its own pattern of distribution. Variants of the Eynon group include Inions (found in Montgomeryshire: Welshpool) and Onions, found especially over the English border. We may see how these evolved from, e.g., 1673 John ap John ap Enian (St Asaph Probate).

1813-37 (V): Very much a name of south Wales, and south-west Wales in particular (Pembrokeshire: Dungleddy 1.11% and Narberth 1.05%). It is virtually absent from north Wales.

FAITHFULL Although this is an English surname in its own right, it is also possible that it is Welsh patronymic, from a forename popular among Puritans.

1813-37 (VI): Found in very small numbers (never greater than 0.03%) in some parts of south Wales.

FELIX From Latin *felix* 'lucky', it was a New Testament name and later a saint's name, but perhaps sits best with those unusual 'classical' revivals found here and there in, especially, 18C Cardiganshire.

1813-37 (VI): Mainly found in north Cardiganshire where it has a maximum incidence of 0.37%. It is also found in a narrow band stretching down to the industrial areas of east Glamorgan (Miskin and Kibbor).

FENNA This name in this form, and as Phenna, has a characteristic look of north-east Wales. Hanks & Hodges (1988) give Fenner as a variant of Fenn, a loc. name for someone living in a low-lying, marshy area, and it seems probable that the endings in '-a' are simply local variants of a name which drifted into Wales from north-west England. However, a study of the distribution of Fenna/h and Phenna/h by Edward Phenna (Lasker & Mascie) leads him to believe that there is no connection with Fenner; he prefers a south Denbighshire origin, though no

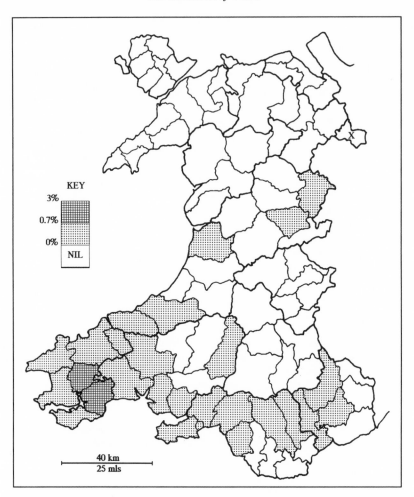

**Fig. 5-3: Distribution and incidence of the surname EYNON/EINON
Maximum incidence – Pembrokeshire, Dungleddy 1.11%**

etymological evidence is suggested and the TD distribution tends to support our own interpretation.

1813-37 (VI): Chiefly confined to the border hundreds of north-east Wales, it is at its maximum in Flintshire (Mold, 0.13%).

Guppy: (Fenner) Essex, 0.15%.

FOLLAND Folant is the W form of Valentine (Hanks & Hodges, 1990) and Folland, found in Pembrokeshire, is therefore one of those rarer patronymics which have survived as a surname in this 'border' area. Vallant is a variant, found in Monmouthshire.

1813-37 (VI): Confined to one area of Pembrokeshire (Rhos, 0.32%) with the exception of a minor occurence in Monmouthshire (Caldicot, 0.05%).

FOULKES From English forename of CG origin, introduced by the Normans; a shortened form of compound names containing *Folc*, cognate with 'folk'. In modern times it is used only in a handful of English families, but it clearly had significant popularity still in Wales in surname-forming times. In 15C pedigrees, Fulk averages <0.25% throughout Wales, with its chief manifestation at 1% in Rhos & Rhufoniog (Bartrum, 1981). As a result of two interconnected factors – 'ff' in older English hands being equal to modern 'F', and 'Ff' in Welsh having the voiced pronunciation (i.e. as in 'fish') – the name is sometimes spelled Ffoulkes, Ffowkes, etc. In Pembrokeshire, though uncommon, it appears as Volk. Many English variants are given in Reaney (1980), including the diminutive Fuge, which appears in Glamorgan. (*WG2* xii; Dwnn i; Griffith, Nicholas.)

1813-37 (IV): A name with considerable prominence in north-east Wales (Denbighshire: Isdulas 2.39%; Rhuthun 1.29%; Isaled 1.03% and Flintshire: Rhuddlan 1.34%; Coleshill 0.87%). It is also found in significant numbers in Montgomeryshire (Llanfyllin 0.81%), but is generally absent from much of south Wales.

Guppy: North Wales, 0.25%.

FRANCIS A patronymic name, that of the saint who founded the order of Franciscan friars. Hanks & Hodges (1990) say it was 'introduced into England in the early 16th century'. However, it was already known in Wales in 15C, when it existed in small traces in five areas, from Powys southwards and westwards (Bartrum, 1981). It also exists as an English surname, from 'Frenchman' (Cottle). The IGI has references to christenings in 1602 (Monmouthshire), 1611 (Montgomeryshire) and 1612 (Glamorgan), whilst there is a reference to Ffranch ap John Williams in Conwy (Caernarfonshire) in 1577. Therefore, it has been in Wales long enough to become a patronymic surname in several areas. It is found in some 17C Glamorgan registers as Phrancis, but this does not seem to have permanently affected the surname-spelling. (*WG2* xii.)

1813-37 (IV): One of those names to be found generally throughout Wales, but only occurring in significant numbers in Pembrokeshire (Dewisland 1.10%), Carmarthenshire (Kidwelly 0.73%), Glamorgan (Neath 0.79%) and Montgomeryshire (Caereinion 0.99%).

Guppy: South Wales, 0.44%; Monmouthshire, 0.45%.

GABRIEL The names of the archangels have never been popular given names in Wales: Michael (see MICHAEL) reaches the greatest numbers, Raphael remains undetected by this survey, whilst Gabriel was rare, giving rise to only a handful of patronymic names. It is found as a given name, for example, in 18C Llanbadarn Fawr, Cardiganshire. (See also Fig. 6-1.)

1813-37 (VI): Found in parts of south Wales and north Wales but to no specific pattern or in any significant concentration (maximum occurrence, Merionethshire: Estimaner 0.15%). It is wholly absent from mid Wales.

GAMES This is a W adj. name, from *gam*, the mutated form of *cam* 'crooked, bent'. Gam appears as an epithet after many personal names in early documents but, to quote *WS*, 'the family of the famous Dafydd Gam of Breconshire seems to be the only one with a surname derived from [it]'. Several authorities are quoted for the interpretation of the epithet as meaning 'squinting'. (*WG1* xxv, *WG2* xii, Dwnn i, ii, *DNB*, *DWB*, Nicholas.)

1813-37 (VI): Almost totally confined to east Breconshire (Talgarth, 0.31%; Crickhowell, 0.24%) and adjacent areas; however it also occurs in one area of Pembrokeshire (Dungleddy, 0.14%).

GAMMON Gammon is probably derived from a nickname, either OFr. *gambon* 'ham' or for 'one fond of games' (Reaney, 1961). It seems likely that the Gower family of this name originated in the West Country of England, possibly Devon. (*WG2* xii.)

1813-37 (VI): A name local to the Gower/Swansea area of west Glamorgan. It has a significant incidence in Gower (0.53%).

Guppy: Devon, 0.18%.

GEORGE (See Fig. 5-4.) Introduced by Crusaders, this forename had relatively little popularity in England before the accession of the Hanoverian kings, after which it blossomed in common use. It may well have done the same in parts of Wales; however, as a Welsh patronymic name it can be traced back before the early 18C. As a forename it forms a small trace (<0.25%) but is nevertheless found throughout Wales in 15C and was 1% in Gwent & Morgannwg (Bartrum, 1981). The use of such a given name by those of pedigree status may well have

98

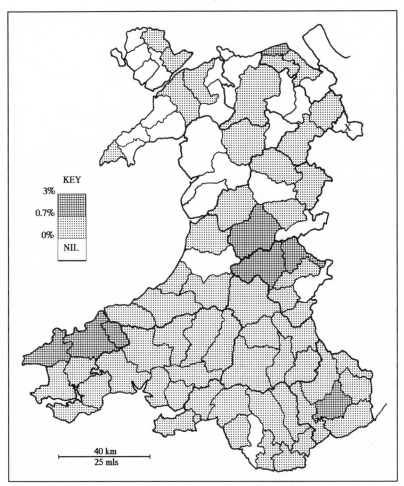

KEY

3%

0.7%

0%

NIL

40 km
25 mls

Fig. 5-4: Distribution and incidence of the surname GEORGE
Maximum incidence – Pembrokeshire, Cemais 1.82%

99

been followed by humbler people, and this is likely to be the explanation of its popularity in north Pembrokeshire (especially Cemais hundred) where the name was in use in 16C by the family of Owen of Henllys (Charles, 1973). The IGI has 17C entries for most Welsh counties, with early examples (16-17C) from the PR of Conwy (Caernarfonshire). 1774 Cilgerran: David John David George/ mark of David George (PemMarr) is an example of late patronymic use.

1813-37 (IV): A name found generally throughout south Wales but only spasmodically in north Wales. In south Wales it is only found in significant numbers in north Pembrokeshire (Cemais 1.82%; Cilgerran 1.19%; Dewisland 1.12%) and in a small area of Monmouthshire (Usk 1.00%). In north Wales its incidence in one part of Flintshire (Prestatyn 1.10%) stands out in an area where its general occurrence is below 0.1%.

Guppy: South Wales, 0.34%; Monmouthshire, 0.66%; Gloucestershire, 0.11%; Herefordshire, 0.20%, Shropshire, 0.17%.

GETHIN W adj. name from *cethin*, 'ugly, hideous', but possibly 'swarthy' in this context. It has been taken up as a first name in modern times, either as a back-formation from the surname or simply because the *sound* of the Welsh word was liked, regardless of its meaning. In early registers, the unmutated form is found quite often (e.g. 1613 Edward Kethin, Penally (Muster). Nevern PR: 1669 Elinor Kethin buried). Gethin is sometimes confused with Gutyn and its variants (see GITTINS).

(*WG2* xii.)

1813-37 (VI): A name which is only of significance in west Glamorgan (Neath, 0.34%), though it is to be found in small numbers in parts of Monmouthshire.

GIBBS An English patronymic surname from a diminutive of the forename Gilbert. It is found in Gower, and GTC 488 has a pedigree of Gibb of Norton. Gilbert has several pet-forms, leading to surnames, including Gibbon and Gibbons, long-established in anglicised areas such as Pembrokeshire. Gibbon as a forename is found in 15C only in very small traces (<0.25%) in three quite separate parts of Wales: Caernarfon, Powys Fadog and Gwent & Morgannwg (Bartrum, 1981), but its use in this way suggests a direct patronymic origin for some family names. The family of Gibbon of Trecastle, Glamorgan, is said to have taken its surname from Richard ap Gibbon ap Llywelyn, a descendant of Einion ap Collwyn. Gibby is another variant (though it is has been attributed to the Welsh forename *Cybi* and some may have that origin). Even in present-day Pembrokeshire, men called Gilbert may be addressed as Gibbah – there is a strong dialect tendency to add '-ah' or '-y' to the root of names and this can be seen in the formation of surnames in early modern times.

(*WG1* xxv, *WG2* xii, Dwnn i, Nicholas.)

1813-37 (V): This name is almost totally confined to the coastal hundreds of south Wales between Neath and Rhos and also parts of Monmouthshire. Only on Gower is it found in significant numbers (0.96%); elsewhere it never exceeds 0.2%.

Guppy: Gibbs: widespread southern/midland England; South Wales, 0.22%; Gloucestershire, 0.60%; Herefordshire, 0.14%. Gibbon: not counted in Wales; Gibby: South Wales, 0.12%.

GITTINS, GITTOES Guto and Gutyn are the hypocoristic or pet versions of Gruffydd (see GRIFFITHS) and have given rise to patronymic surnames in their own right. In 15C Guto is found (in very small numbers, since the *formal* name would tend to be preferred) in the southern areas of Wales, while Gutyn, in similar numbers, was favoured in the north (with some overlap in Powys) (Bartrum, 1981). The sound of the first syllable is short 'i' and the surnames derived include Gittah, Gittoes, Gittins, Gittings, etc.

(*WG2* xii.)

1813-37 (V): These surnames are largely confined to the English border north of Painscastle (Radnorshire). They are most commonly found in Montgomeryshire (Newtown 1.08%; Caereinion 0.99%; Llanfyllin 0.87%) and Radnorshire (Radnor 0.73%).

Guppy: North Wales, 0.20%; Shropshire, 0.41%.

GOODWIN An English surname from the OE forename *Godwine* (from elements meaning 'good' and 'friend'). Famous from before the Norman Conquest as the name of the father of the English king Harold, it continued in use into the English surname-period. Reaney (1980) gives details of an English family in which this patronymic name settled *c.*1250. Therefore, it came into Wales ready-made as a surname, perhaps from the west Midlands area, since its Welsh home is Montgomeryshire. John Goodwin, 18C Quaker, was of Trefeglwys (E.R. Morris, 1982). Goodwyn is a common variant, while Goodin is found once in the period of our survey.

1813-37 (V): Again a surname which is largely confined to the English border. It is most common in Montgomeryshire (Newtown 0.78%).

Guppy: counts this spelling in several English counties, including Cheshire 0.30%, Derbyshire 0.40% and Herefordshire 0.17%, all possible influences.

GOUGH is an adj. name from W *goch*, the mutated form of *coch* 'red' (i.e. red-haired, red-complexioned). The final guttural sound caused problems to the non-Welsh speaker and to scribes. Goch became Gogh, then Gough, then Goff; or Gooch, Goudge. Some of these forms now look English, and have been long assimilated across the border.

(*WG2* xii, Dwnn i, Nicholas.)

1813-37 (VI): Found spasmodically throughout Wales but always in small numbers (less than 0.3%). The main incidence is in Montgomeryshire and Monmouthshire.

Guppy: counts Gough only in the English counties of Buckinghamshire 0.20%, Herefordshire 0.24%, Shropshire 0.29% and Wiltshire 0.27%.

GRAVENOR Gravenor and Grosvenor are variant spellings of the same name (from OFr. for 'great hunter'), the first of the name in England being Gilbert le Grosvenor, a kinsman of William I. As the family name of the dukes of Westminster, with estates in Cheshire, it presumably came into Wales from that county. It is found in 13C documents in Cheshire, Lancashire and Staffordshire. (*WG1* xxv, *WG2* xii.)

1813-37 (VI): Mainly to be found in Radnorshire (Knighton, 0.31%), it also occurs in Montgomeryshire and Monmouthshire.

GRIFFITHS A patronymic name from OW *Grippiud*, later *Gruffudd*; the modern standard Welsh is Gruffydd (pron. approximately as its English equivalent, Griffith). It was the name of princes and leaders, notably Gruffudd ap Llywelyn (d.1063), who ruled over all Wales for a time. It was a common forename in 15C pedigrees, averaging 6% throughout Wales, and rising to 9% in Meirionnydd – it was generally more common in the north (Bartrum, 1981). Griffith/s became a widespread patronymic surname. As usual, in speech the *dd* sound was weak, and Griffies/Griffis are not uncommon variants. In documents the name is often abbreviated to 'Gr:', while 'Gruff:' (i.e. Griff) is also found. The latinised version of the forename in documents is usually *Griffinus*; Griffin is found as an alternative to Griffith in documents, often for the same person. However, Griffin was an English surname too (of Breton origin) and is also found in Ireland, so should be treated with caution (Guppy does not count it in Wales). White (1981) writes, 'though of Welsh origin [Griffin and Griffiths] are recorded in Cornwall for at least four centuries'. Guto is the pet-form of Griffith as a forename and formed several surnames (see GITTINS, GITTOES). (*WG2* xii, Dwnn i, ii, Nicholas.)

1813-37 (I): Found throughout Wales. There are significant concentrations along the whole length of the Llŷn peninsula (in the range 5% to 9%) and in north Pembrokeshire (Cemais 5.5%).

Guppy: North Wales, 2.90%; South Wales, 2.20%; Monmouthshire, 1.10%; Cheshire, 0.30%; Gloucestershire, 0.27%; Herefordshire, 1.36%; Shropshire, 1.00%.

GRONOW represents a colloquial form of the W personal name *Goronwy*, and is one of the main forms in which this surname has evolved in the patronymic system. As Gronwy it appears in the list of forenames in use in 15C pedigrees, forming a small trace through Wales generally (<0.25%), and reaching 1% in parts of north-west Wales (Bartrum, 1981). However, it seems to have had a greater effect in the border areas, leading to variants such as Grono and Grunna(h) and, notably, to Green(a)way, Greenhow, Greeno, etc. Because of the inevitable addition of 's' to most patronymic names, such English-looking names as Greenhouse are another outcome. Many of the Gronow-names moved over the English border and are found plentifully in the registers of Shropshire and Herefordshire.

(Dwnn i.)

1813-37 (VI): This name, in all its variations, is only to be found in south Wales where there are several areas of noticeable incidence, namely: Pembrokeshire (Cemais, 0.36%), Breconshire (Talgarth, 0.31%), Radnorshire (Painscastle, 0.31%) and Glamorgan (Newcastle, 0.28%).

Guppy: Greenaway: Cornwall, 0.08%; Wiltshire, 0.13%.

GUNTER Based on a CG forename meaning 'battle-army', this surname came into Wales with Peter Gunter, a follower of Bernard de Neufmarché in the conquest of Brycheiniog. Their early home, Tregunter, took their name. Nicholas writes that they spread widely and had many estates in the county '... but their tendency was downwards: no Gunter is found in the shrievalty of the county after 1689, when John Gunter of Trevecca served'. Nevertheless, the act of spreading wide guaranteed the survival of the family name.

(*WG1* xxv, *WG2* xii, Dwnn ii, Nicholas.)

1813-37 (VI): A name which is local to Breconshire (Crickhowell and Penkelly both 0.16%) and Monmouthshire (Trelleck, 0.29%).

Guppy: finds it only in Berkshire, 0.15%; Gloucestershire, 0.17%.

GUY English patronymic name from Fr. form of CG name *Wido*, of unclear origin; an alternative meaning, though rare, is the English occ. name for 'guide'. From its numbers in the IGI, it was a widespread surname in England, though Guppy finds it only in Buckinghamshire, Dorset and Yorkshire (East and North Ridings). *1813-37 (V):* A highly localised name found only in west Glamorgan (Gower 0.72%).

GWALCHMAI This is a patronymic name from W *Gwalchmai*, an early forename – it is the name of an Arthurian character, Gwalchmai fab Gwyar, and of the 12C poet Gwalchmai ap Meyler (*DWB*) – from *gwalch* 'hawk', + *mai* 'field', though it is often interpreted as 'hawk of May' (see *WS* for reasoning). (Gwalchmai is also an Anglesey place-name, but this is not likely to have contributed to the surname.) In the Middle Ages the use of the forename Gwalchmai seems to have been rare, but it became a surname in a few areas. The name is not in 1574 Mgy Muster, but may have been revived in that area later.

Owen Gwalchmey was in p. Llanycefn (Pem, Dungleddy) in 1613 (Pem Muster), and Owen Gwallmay who was there in 1670 (HTPem) is clearly a kinsman, as was probably Evan Gwallmay in Llawhaden in the same hundred, though the name does not seem to have survived in that area to modern times.

1813-37 (VI): A name local to Montgomeryshire (Newtown, 0.16%).

GWILT W adj. name from *gwyllt* 'wild'. This epithet has formed a surname which is probably more numerous over the English border. Occasionally it is spelt Quilt, even in Wales. Worthy of note is the appearance of the name in the PR of Llannarth, Cardiganshire, in 1771. John Gwilt of that parish gave his name to a topographical feature, Banc Siôn Cwilt (= Quilt).

1813-37 (VI): Mainly confined to Montgomeryshire (Kerry 0.53%).

Guppy: Shropshire, 0.31%.

GWYNNE (See also Fig. 4-18.) The group of surnames Gwyn, Gwynn, Gwynne are adj. from W *gwyn* 'white', in this context 'fair of hair or complexion'. The dark-haired and dark-complexioned majority clearly found it convenient to add a distinguishing epithet to some individuals with these characteristics. In their mutated forms, these names become the surnames Wyn, Wynn, Wynne (see WYNNE). *WS* draws to our attention that Gwyn was also a male forename and gives examples of its use (as Gwyn and Wyn) in early documents. Although Gwyn has been revived as a forename in modern times, it was only a very small trace (<0.25% overall) in 15C (Bartrum, 1981). The later distribution of Gwynne and Wynne are treated separately here, but in earlier periods the names could be interchangeable in the same family.

(*WG1* xxv, *WG2* xii, Dwnn i, ii, Nicholas.)

1813-37 (V): This surname is chiefly found in south Wales and is rarely found north of Radnorshire. It is at its most frequent in Glamorgan (Gower 1.35%) and in Radnorshire (Painscastle 0.91%; Colwyn 0.77%).

Guppy: Monmouthshire, 0.17%.

GWYTHER A patronymic name from W *Gwythur,* which was derived from the Latin *victor.* It is a good example of a Welsh name which has survived in anglicised areas because surnames formed there earlier, at a period when the forename was still in use. In one of its centres, Pembrokeshire, it was probably used in the border areas between English and Welsh speech, but moved to the English-speaking Castlemartin hundred, where Gwyther families have been long established in Manorbier and Pembroke: Richard Gwyther was reeve of Pembroke in 1516; Watkin Guyther was at Hill, Manorbier, from at least 1543 (the Gwyther family remained in that parish until late 19C). Wither/s, found in eastern border counties, appears in some cases to be a variant from the mutated form of the name.

1813-37 (V): Very much a Pembrokeshire name where it has a particular concentration in the Castlemartin hundred (1.13%). Occasionally found in south Carmarthenshire and south-east Wales.

HAINES This is a surname for which a Welsh origin is often claimed. One interpretation is that it derives from the personal name *Einws*, a diminutive of *Einion* (see EYNON); another, described in *WS* as 'less unlikely', finds its origin in W adj. *hen* 'old'. *WS* has examples of *hen* used after first names, when it normally precedes a noun, but we then have to accept that 's' was consistently added to an adj. name. We find it seemingly in this form in Mgy Muster: Lewys ap Owen Heyns (followed by Morys ap Owen Hyre). The possibility of an English loc. name has, however, also to be considered. Ekwall (1960) indicates an OE vocabulary-element meaning 'hedges, enclosures'. The surname remains enigmatic and more early examples of its use are needed before conclusions can be safely drawn.

(*WG1* xxv, *WG2* xii, Heynes of Stretton.)

1813-37 (VI): Mainly to be found in south-east Wales but occasionally found elsewhere. It has its greatest incidence in Radnorshire (Painscastle, 0.45%).

Guppy: Haines: Herefordshire, 0.09%; Oxfordshire, 0.12%; Somerset, 0.11%. Haine: Somerset, 0.15%. Hayne: Cornwall, 0.09%. Haynes: Derbyshire, 0.07%; Herefordshire, 0.09%; Huntingdonshire, 0.25%; Northamptonshire, 0.25%; Oxfordshire, 0.54%; Shropshire, 0.17%; Staffordshire, 0.10%; Warwickshire, 0.20%, Worcestershire, 0.18%. Guppy's references are given in full.

HALL is a common English surname (16th most common in England and Wales in 1853), which originally described someone who worked at, and so dwelt in, a hall (but see also HOWELLS). In Pembrokeshire, Walter de le Halle is a juror in 1376 (H. Owen, 1911-18, iii 101); Thomas Hall of Tenby appears in LS 1543; there are three heads of household in the southernmost (Castlemartin and Narberth) hundreds in 1670 HTPem.

(*WG2* xii, Nicholas.)

1813-37 (V): A name found right across south Wales but generally in small numbers. It is, however, particularly prominent in south Pembrokeshire (Castlemartin 0.72%).

Guppy: South Wales, 0.22%; Monmouthshire 0.28%; widespread in English counties, including Cheshire, 0.40%; Gloucestershire, 0.36%; Herefordshire, 0.41%; Shropshire, 0.31%.

HAMER (See Fig. 5-5.) This name is derived from a place in Lancashire, an ecclesiastical district in p. Rochdale, and is a surname in that area from at least

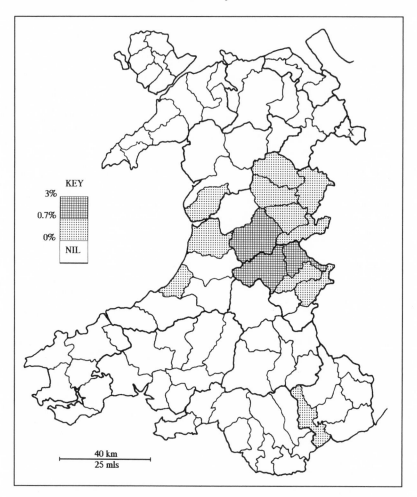

KEY

3%

0.7%

0%

NIL

40 km
25 mls

**Fig. 5-5: Distribution and incidence of the surname HAMER
Maximum incidence – Radnorshire, Rhaeadr 2.46%**

14C. It is found in Shropshire in the early 17C. By 1627 it appears in Llandinam (Montgomeryshire) and it was common in 18C Radnorshire (Peate, 1986).

1813-37 (V): A name which is almost wholly confined to Montgomeryshire (Llanidloes 0.72%) and Radnorshire (Rhaeadr 2.46%; Knighton 2.29%).

Guppy: Hamar, 'occasionally spelt Hamer': South Wales, 0.17%; Herefordshire, 0.11%; Shropshire, 0.33%.

HARRIES, HARRIS The surnames Harris and Harries represent 'son of Harry/Henry'. Though the same names in origin as Harry, they are sufficiently numerous to require separate statistical treatment.

(*WG2* xii, Dwnn i, Nicholas, *WWHR* viii.)

1813-37 (III): This is a name which is largely confined to the counties of Pembrokeshire (Dewisland 3.70%), Carmarthenshire (Kidwelly 2.18%) and Monmouthshire (Usk 2.63%). It becomes increasingly less common the further north in Wales one goes, and is virtually non-existent in Anglesey, Caernarfonshire and Merionethshire. Its incidence in Glamorgan is generally low but this is compensated for by the relatively high incidence of the variant HARRY (q.v.).

Guppy: North Wales, 0.20%; South Wales, 1.20%; Monmouthshire, 1.60%; Gloucestershire, 0.43%; Herefordshire, 0.47%; Shropshire, 0.20%. 'Harries is a not uncommon form in South Wales'.

HARRY Harry (W *Harri*) was the common med. and early modern pronunciation of Henry, closely resembling the French pronunciation in which this CG name was first heard in Britain. The name of Norman and English kings, it was popular generally in med. times, and spread quickly to Wales. In 15C, Harri/Henry were significant in Deheubarth (3%), and averaged 1% throughout Wales (Bartrum, 1981). In some areas, Harry itself was adopted as a surname; occasionally Harrhy is found. Henry also exists as a surname. Harry and Henry in their unpossessive forms were names to which *ap* was easily attracted and we have Parry (see PARRY) and Penry widespread as a result. Henry appears as Hendry as an ignorant spelling in registers. Pendry may well follow the standard pattern, as ap Hendry, but *WS* says that *pen(y)dref* (top end of the town) 'should not be excluded completely from being a possible source'.

1813-37 (IV): A south Wales name found throughout Carmarthenshire (where HARRIES/HARRIS is also quite strong), Glamorgan and east Monmouthshire. Its incidence seldom rises above 1% and is at a maximum in the vale of Glamorgan (Cowbridge 1.5%).

Guppy: South Wales, 0.17%.

HATFIELD This is an English loc. name and there are places called Hatfield in half a dozen or more counties. However, its appearance in Montgomeryshire can be fairly closely dated to 1576, when a group of men who came from Derbyshire settled in Llangurig (*WHF*, 67). The hamlet of Hadfield in p. Glossop, in its early forms – which would relate to surname-forming times also – is *Hatfeld*, *Hattefeld*, and this seems a plausible origin for this family.

1813-37 (VI): A surname of north Radnorshire (max: Knighton, 0.62%).

Guppy: records it only in Derbyshire, 0.07%; Nottinghamshire, 0.16%.

HAVARD (See Fig. 5-6.) Bernard de Neufmarché, the Norman conqueror of Brycheiniog, gave the manor of Pontwilym to Sir Walter Havard (Jones, *Brecknock*); a reasonable case is made for his surname being from nearby Hereford (P. Morgan, 1995). Nicholas gives his name as Walter Havre de Grace (from Le Havre in Normandy) and there was an ON name responsible for the English surname Haward and cognate with Howard. The consequent great Breconshire family was responsible for the spread of the name locally; also descended from them were the Havards of Glamorgan (GTC) and those who married into Carmarthenshire (F. Jones, 1987) – from the latter probably derive the small numbers of 18C Havards in Cardiganshire and Pembrokeshire, though an alternative theory derives *their* name from Haverford (P. Morgan, 1995). For Havard pedigrees see *WG2*; for Radnorshire see Dwnn ii, 264. Of the name in Glamorgan, GTC writes that in PRs of or around Llantrithyd the name sometimes becomes Herward and Howard.

(*WG1* xxv, *WG2* xii, Dwnn i, ii, Nicholas.)

1813-37 (IV): This name is found in two distinct (and separate) clusters in south-east and south-west Wales. It is much stronger in the former – mainly Radnorshire (Colwyn 1.23%; Painscastle 1.06%), Breconshire (Defynnog 1.35%; Penkelly 0.71%) and Monmouthshire. In the latter region – mainly Pembrokeshire – it is in much smaller numbers – always less than 0.3% (Cemais 0.29%).

HEILYN A surname of W patronymic origin: though common at one stage (*WS*), by 15C it appears only as a small trace (<0.25%) in two areas, Rhos & Rhufoniog and Deheubarth. As a surname it is spelled Heylyn, etc, and with *ap* attached, it becomes Palin.

(*WG1* xxv.)

1813-37 (VI): Has a minimal occurrence in east Denbighshire (Chirk 0.03%).

HERBERT It is not possible in a small space to summarise the history of the great Herbert family groups, including the earls of Pembroke and the earls of Powis, which have offshoots in many parts of Wales. *DWB* has long entries for them, plus several on individuals. Nicholas has a useful summary, while GTC has a master-chart of the interconnections, and 59 pages of separate genealogies. Herbert was a CG forename (also used as a surname in England). We may note

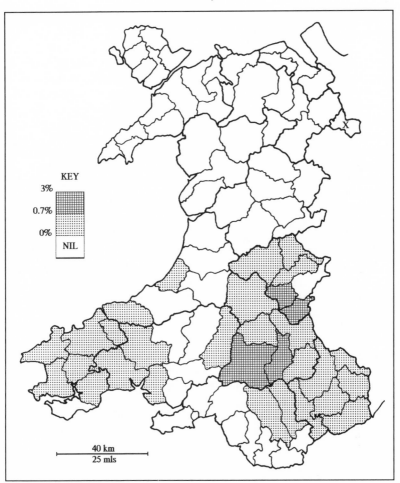

Fig. 5-6: Distribution and incidence of the surname HAVARD
Maximum incidence – Breconshire, Defynnog 1.35%

that William Herbert, earl of Pembroke (d.1469) was the son of Sir William ap Thomas.
(*WG1* xxv, *WG2* xii, Dwnn i, ii.)
1813-37 (IV): This name is found in most hundreds south of a line from Machynlleth to Welshpool but almost always in small numbers. It is at its most prominent in Cardiganshire (Upper Ilar 0.74%) and Radnorshire (Radnor 0.73%).
Guppy: Monmouthshire, 0.33%; Gloucestershire, 0.24%.

HIER, often Hire, is an adj. surname, from W *hir*, 'tall, long'. David Hire is listed in 1613 in Cemais (Pem Muster); Hire appears in 1670 in Castlemartin and Rhos hundreds (though Hyer is the more numerous spelling), and in Rhos and Dungleddy.
1813-37 (VI): Mainly to be found in Pembrokeshire (Rhos 0.27%), but also has a limited presence in parts of Monmouthshire.

HOOSON is a variant of Hughson, a northern English form which is not native to Wales. Ellis (1994) provides evidence that the name entered Flintshire from Derbyshire: William Hooson, author of *The Miner's Dictionary*, published in Wrexham in 1747, and a Derbyshire man, settled in Halkyn, as did his nephew and heir, Thomas Hooson, a prominent lead-mine agent. 'There are many descendants of this, and other branches of the family, in the area.'
1813-37 (VI): Mainly confined to Flintshire (Coleshill 0.32%) and only found occasionally elsewhere.

HOPKINS (See also Fig. 4-12.) Patronymic name from an English forename which was adopted too late to contribute significantly to surnames in England but was borrowed widely in Wales. It was formed from a diminutive form of Robert, Hob, plus the hypocoristic suffix '-kin'. In 15C it amounts to 1% of pedigree forenames in two areas: Deheubarth and Gwent & Morgannwg (Bartrum, 1981). It was in very common use as a given name in a number of Glamorgan parishes in 17C and early, e.g. frequently in 17-18C Cilybebyll, Llansamlet BT, and, in that area, often remained as Hopkin (without 's') as a surname. With *ap*, Hopkin becomes the less common Popkin and then Popkins, found in HTGlam.
(*WG2* xii.)
1813-37 (III): This is very much a Glamorgan name; albeit with a distinct presence in central Monmouthshire (Usk 1.57%) It is only found incidentally (and to no particular pattern) elsewhere. In Glamorgan it ranges from 0.6% in the Miskin hundred to 2.9% in the Llangyfelach hundred.
Guppy: South Wales, 1.08%; Monmouthshire, 0.22%; Gloucestershire, 0.43%.

HOSKINS This name may be English in origin, as it is generally considered to be a Devon name (with consequent possible movement towards Wales), formed as a diminutive of OE names beginning in 'Os-' (cf. Osgood, Osborn) with illiterate

'H' attached. However, Hoesgyn is found as a forename in 15C in very small traces, widely separated (Caernarfonshire & Anglesey, Deheubarth, and Gwent & Morgannwg) (Bartrum, 1981). Reece ap Hoskin was portreeve of Manordeifi in 1481 (H. Owen, 1911-18, ii 43). This type of example and, in particular, the survival of Hoiskin, Oiskins and Poiskin in Monmouthshire tends to suggest a Welsh patronymic origin for the early modern surname. *WS* suggests that it may be a form of Hodgkin (diminutive of Hodge, from Roger), quoting Adam Hochekyn (BBStD 296). GTC 490 has a pedigree of Hoskyn of Underhill, Gower.

1813-37 (V): Found intermittently along the English border as well as in east Denbighshire and west Glamorgan where, in Gower, it has an incidence of 1.25%. Generally, however, it has a low incidence.

Guppy: found Hoskin and Hosking in Cornwall 0.65% and Devon 0.14%, and Hoskings and Hoskins in Somerset 0.12% and Monmouthshire 0.28%.

HOWE This name and its variant spellings How and Howes are common enough English surnames derived from a diminutive of Hugh (as an English forename); alternatively, it may come from a place-name element meaning 'hill' or 'burial-mound'. Bearing in mind its location in south Wales, near to English influences, it is quite likely that it came in from, say, the English West Country.

1813-37 (VI): Almost totally confined to Monmouthshire and Glamorgan. Its general incidence is very low (less than 0.2%) but in the Ogmore area of Glamorgan it is held by 0.69% of the population.

Guppy: has it in Bedfordshire, Derbyshire, Huntingdonshire, Northamptonshire and, most frequent and probably most significantly, in Somerset 0.24%.

HOWELLS Patronymic, from the W forename *Hywel*, generally pronounced Howel (as in 'towel') and written in anglicised form as Howell. In some areas, Hywel was pronounced 'Hew-el' and this contributed to its absorption of the CG forename Hugh, so that Hugh and Hywel were considered equivalents. Griffith (1914) 165, has Howel alias Hugh Nannau. HUGHES and Howells, therefore, have a history in common. See *WS* 20, for more on the change from Hywel to Hugh. Hywel was written Hoel/l, Holl, in some areas and so could be pronounced Hole. (However, Hole entered the Swansea area separately from the West Country of England.) *WS* gives an example of Richard Howell and Richard Hall being the same person. As with other names beginning with 'H', *ap* attached itself with ease, and POWELL forms a large body in itself.
(*WG2* xii, Dwnn i, Nicholas.)

1813-37 (III): This is very much a name of the south Wales coastal belt from Dinas Powis in Glamorgan to Cemais in Pembrokeshire. Over this area it covers more than 1% of the population and has its maximum incidence in

Carmarthenshire (Derllys 2.65%). There are small concentrations in Montgomeryshire (Cyfeiliog 1.17%) and Cardiganshire (Ilar Upper 0.95%), but the name is virtually non-existent in Anglesey, Caernarfonshire and Denbighshire.

Guppy: counts Howell and Howells separately – Howell: North Wales, 0.15%; South Wales, 0.66% (and Norfolk, 0.22%); Howells: South Wales, 0.44%; Monmouthshire, 0.89%; Herefordshire, 0.28%; Shropshire, 0.31%.

HUGHES This surname is derived from a patronymic name of CG origin. Though Hugh was not a native Welsh forename, the mere fact of its use inevitably led to the formation of a surname. Moreover, it was considered to equate to W *Hywel*, and this interchangeability produced an abundant surname (see also HOWELLS). Modern bearers of the surname often choose to spell it Huws. As a med. name in wide use in England, Hugh evolved many diminutive forms. HULLIN is one such name with a significant history in Wales. See also PUGH.

(*WG2* xii, Dwnn i, ii, Nicholas.)

1813-37 (I): This is very much a name of north Wales and especially Anglesey where (at 10% to 13.5%) it occurs at more than ten times the frequency found generally in south Wales. Nevertheless it is found throughout Wales and it is only in the Radnor hundred that it is totally absent.

Guppy: North Wales, 3.50%; South Wales, 0.76%; Monmouthshire, 0.40%; Cheshire, 0.24%; Gloucestershire, 0.14%; Herefordshire, 0.72%; Shropshire, 0.65%.

HULLIN Reaney (1980) notes many surnames ending in '-en', from 14C in Warwickshire and Worcestershire, where the suffix was added to pet forms of personal names common among peasants. One of these names was Hugh + '-el' and '-en' to form Hullen, Hullin. The name seems to have been borrowed early as a diminutive of Hywel (see HOWELLS), and many early examples are listed in *WS*, including clear use of Hoell and Hullyn for the same man. Ap Hullin is also found. Quoting J.B. Davies, Glamorgan local historian, *WS* says that Hullyn was a common name amongst 16C copyholders in parts of Glamorgan. This may be sufficient to explain its later frequency as a surname in Gower.

1813-37 (V): Has a distinct (and isolated) concentration on Gower (0.82%). Also found incidentally in Monmouthshire and east Glamorgan.

HUMPHREYS (See Fig. 5-7.) *WS* says that Humphrey is not often found early in Wales (that is, as a given name) and started rather late. In 15C it is recorded in small traces (in all but south-east Wales), reaching 1% only in southern Powys (Bartrum, 1981). Nevertheless, it has produced a numerous surname. Although the failure to sound 'h' is not typical of the North Wales areas where this name is most often found, the form Wmffre exists. Pumphrey (*ap* + Humphrey) is a form

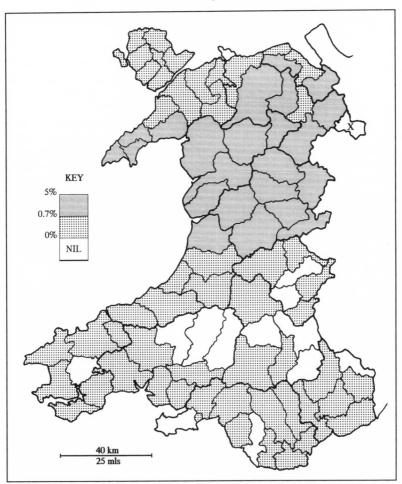

Fig. 5-7: Distribution and incidence of the surname HUMPHREYS
Maximum incidence – Denbighshire, Isaled 3.45%

found largely in English border counties, as is Bumfrey (*ab* + Umfrey), though the latter is, for instance, seen in Conwy PR, 1542 (*WS*).

(Dwnn ii, Nicholas.)

1813-37 (III): This name is to be found consistently throughout Merionethshire, Montgomeryshire, north Cardiganshire, the Llŷn peninsula and parts of Denbighshire (most notably Isaled 3.5%). It is virtually non-existent in south Wales.

Guppy: North Wales, 0.75%; Gloucestershire, 0.20%; Herefordshire, 0.14%; Shropshire, 0.30%.

HUSBAND An English occ. surname, meaning a householder or husbandman, which is of considerable antiquity and widespread in Pembrokeshire: in 1532, David Husband was a tenant at Newton, near Narberth, while John Husband was of Arnoldshill, p. Slebech; by 1560 the name is found in Pembroke (Slebech). In 1613 Muster it is found in Dungleddy, Narberth and Rhos hundreds; in 1670 (HTPem) families remain in those areas, while five heads of household are listed in Castlemartin hundred.

1813-37 (VI): Mainly found in Pembrokeshire (Castlemartin 0.09%) and west Carmarthenshire, but nowhere in significant numbers.

HUSSEY This is probably an English occ. surname from ME *huswif,* the mistress of a household (rather than loc. from Houssaye in Seine-Maritime) in Pembrokeshire, in view of these sightings: 1563, Thomas Husswie of Langum (Llangwm), yeoman (Bronwydd Deeds); 1656, Lewis Huswiffe, tailor (Charles, 1967); 1669, Abraham Huswife, tailor of Haverfordwest (Charles, 1960). In 1670 HTPem, Thomas Hussey lived in Rosemarket, Rhos hundred – dialect pron. would take care of the change – and thereafter the Husseys (sometimes Huzzey) are well represented in the registers of Burton and nearby parishes in 18C.

1813-37 (VI): Mainly confined to Glamorgan (Cowbridge 0.16%) and Monmouthshire (Usk 0.23%).

Guppy: found it only in Somerset and Wiltshire.

ISAAC This biblical forename, the name of the son of Abraham and father of Esau and Jacob, is found in England in DB. It is found in a very small trace in one area only in 15C Wales, in Brycheiniog (Bartrum, 1981). The Welsh use of biblical names after the Reformation meant that Isaac then entered the patronymic naming system in a few areas. (See also Fig. 6-1.)

(*WG2* xii; Griffith.)

1813-37 (VI): Amongst the most prominent of the biblical names in Wales. It is found over most of south Wales and has a maximum incidence in Carmarthenshire (Caio, 0.35%). It also occurs in significant numbers in north

Merionethshire (Penllyn, 0.45%), north Montgomeryshire (Llanfyllin 0.22%), and on the tip of the Llŷn peninsula (Cymydmaen 0.23%).

ITHELL The W given name *Ithael, Ithel*, was in OW *Iudhael*. It was in use in 15C in a trace (>0.25%) throughout Wales, but figured chiefly in Tegeingl & Dyffryn Clwyd (2%) and Powys Fadog (1%) (Bartrum, 1981). Occasional examples are found in west Wales: 1600 Elizabeth Bethell, Prendergast (St David's Probate). It developed into a surname with several variant spellings, e.g. Eathell, Ethell, and, with the particle *ab*, Bithell, Bythell, Bethell, etc. Examples from St Asaph Probate include: 1668, John Bythell, Nerquis; 1669, John Ithell, Northop; 1683, Jane Beethel, Northop. In its various forms it travelled early into England. An example of the name in English usage, in a notably 'unspoilt' Welsh form, is Richard Abethell, Master Shipwright at the Royal Naval Dockyard, Pembroke, in 1851 (born Deptford, Kent).

(*WG2* xii.)

1813-37 (VI): Found in several parts of Wales but to no identifiable pattern. It has its maximum incidence in Flint (Mold 0.27%; Coleshill 0.18%) and Radnorshire (Radnor 0.18%).

JACOB This biblical given name, that of the son of Isaac and Rebecca (Genesis), was little used before the Reformation. Its history as a forename is blurred in that PRs in Latin used *Jacobus* for both Jacob and James. Most examples of *Jacobus* refer to James, which was much the more common, but Jacob grew sufficiently popular in its own right to develop into a patronymic surname, usually as Jacobs. (See also Fig. 6-1.)

1813-37 (VI): A surname found consistently over a major part of south-west Wales up to, and including, north Cardiganshire. It has its maximum incidence in south Cardiganshire (Moyddyn, 0.21%).

JAMES is a very significant patronymic surname in Wales (although, ironically, it does not merit an entry in *WS*, being non-Welsh in origin). It appears as an English surname in 12C (Reaney, 1980), and was of course patronymic, but did not become numerous in England. It is tempting to attribute the large numbers of the name in some areas of Wales to the popularity of the Stuart royal house. However, this not the main explanation, for James as a forename appears in 15C, being 1% of all Wales (Bartrum, 1981). It therefore had a significant early base, clearly because it was the name of saints, which would have been enhanced by later royal usage – not necessarily Jacobite in sympathy. In Latin registers, *Jacobus* served for Jacob and for James – mostly for the latter (which originated in the variant spelling *Jacomus*). Jacob, however, had its own separate existence after the Reformation and produced a surname, (see JACOB).

(*WG2* xii, Dwnn i, Nicholas.)

1813-37 (II): The occurrence of this name is almost exactly the opposite to that for the surname HUMPHREYS. (See Fig. 5-7.) It is very much a surname of south Wales but is not in the first rank of common surnames. The only area of significant concentration is centred on north Pembrokeshire (Cilgerran 6.3%; Cemais 5.4%) and south Cardiganshire (Troedyraur 5.4%). It is almost totally absent in north Wales.

Guppy: North Wales, 0.25%; South Wales, 1.85%; Monmouthshire, 1.70%; widespread in several English counties.

JARMAN Jarman is a variant of German, from the Latin *germanus*, 'kinsman'. An older pronunciation of modern English '-er' is '-ar' (cf. clerk, Derby, Hertford, in English pronunciation), and the same name is found as Jermin, Jermyn/e. Examples of the latter are found in Pembrokeshire: Alson and John Jermyn are in Gumfreston (Pembrokeshire) in 1543; the name is found widely in Narberth hundred throughout 17C. In the eastern border counties, the name is also long-established: Giles Jerman, Trefeglwys, Montgomeryshire, appears on a 1596 tax list (E.R. Morris, 1982) and the name spread in Montgomeryshire and Radnorshire.

1813-37 (V): Found fairly widely across mid Wales and down into Monmouth-shire. It is particularly prominent on the border between Montgomeryshire (Llanidloes 2%) and Radnorshire (Rhaeadr 0.7%).

JASPER As a forename, this is the English version of Caspar, traditionally one of the Three Kings of the Nativity story. The others were Balthasar and Melchior (the latter a name found in early 17C Pem). Their remains were supposed to have been moved to Cologne in 12C, leading to the popularity of Caspar in Germany (Withycombe, 1977*)*. Jasper became an English surname in small numbers. In 15C Wales, the forename Jasper is found in very small traces in north-west Wales and Powys (Bartrum, 1981). Owain Tudor (*c.*1400-61) and his wife Catherine de Valois, widow of Henry V of England, named their second son Jasper; he was to become earl of Pembroke and uncle of Henry Tudor (Henry VII) and a man who had a great impact on Welsh affairs. Perhaps he inspired the localised popularity of Jasper, for it entered the patronymic system in a small way. It is still found in 17-18C: 1689 Jasper Thomas. Llangadwaladr; 1724 Jasper ap Evan, Llangollen (St Asaph Probate).

1813-37 (VI): Almost totally confined to south-east Wales with a maximum incidence in Breconshire (Crickhowell, 0.20%).

Guppy: Cornwall, 0.20%.

JEFFREYS This is the usual surname spelling from the forename Geoffrey, a CG name brought by the Normans. It is found in small numbers in every region in 15C (Bartrum, 1981), reaching 1% in north-west Wales so, though this is also a recognised English surname, Welsh examples are likely to be patronymic. In 1574 (Mgy Muster) Geffery ap Rees (Machynlleth [Cyfeiliog] hundred) and men in Deuthwr [Ystrad Marchell] hundred have the forename, and there is William Gefferys (also Deuthwr). Jefferson is a derivative of the same name, but follows the (mainly northern) English pattern of adding '-son' – the single entry in Wales found in our survey (Monmouthshire, Wentloog) is perhaps worthy of mention because of Thomas Jefferson's family tradition of a 17C connection with Wales (*DAB*; T.R. Roberts, 1908), though it could hardly be further from the Snowdon of the tradition.

(Nicholas; *WG1* xxv, *WG2* xii – Jeffreys of Brecon and Abercynrig.)

1813-37 (VI): The name occurs fairly extensively across Wales with particular concentrations in Denbighshire (Isdulas, 0.22%) and Flint (Mold, 0.13%). However, it is mainly to be found in Monmouthshire (Skenfrith, 0.50%; Raglan, 0.43%) and west Glamorgan (Gower, 0.29%).

Guppy: Monmouthshire, 0.28%.

JEHU A biblical name from Hebrew 'Jehovah is he', used by a few Puritan families (Withycombe, 1977). Unusually for Welsh patronymic surnames, Jehu families around the world have been traced to a single person, Jehu ap Richard, (*c.*1575-1647), carpenter and joiner of Llanfair Caereinion, Montgomeryshire, whose sons took his first name as a surname. (See also Fig. 6-1.)

1813-37 (VI): A Montgomeryshire name centred on the Caereinion area (0.52%).

JENKINS Of this as a first name in England and Wales, Hanks & Hodges (1990) say it is a 'transferred use of the surname, which is derived from the med. given name Jankin', which is to put the cart before the horse in Wales. Jankin, then Jenkin, a pet form of John, was adopted early in Wales as a forename. It formed 2% of the 15C names listed in Bartrum (1981) and became popular in some areas. In due course, it became a surname of patronymic origin. Siencyn reflects the Welsh pronunciation.

(Nicholas.)

1813-37 (III): Very much a surname of south and south-west Wales, it is almost totally absent from north-west Wales. There are concentrations in Cardiganshire (Lower Ilar 5.2%) and Glamorgan (Neath 5.4%; Ogmore 5.3%).

Guppy: NW, 0.30%; South Wales, 2.20%; Monmouthshire, 2.20%.

JERVIS The forename Gervaise, yet another CG name introduced by the Normans, was in use in med. Wales, though it is found in a very small trace only in Powys Wenwynwyn (15C Bartrum, 1981). As Gervys, it is the second name (without *ap*) of two men in 1574 Mgy Muster (Poole hundred), and has been noted in other parts of the county in early 17C (E.R. Morris, 1982). The name is also spelt Jarvis, which represents the older pronunciation. Jervis is also long-established as an English surname.

1813-37 (VI): Found along the English border but strangely absent from Radnorshire. It has its maximum incidence in Montgomeryshire (Cyfeiliog, 0.66%) and in Flint (Bromfield, 0.41%) but has a generally low incidence elsewhere.

Guppy: North Wales, 0.15%; Shropshire, 0.11%; Staffordshire, 0.14%.

JOB Though the story told in the Book of Job is a favourite subject of med. drama in England (Hanks & Hodges, 1990) there is no early indication of the name being used in Wales. Like so many OT names, Job came into use as a forename in Wales after the Reformation, subsequently entering the patronymic system in several areas. (See also Fig. 6-1.)

1813-37 (VI): Found intermittently throughout Wales without any clear pattern or in any significant concentration. Maximum incidence in Carmarthenshire (Elvet, 0.15%) and Caernarfonshire (Cymydmaen, 0.15%).

JOHN The biblical name John (from Hebrew *Johanan* 'God is gracious') has been universally popular in the Christian world, giving rise to numerous forenames and surnames – Wales is no exception. The name came first to Wales as Latin *Johannes*, becoming W *Ieuan*, and this is the version found in early lists (e.g. 13C Mer LS). The version John was borrowed from English after Norman influence made it popular there. In 15C, Ieuan formed 8% of all forenames in pedigrees, but John had already reached 12% (Bartrum, 1981). John became a patronymic surname in early modern times in its own right, but also, famously, led to JONES, i.e. 'son of John'. In the form Ieuan it led to EVANS and its variants. The letter 'J' is absent from the Welsh alphabet, the name John being said and written as *Siôn* in W, and this has given rise to the surname Shone, found in north-east Wales.

(*WG2* xii; Dwnn i, re Johns.)

1813-37 (III): Very much a surname of the coastal belt of south and west Wales. It exists in significant numbers in Pembrokeshire (2% to 5%) and spills over into the adjacent hundreds of Cardiganshire and Carmarthenshire. However, the real concentration of the name is in Glamorgan (Cowbridge 5.7%; and Ogmore and Dinas Powis both 5.6%). Not surprisingly the presence of this surname directly reflects the relative absence of the surname Jones.

Guppy: lists John and Johns separately – John: South Wales, 1.10%; Monmouthshire, 0.28%; Johns: South Wales, 0.27%; Monmouthshire, 0.17%; also found in Devon and Cornwall.

JONES (See also Fig. 4-3.) This, the most common Welsh patronymic surname, was derived from the forename John (see JOHN). As Jones it followed the

English pattern early, being found in Huntingdonshire in 1279 (Reaney, 1980) and in several other English counties by 14C. Therefore we may conclude that Jones *began* as an English surname (cf. James). Welshmen migrating into England might assume this name (or have it attributed to them) in place of ap John. Awareness of the English surname-system filtered down through Welsh society, so that in due course many whose patronymic name had been John might become Jones (see Fig. 3-1). In Gower (Glamorgan), Jone is found in a number of parishes, but this is a back-formation from Jones – it is interesting to compare this with the common lack of possessive 's' in other names (e.g. David, Hopkin, Watkin) in parts of that county.

(*WG2* xii, Dwnn i, ii, Nicholas.)

1813-37 (I): This name is not merely in the first rank of common surnames but it leads that rank for frequency by a considerable margin. In much of north and mid Wales it occurs with such frequency as to support the observation of the Registrar General that it confers a perpetual incognito on those who bear it. However, over Wales as a whole its incidence varies considerably, from over 30% in north Wales (Penllyn 30.7%) to levels along the coast of south Wales, where it is very much in the lower ranks of surnames (Pembrokeshire, Dewisland 1.06%; Glamorgan, Cowbridge 2.93%).

Guppy: North Wales, 15.00%; South Wales, 6.50%; Monmouthshire, 6.50%; in numerous English counties, of course, with those bordering Wales being the most significant.

JOSEPH Joseph is yet another example of a biblical name unfamiliar in med. Wales but taken up after the Reformation. It seems likely that it represents Joseph the son of Jacob and Rachel (OT), rather than any of the three NT bearers of the name. After its relatively late adoption it became an infrequent but not uncommon patronymic surname. (See also Fig. 6-1.)

1813-37 (VI): A surname which is found right across south Wales with the exception that it is totally absent from Pembrokeshire. It usually has a low level of incidence but is fairly strong in parts of Glamorgan (most notably Newcastle, 0.61%).

Guppy: South Wales, 0.22%.

KENDRICK This is the most usual version of the W forename *Cynwrig* (pron. with two syllables), a popular med. name. It is found only in north Wales in 15C pedigrees, rising to 1% in Gwynedd Is Conwy, and developed into a patronymic surname chiefly in that area (Bartrum, 1981). K.Ll. Gruffudd (1980) illustrates the way in which this name has similar distributions in 1580-1680 (based on probate records) and in 1980 (TD). The concentration in both periods is in the

Hawarden/Mold/Hope area; our survey, in an intermediate period, also confirms these findings. The surname is found widely in the English border counties. (*WG2* xii; Griffith.)

1813-37 (VI): Mainly centred on Flint (Mold, 0.17%), Denbighshire (Bromfield, 0.31%) and north Montgomeryshire (Llanfyllin, 0.16%) it is only occasionally found elsewhere.

KINSEY This is an English surname of patronymic origin, from an OE forename, from *cyn* + *sige* 'royal victory', generally used in the English west midlands. As such it was a surname long before it came into Wales.

1813-37 (VI): Occurs along the English border of mid Wales. It has its maximum incidence in Montgomeryshire (Llanidloes, 0.64%) and in Breconshire (Talgarth, 0.52%).

Guppy: Cheshire: 0.39%.

KNEATH is a name of misleading appearance to modern eyes, when readers expect initial 'kn ' to be pronounced 'n' and that the name should sound like that of the Welsh town Neath. Instead, it derives from the W personal name *Cynaethwy*, leading to the colloquial forms, Cnaitho, Cneitho (cf. Goronwy, Gronow – see GRONOW), eventually becoming Cnaith and, under the influence of English orthography, Kneath (originally pronounced to rhyme with 'great'). Knaveston, in p. Brawdy, Pembrokeshire, is an example of a place-name based on the root-word, being *Canaytherystoune* in 1287; the W version is Treganeithw (Charles, 1992, 200), 'Canaethwr's farm'.

(GTC 491 has Knayth of Nicholaston, Gower, pedigree from early 17C.)

1813-37 (VI): Found only in a small part of west Glamorgan (Gower, 0.68%; Swansea, 0.23%).

KNETHELL through most of its history would have had its initial letter sounded, the patronymic name being from *Cynddelw* and its variants, this traditional Welsh personal name being best known as that of a great 12C poet (*DWB*). The final '-w' was not sounded, so that the stress fell on the first syllable, '*cyn-*'. The inevitable loss of the final '-w' in written forms led to several English-looking names as this rare forename (it does not feature in 15C pedigrees) contributed patronymic surnames: Kendal(l) and its variant spellings form one group, whilst Knethell is found distinctively in early modern Pembrokeshire: 1613 David Knethell, Monkton; 1619 Balthazar Knethell, Haverfordwest; 1624 Hugh Knethell, Haverfordwest (St David's Probate); 1670 HTPem, Castlemartin hundred. No doubt examples could be cited from other counties.

1813-37 (VI): Found at a low level of incidence (max. 0.05%) in Gower and in the Kidwelly Hundred.

KYFFIN The W common noun *cyffin* (pron. 'cuffin') means 'border, boundary' and therefore could form independent place-names in more than one area, including Cyffin, a township in p. Llangadfan, Montgomeryshire. Of one Madog Kyffin, *WS* quotes from Griffith, 'He took the surname Kyffin ... , being nursed in a place of that name in Llangedwyn [Denbighshire]'. Richard Kyffin (*c.*1480-1502), dean of Bangor, with an entry in *DWB*, is thought to have been rector of Gyffin in the diocese of Bangor. Other *DWB* entries are Edward Kyffin (1558-1603), cleric and composer of metrical psalms, and Morris Kyffin (*c.*1555-98), writer and soldier, and perhaps brother of Edward – they are probably of an Oswestry family. The name has spread further over the border, giving rise to variants such as Cuffin, Keffin, Kephin, Kiffin (see *WS*); Hanks & Hodges (1988) has also Caffyn, Coffin.
(*WG2* xii; Dwnn; Griffith, Nicholas.)
1813-37 (VI): A name of north-east Wales. It has its main incidence in Denbighshire (Isdulas, 0.52%).

LANDEG is an adj. name, the mutated form of *glandeg*, used after a personal name to mean 'handsome, good-looking'. It is an unusual surname, found in a limited area. In 1670, HTGlam, it appears as Landeck in Llangyfelach hundred (Clase parcel), relating to three individuals; Swansea hundred (High Street; Bishopston; Oystermouth, as Landcock); Edward and Roger Landeck are constables, the former being also a collector.
(*WG2* xii.)
1813-37 (VI): A name which occurs in only small numbers (maximum 0.04%) in contiguous hundreds in west Glamorgan and east Carmarthenshire.

LAUGHARNE is derived from a W place-name, being the anglicised version of Talacharn (Carmarthenshire); in Welsh the penultimate syllable is stressed, leading to the weak first syllable being lost, whilst further anglicisation has eliminated the 'ch' sound in the middle – the surname is pronounced Larne. Richard de Thallazharne was reeve of Haverford in late 13C; members of this family holding similar positions were variously de Lacharn, de Talacharn, de Lagharn; by late 14C they are Lacharn, Lagharn. They later became the distinguished family of Laugharne of St Bride's (H. Owen, 1902; Dwnn) – Fenton connects them erroneously with Cornwall. Other branches are found in Castlemartin and Dewisland hundreds in 1670 HTPem.
(*WG2* xii, Dwnn i, ii.)
1813-37 (VI): Found only incidentally in the Derllys hundred which contains the parish of Laugharne. It is rather more prominent in Pembrokeshire (Cemais 0.16%; Rhos 0.15%). The only other presence is a minor one in west Glamorgan (Swansea 0.02%).

LEWIS (See Fig. 5-8.) This patronymic name comes from an English (clerical) approximation of *Llywelyn* (see also LLEWELYN). Frequently the first syllable of the latter was pronounced 'Lew' in anglicised areas. As an English given name, Lewis is a form of the French *Louis*, from the CG name which became Ludwig (Latin *Ludovicus*). The Frankish leader Clovis bore the same name. Lewis in Wales is *relatively* modern, e.g. Mer LS (Index) has Llywelyn but not Lewis. However, by 15C Lewys (W spelling) 'shadows' Llywelyn in most parts of Wales (ranges from 1 to 3%, overall 2%) (Bartrum, 1981). The use of both Lewis and Llewelyn for the same person may be easily illustrated, e.g. (15C) Lewis Glyn Cothi = Llywelyn y Glyn (*DWB*); much later (18C) Lewis Morris = Llywelyn Ddu o Fôn. Many examples are cited in *WS* as are changes from Llywelyn to Lewis in pedigrees The Latin form *Ludovicus* has produced another surname in LODWICK .

(*WG1* xxv, *WG2* xii, Dwnn i, ii, Nicholas.)

1813-37 (I): This is a prominent surname in south and mid Wales although it also occurs with reasonable frequency in Anglesey (up to 2.3%). There are concentrations of the name in Radnorshire (Rhaeadr 6.2%), Carmarthenshire (Derllys 6.3%; Kidwelly 5.5%; Cathinog 5.2%), Glamorgan (Caerphilly 5.0%) and Monmouthshire (Wentloog 5.0%).

Guppy: North Wales, 1.50%; South Wales, 3.30%; Monmouthshire, 4.00%.

LEYSHON A patronymic surname with a localised modern distribution which reflects its earlier popularity. It is from the W forename *Lleision* (local pron. replaces the initial sound with single 'l'). It is not a derivative of Lewis as has been suggested (Cottle). In 15C there is a small trace (<0.50%) in Deheubarth and 1% in Gwent & Morgannwg (Bartrum, 1981). Lleision, Leyshon, Leyson were widely used in early modern Glamorgan parishes (IGI, Glam Marr), so entering the patronymic system. A large number of people with this family name appear in HTGlam; GTC has several references to Leyshon families of Glamorgan.

1813-37 (V): A surname which is confined to an area which takes in south-east Carmarthenshire, the whole of Glamorgan, south-west Monmouthshire and the Penkelly hundred in Breconshire. It cannot be ranked as a common surname and appears in Rank V only by virtue of achieving an incidence of 0.7% in a small part of the vale of Glamorgan (Ogmore and Cowbridge).

LLEWELYN (See also Fig. 4-13.) *Llywelyn* is a W forename of considerable antiquity and, as the name of great princes, of steady med. popularity. In 15C it is found in every region of Wales, ranging from 2% to 5% and averaging 3% (Bartrum, 1981), a base from which a significant patronymic surname could be expected to spread throughout Wales. Its derivation is from a British name

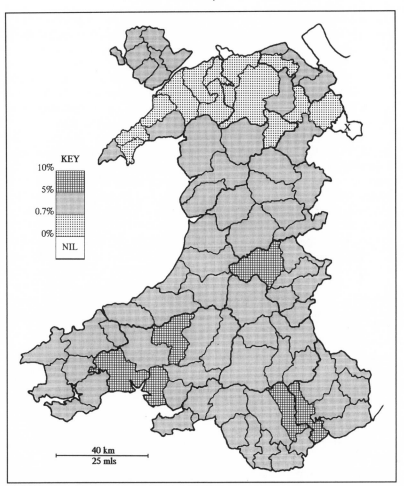

Fig. 5-8: Distribution and incidence of the surname LEWIS
Maximum incidence – Carmarthenshire, Derllys 6.30%

Lugobelinus, the first element being a divine name (and not equivalent to W *llew* 'lion', as has been popularly believed), the second element being the same as in *Cunobelinus* (Cymbeline). Llywelyn always presented clerks with problems and the variant spellings of the patronymic surname which emerged are numerous: in 18C Pembrokeshire it is found as Lewelin, Lewhellin, Llewelin, Llewellin, Llewelling, Llewellyn, Llewelyn, Llewheling, Llewhellin, Llewhelling, etc – the headword has been chosen as a reasonable compromise. These forms rarely take 's', though there are some examples, for instance, in Brecon Probate. The common 'll' in the middle is misleading, since the sound is English 'l', not W '*ll*'. Frequently, especially in anglicised areas (where the name is often fairly common, e.g. Pembrokeshire), initial 'll' is pronounced 'l'. The stress, of course, is on the second syllable, which has led to Whellin, Welling, Wellins, Hillin/g, all with or without a final 's' (e.g. St David's Probate: 1602 John Hilling, Stackpole; Pem Marr: 1725 Pembroke St Mary, Richard Whelling). Though the forename may be found in Latin documents as *Leolinus* (perhaps the origin of Loveling, Lovell, etc), it was, for much of the period of Welsh surname-formation, equated to Lewis (see LEWIS) and latinised as *Ludovicus*. A pet form of Llywelyn, Llelo, which is found in 15C pedigrees (Bartrum, 1981) in a small trace (<0.25%) only in two areas, Powys Wenwynwyn and Rhwng Gwy a Hafren, has produced a surname Lello, Lellow, Flello, etc. This group of names is not evident in our survey and seems to have its modern focus in the English border counties.

(Nicholas.)

1813-37 (III): Rather surprisingly (in view of its prominence as a med. given name) it is totally absent from the whole of north and mid Wales. It is found generally throughout south Wales often in significant numbers: Pembrokeshire (Dungleddy 1.99%), Glamorgan (Dinas Powis 2.88%).

Guppy: South Wales, 0.85%; Monmouthshire, 0.40%.

LLOYD From W adjective *llwyd* meaning grey/brown, originally, but in some families settled as a surname early, so that the significance of the epithet is not often obvious. It was not mutated after a personal name, thereby being distinguished from the vocabulary word (in med. use) for 'holy'. Although this is the surname quite early of a number of distinct families in several areas, that it was occasionally used as a forename is shown by examples in *WS*. This, however, is unusual and rarely applies to humble families. The name was widely pronounced 'Loyd' and this spelling sometimes appears in registers. Even so, that it was also correctly pronounced with *ll* is clear from the other names which have branched out from it: Floyd, Flood show at least a willingness to attempt to render the sound: 1785 Llanfihangel Penbedw, Elinor Lloyd alias Flwyd (Pem Marr). Nowadays, bearers choose sometimes to spell their name Llwyd.

(*WG1* xxv, *WG2* xii, Dwnn i, ii, Griffith, Nicholas, *WWHR* viii.)

1813-37 (II): A surname which is very much in the second rank of common surnames. It is largely confined to mid and north-east Wales where its greatest incidence is in Radnorshire (Cefnllys 4.00%), Merionethshire (Ardudwy 3.34%) and Denbighshire (Iâl 3.58%). In north Wales (Caernarfonshire and Anglesey) and in south Wales (Carmarthenshire, Glamorgan, Monmouthshire and south Breconshire) it is held by a small proportion of the population – often by less than 0.5%.

Guppy: NW, 1.00%; South Wales, 0.93%; Monmouthshire, 0.60%; western English counties, including Herefordshire, 0.68%; Shropshire, 0.60%.

LLYWARCH A W patronymic name which has remained true to its correct form, though it is also found as Llowarch. (*WS* has many variants found in early records.) It is found only in one area (Deheubarth) in a very small trace (<0.25%) in 15C (Bartrum, 1981), so may have enjoyed an early modern revival.

1813-37 (VI): Found in small numbers in parts of Montgomeryshire (Caereinion, 0.14%).

LODWICK has developed from Latin *Ludovicus*, for Lewis and Llewelyn, and so has entered the patronymic system, forming another surname. See also LEWIS, LLEWELYN.

1813-37 (VI): A surname which is largely confined to Cardiganshire (where it has its greatest incidence – Pennarth, 0.36%) and Carmarthenshire. It is only found incidentally elsewhere.

LOUGHER This is a W loc. name, found more frequently than many of its type; its area of influence reflects the locality of the river Llwchwr, the boundary between the counties of Glamorgan and Carmarthen. About a dozen heads of families appear in HTGlam in Neath, Newcastle, Ogmore and Dinas Powis hundreds; several of these are of good status though, as is often the case, people of the same name appear among the poor. The hearth tax entries have the spellings Louger, Lougher and (once) Llougher. Usually, the surname is pron. with single 'l' and with guttural 'gh'. Locker is a logical variant, also found in Glamorgan.

(*WG1* xxv, *WG2* xii, Dwnn i, GTC, Nicholas.)

1813-37 (VI): Found only in Glamorgan (that is to the east of the River Lougher) and has its maximum incidence at a point furthest from the river: Dinas Powis (0.65%).

LUCAS This is the Latin version of the forename Luke, the name of the Evangelist and beloved physician. The Lucas family of Gower is well documented from the second half of the 15C (Lucas, 1986); 17C members of the family used the arms of the East Anglian family of Lucas though no evidence of connection has been found and the western part of England seems a more likely area of origin. Several men called 'Licas' are listed in 1574 Mgy Muster. Luke is to be found, a patronymic surname in some areas such as Pembrokeshire.

1813-37 (V): Largely confined to mid Wales and Monmouthshire/Glamorgan, it is generally found at low incidence. It has its greatest incidence (and a significant one) in west Glamorgan (Gower 0.82%).

Guppy: found it in Cornwall and Somerset, among others.

LUMLEY This is an English place-name from county Durham. Of its origin as a surname, Hanks & Hodges (1988) write 'This is the surname of a noble English family, who according to tradition are descended from a certain Li(g)ulf, who lost his estates in Northumberland at the time of the Conquest'. The name was first recorded in 12C when Robert de Lumeleye witnessed a charter. The Lumleys were later viscounts (Irish peerage, created 1628) and earls of Scarbrough (English peerage, created 1690). A branch of this family is believed to have moved into Wales in 16C when it intermarried with (among others) Williams of Denbigh and, in the next generation, the Salusbery family. It is clear from numerous entries in Merionethshire PRs (IGI) that related eminent families used Lumley as a given name and that this practice was copied by humbler families. In turn the name was used in the patronymic system and it is far from unusual to come across 'Lumley Lumley' in PRs or on tombstones.

1813-37 (VI): Mainly found in Montgomeryshire (Cyfeiliog, 0.40%) and surrounding hundreds in Merionethshire and Cardiganshire.

Guppy: only in Yorkshire.

MABE From W *mab,* 'son', this word was used as an epithet after, in particular and most relevant here, a personal name. Early examples are given in *WS* and it is generally agreed that the usage which developed into a settled surname was peculiar to south-west Wales. Llewelyn Mabe Gruffuth ap Llewelyn, husbandman of Llawhaden, Pembrokeshire (1499, Picton Castle) may or may not have passed this form to his descendants, but he must have been typical of those who did. That there were a number of men in the county known as Mabe is clear from place-names: Mabes land in p. Camrose (1542, H. Owen, 1911-18, i 81); Mabes Gate, p. St Ishmaels; Mabes Mill, p. Narberth (both 18C, Picton Castle, quoted in Charles, 1992). In 17C Mabe is in Narberth and Rhos hundreds in very small numbers (Pem Muster; HTPem). Mapes, found occasionally in England, may have the same origin.

1813-37 (VI): Almost totally confined to Pembrokeshire (Narberth, 0.11%).

MADDOCKS *Madog* is a W forename of antiquity, the name of princes and leaders, including Madog ap Gruffydd (d.1236), lord of Powys (from whom the area known as Powys Fadog took its name). Though common enough as a med. given name, its popularity was not as great as, say, Llywelyn, and in 15C its greatest numbers were in Powys Fadog (2%) – it was generally favoured more in north Wales than south, averaging 1% throughout (Bartrum, 1981). As a patronymic surname, its pronunciation followed a standard process, Madog > Madoc, which in turn was written Madock, Maddock; when the genitive 's' was added, Maddocks easily became Maddox. The possible hypocoristic forms of Madog are dealt with fully in *WS*, of which Maddy has appeared in our survey. (*WG2* xii, Nicholas.)

1813-37 (VI): Found in north-east Wales, Monmouthshire and the coastal hundreds of south Wales from Glamorgan (Newcastle 0.47%) to Pembrokeshire (Dewisland 0.34%). Generally it has a low incidence.

Guppy: South Wales, 0.27%; also found in Cheshire, Herefordshire and Shropshire. Maddy: Herefordshire (0.14%).

MASON This is an English occ. surname, widespread in England and found in Wales quite early as a result of in-migration, probably from the English Midland counties. The editor of the 1574 Mgy Muster comments on its long existence in Welsh-speaking Montgomeryshire: in 1574 there were Maredudd and William Mason in Caus hundred, Rynold Mason in Deuthwr [both in Ystrad Marchell], and even David ap Mason in Mathrafal – these names give an impression of men who were not very recent incomers. The surname spread west and many examples are to be found in 18C Cardiganshire and in some parts of north Pembrokeshire. The surname is sometimes found as Masson, which reflects the Welsh pronunciation. (Dwnn ii, Griffith.)

1813-37 (V): The name is found in pockets throughout Wales. It is generally absent from Caernarfonshire, Merionethshire, Breconshire and Carmarthenshire. It has its greatest incidence in Cardiganshire (Geneu'r Glyn 1.14%).

Guppy: found in 20 English counties.

MATHIAS This surname shares its origin with MATTHEWS. As a patronymic name it derives from the forename which is the NT Greek form of Matthew, Matthias being the version used for the disciple of Jesus. A small trace (<0.25%) is found in Deheubarth in 15C, with none elsewhere (Bartrum, 1981). Mathias is the most common spelling found, though Matthias is a close variant, used interchangeably. As a surname, Mathias is easily and frequently confused with Matthews, the two being used for the same person or family at times. For one Mathias family of Cemais, Pembrokeshire, see COLE.

1813-37 (V): Chiefly found in Pembrokeshire (Dungleddy 1.34%, but the majority of hundreds are over 0.7%) and to a much lesser extent throughout Carmarthenshire. It is also found in pockets elsewhere.

Guppy: South Wales, 0.22%.

MATTHEWS Matthew, as the name of one of the evangelists in the New Testament, had moderate popularity in med. Wales. It is found in 15C in small numbers in several parts of Wales, but in the south rather than in the north, east rather than west Wales (Bartrum, 1981). It led to the development of a common patronymic surname, spelled variously Mathew, Matthew, Matthews. MATHIAS was often considered interchangeable. The Mathew family of Glamorgan (with a longer-settled surname) is well represented in pedigrees. See J.B. Davies (1975) for an accessible article about them.

(*WG1* xxv, *WG2* xii, Nicholas.)

1813-37 (IV): The name is found spasmodically throughout Wales but rarely in large numbers. It is at a maximum in Glamorgan (Dinas Powis 1.4%; Llangyfelach 1.2%).

Guppy: South Wales, 0.17%; Monmouthshire, 0.49%.

MAYBERY The Maybery family which provided pioneers of the South Wales iron industry came from Worcestershire, starting when Thomas Maybery acquired the Brecon furnace and Pipton forge in 1753 for his son John; the latter leased mineral properties in Hirwaun in 1757 and the Tredegar forge in 1764. John Maybery (d. 1784) formed a connection by marriage with the Wilkins family of Breconshire, and thus with the law and public life, to which fields their descendants turned (NLW Annual Report 1953). Their papers (13C-19C) are held at NLW. There are some sightings of the name which seem to be too early or too illiterate to be part of the same family: 1766 Manordeifi, Jane Maybry married; 1781 Clydey, Evan Mibry married (both by mark – Pem Marr). Possibly there was an earlier connection than that outlined above.

1813-37 (VI): A surname which occurs in small numbers throughout Monmouthshire and the valleys of Glamorgan (but not the Vale of Glamorgan). There are only isolated occurrences elsewhere. It has its maximum concentrations in Monmouthshire (Caldicott 0.14%) and Glamorgan (Llangyfelach 0.18%).

MENDUS It seems probable that this was the name of *advenae* in north Pembrokeshire. William Mendus was portreeve of Newport in Cemais in 1503 (Poyston), whilst Lewys Mendus was a juror there in the same year and there are several other sightings in the first half of the 16C (LS; H. Owen, 1911-18). The story that this name came to the county at the time of the Spanish Armada is, therefore, not true. Nevertheless, its origin – without further evidence – is obscure and one must note that Mendes, Mendoza, etc, in Spain have a common given name as their root. In 1670 (HTPem), Mendus is found in Rhos hundred (Rosemarket), Mends in both Narberth (Begelly) and Castlemartin hundreds (Pembroke and Monkton); Mende (Castlemartin) and Menday (Rhos) appear to be variant spellings of the same name, and it is also found in documents as Mens. Meands and Means are further variants.

(*WG2* xii.)

1813-37 (VI): Chiefly confined to the Pembrokeshire/Carmarthenshire border it is at its greatest incidence in the former county (Narberth 0.11%). It also occurs on the Glamorgan/Monmouthshire/Breconshire border.

MEREDITH (See also Fig. 4-17.) *Maredudd* is a W forename of considerable antiquity, come down to us with relatively little change. Its final element *-udd* means 'lord' as in Gruffudd (see GRIFFITHS). In 15C pedigrees, Maredudd averages 1% of forenames over Wales generally but reaches its highest figure (5%) in Rhwng Gwy a Hafren (Bartrum, 1981). In Welsh, and for the surname in Wales, the stress is on the penultimate syllable, Mer-ed'-ith. This fact affects the variants and mis-spellings to be found in PRs, so it is important to ignore the pronunciation which seems to strike the name as soon as it leaves Wales (stress on the first syllable, which allows 'Merry' to seem a suitable shortening). 'Mredith', following W pronunciation, (1613 Pem Muster, Cemais hundred, John Mredyth) becomes Redith and, with *ap*, Predith, Preddy, Priddy. The pet form of Maredudd/Meredith is Bedo, which has led to the development of the surname group Beddow/Beddoes. In 15C pedigrees, Bedo is found in very small numbers in several parts of Wales, but reaches 2% in Rhwng Gwy a Hafren. By a process of 'back-formation' Eddow/es has emerged from this group of names – that is, at some point it as been assumed wrongly that Beddows = ab Eddow.

(*WG2* xii, Dwnn i, ii.)

1813-37 (III): The surname Meredith has a distribution/incidence which is probably the most interesting of all the surnames of Wales. These two characteristics are shown in Fig. 4-17 and they have also been described fairly fully in Chapter 4. The main concentrations in south Radnorshire are in the hundreds of Radnor, 2.4% and Colwyn, 2.2%. The inclusion of the variant Beddow extends the pattern across the Glamorgan/Carmarthenshire border but otherwise has relatively little effect. The pattern shown in Fig. 4-17 would lead to the conclusion that this surname is likely to occur in significant numbers in the English counties of Shropshire, Herefordshire and Gloucestershire, and this is indeed found to be the case in other studies (most notably Guppy – see below).

Guppy: North Wales, 0.15%; South Wales, 0.17% Monmouthshire, 0.26%; Gloucestershire, 0.18%; Herefordshire, 0.61%; Shropshire, 0.30%.

MEYLER The W personal name *Meilyr*, the name for instance of med. poets (e.g. *DWB:* Meilyr Brydydd, *c.* 1100-37) was used very little by 15C, when it appears in only a very small trace (<0.25%) in Deheubarth (Bartrum, 1981). It has led to a surname chiefly in border areas, and not in large numbers. In Pembrokeshire by 17C (Pem Muster; HTPem) it was only in Dewisland, with an odd example in Castlemartin hundred.
(*WG2* xii.)
1813-37 (VI): A name which is only to be found in a small number of hundreds in south-west Wales. It has its maximum incidence in Pembrokeshire (Cemais 0.22%).

MEYRICK The W forename *Meurig* derives from Latin *Mauricius*, which in English became Maurice, Morris. Meurig and Morris were considered equivalent names and their histories overlap (see MORRIS). In 15C Meurig is uncommon, though it was slightly more numerous in south-east Wales than elsewhere (Bartrum, 1981). As a patronymic surname, Meurig became Meiricke, Merrick, Meyrick, etc., and it spread into the English border counties. The Meyrick family of Bodorgan, Anglesey, became prominent in Tudor times and produced offshoots in Meyrick of Fleet and Bush, Pembrokeshire, and of Wigmore, Worcestershire – their connections were to be found in many counties.
(*WG2* xii, Dwnn i, ii, *DWB,* Griffith, Nicholas, McGarvie.)
1813-37 (V): Mainly centred on south-east Wales this surname also occurs at a low level of incidence in Pembrokeshire and in half a dozen other locations scattered over mid Wales. It reaches some prominence in Glamorgan (Ogmore 0.79%).
Guppy: (Merrick) Herefordshire (0.17%), Shropshire (0.12%); Middlesex (0.08%).

MICHAEL Michael, the name of an archangel and saint to whom numerous Welsh churches have been dedicated since Norman times (Mihangel = Michael + angel, mutates to *Fihangel* in Llanfihangel dedications), has not been widely popular as a given name in Wales. Nevertheless it does appear as a small trace in 15C, with a single example each in part of north-east and south-west Wales (Bartrum, 1981). Though its usage grew, it is generally a rare patronymic name in most of Wales.
(Griffith.)
1813-37 (V): Found at low incidence right across south Wales and also in Caernarfonshire and Anglesey. It is particularly prominent in an isolated pocket in Radnorshire (Painscastle 0.76%). A single Mejangel, presumably pronounced Mihangel, is found in Cardiganshire (Genau'r Glyn).

MILES This CG name came to England with the Normans, usually as Milo, and had some popularity there in the Middle Ages, enhanced by the use of Miles as a shortening of Michael. It must have been brought into Wales fairly early and appears in 15C south-east Wales (Bartrum, 1981).
(Dwnn i.)
1813-37 (V): There are three main (and separate) groupings of the name. The largest is in south-east Wales where it reaches a maximum in Glamorgan (Dinas Powis 1.35%). There are also groups in south-west Wales with a maximum in Pembrokeshire (Cilgerran 0.55%) and in mid Wales (never above 0.27%).
Guppy: Monmouthshire, 0.39%.

MILLS This is a very common English loc. surname, chiefly southern, for one who lived at a mill – Mill is a less common variant. In some early English examples, where *Mille, Mylle* appear to be personal names, it may be equivalent to Miles, but evidence for this in Wales is not forthcoming. People called Mills are found in the early 1600s in Llandinam and Trefeglwys, Montgomeryshire (E.R. Morris, 1982). The musical Mills family of Llanidloes, Montgomeryshire, merits five entries in *DWB*.
1813-37 (V): The only significant grouping of the name is found in Montgomeryshire and north Radnorshire. Elsewhere it is only occasionally found. Its maximum occurrence is in Montgomeryshire (Llanidloes 1.39%).
Guppy: South Wales, 0.22%.

MORGAN (See Fig. 5-9.) A W patronymic surname from Morgan (OW *Morcant*), a forename which was popular for many centuries. In 15C it is found in every region of Wales, though in small numbers in the north; in Gwent & Morgannwg it was 4%, in Deheubarth 5%, and in Brycheiniog 6% (Bartrum, 1981). Myths circulate around the name, including that it was the original name of the heretic Pelagius (Morgan is used for that name in the Welsh Book of Common Prayer). The Morgans of Tredegar Park, Monmouthshire, a prominent Welsh family which retained its stature after the Norman Conquest, are the most notable example of a great family which took this surname early (*DWB*) and which had many offshoots.
(*WG1* xxv, *WG2* xii, Dwnn i, ii, Nicholas.)
1813-37 (I): This is a name of south and mid Wales. There is some concentration (in the range 5% to 7.5%) along a straight line stretching from Aberystwyth to just west of Cardiff, with a similar concentration in central Monmouthshire. One of those Monmouthshire hundreds (Wentloog 5.29%) takes in Tredegar Park.
Guppy: North Wales, 1.10%; South Wales, 3.80%; Monmouthshire, 4.00%.

MORRIS Like MEYRICK, Morris is derived from Latin *Mauricius*. It is more favoured as a spelling in Wales than Maurice (which is nevertheless found

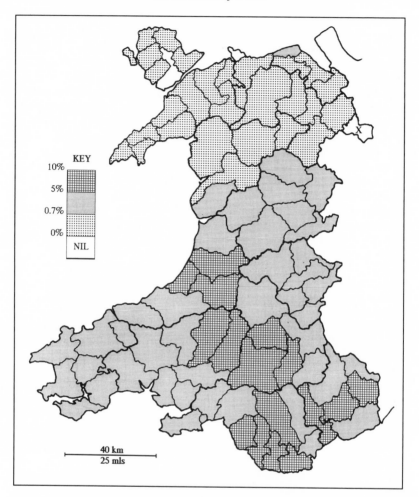

Fig. 5-9: Distribution and incidence of the surname MORGAN
Maximum incidence – Glamorgan, Miskin 7.55%

132

occasionally). The forename Morris was introduced from England (assimilated in Wales because of its approximation to Meurig) – and gave rise to an English surname also. As a forename Morris (in W, *Morus*, *Morys*) is found in greater numbers in 15C than Meurig, which it clearly replaced in popularity. At that date, Morris was general in north and west Wales and especially found in Powys Wenwynwyn (5%), but non-existent in Brycheiniog and rare in Gwent & Morgannwg – it averaged 2% of all Welsh forenames (Bartrum, 1981). Probably the most celebrated of the many Morris families in Wales is that from Anglesey (*Y Morisiaid Môn*), which produced among others Lewis Morris (Llywelyn Ddu o Fôn, 1701-1765), scholar, philosopher, poet and patriot. The father of Lewis Morris and his brothers was Morris ap Richard Morris, their grandfather Richard Morris ap William ap Hugh Griffith (Griffith, 348).

(*WG1* xxv, *WG2* xii, Dwnn i, ii, Griffith, Nicholas.)

1813-37 (II): The main areas in which this surname is to be found coincide with its occurrence as a forename in the 15C (see above). In mid and north Wales, and also in Pembrokeshire, its incidence is generally in the range 1% to 4.2%. It is, however, to be found in every part of Wales and with an incidence never less than 0.2%.

Guppy: North Wales, 0.80%; South Wales, 0.76%; Monmouthshire, 0.78%.

MORSE A variant spelling of MORRIS. Reaney (1995) gives an English example (1382) of the same man being referred to as John Morice and as John Morce. In 1386 John Mors is named as a former holder of land in Llawhaden (Foley) and the same process may have been taking place in anglicised Pembrokeshire; by 17C the surname was widespread in the county.

(*WG2* xii.)

1813-37 (VI): Mainly confined to Pembrokeshire where it has a maximum incidence of 0.60% (Dewisland). There are pockets of the name near Cardiff and on the Monmouthshire/Breconshire border.

Guppy: counted it only in Wiltshire.

MORTIMER The great Norman family of Mortimer was enormously influential in the history of med. Wales (for a map of their Welsh estates, see R.R. Davies). Nicholas writes of the Mortimers of Coedmor and Genau'r-glyn that they were 'worthy of special notice as being ... the only remains of the Norman race in Cardiganshire after the expulsion of the Lords Marcher.' They produced a sheriff of Cardiganshire in 1577, the direct line leaving the county for Carmarthenshire in the following century. Nevertheless, Mortimers were plentiful in some south Cardiganshire and north Pembrokeshire PRs in 18C – though undoubtedly some of these can be explained by the use of Mortimer as given name, which entered the patronymic system in these parts: 1679 Nevern: Felis wife of Mortimer Elston buried; 1687 Mortimer Yong buried (PR).

(*WG1* xxv, *WG2* xii, Dwnn i, ii, Nicholas.)

1813-37 (VI): Found only in south Wales and mainly confined to Pembrokeshire (Rhos, 0.28%).

MOSTYN This is an early example of the use of a Welsh place-name as a surname or, rather, it illustrates the adoption of the names of their estates by a handful of notable families (NANNEY and Pennant). The tale attached to Mostyn, that Thomas ap Richard ap Howell ap Jevan Vychan, Lord of Mostyn (d. 1558), and his brother, Piers, were ordered 'to assume their last name, or that of their residence ...' by Rowland Lee, president of the Council of the Marches, is recounted in detail in *WS*.

(*WG2* xii, *DWB*, Carr, Pennant, Nicholas; Mostyn, 1925).

1813-37 (VI): A name primarily of north-east Wales with a maximum incidence in Denbighshire (Iâl 0.18).

NANNEY This is the anglicised form of Nannau, the name of the residence of a powerful Merioneth family with many branches, adopted by them as a surname in 16C – it comes, therefore, in the same category as MOSTYN and Pennant.

(*DWB*; *WG2* xii, Dwnn ii, Griffith, Nicholas.)

1813-37 (VI): Found only in Merionethshire (Ardudwy 0.09%) and Caernarfonshire (Isgwyrfai 0.08%).

NARBERTH A W loc. surname, from Narberth (W *Arberth*) in Pembrokeshire, which has survived in small numbers to the present day. John Nerberth of Begelly (Narberth hundred) is listed in 1613 (Pem Muster), whilst in 1670 (HTPem) there is a single family in each of Dungleddy (Wiston) and Rhos (Rosemarket) hundreds. Presumably one of these produced, ultimately, John Narbett, builder of one of the very first houses in the 19C 'new town', Pembroke Dock. The name survives still in the St Clears area of Carmarthenshire, as Narbett, and is also found as Narberd (*WM* Deaths, 21 Mar 94).

(*WG2* xii.)

1813-37 (VI): Confined to the southern part of Pembrokeshire and west Carmarthenshire with a maximum incidence in the former county (Dungleddy 0.36%).

NASH may be from the Pembrokeshire parish (or from places in Glamorgan or Monmouthshire), the name formed from OE *atten aesc*, 'at the ash tree', but it is too common an English loc. surname to be sure in all cases. Many modern bearers of the surname claim descent from the landowning family of Llangwm, Pembrokeshire, but poor local records usually prevent proof. The name was very common generally in the county in 17C (HTPem). In south Pembrokeshire the surname was still often written as Ash as late as 18C: Bosherston 1703, John Ash; Richard Ash; 1713, Lettice Ash; 1714, Jane Ash; 1735, John Ash of Stackpole Elidir; 1767, Robert Nash; 1789, Henry Nash witness (PemMarr). There are two famous Nashes in *DWB*: John Nash (1752-1835), the architect; and Richard Nash (1674-1761, 'Beau Nash').

(*WG2* xii, Dwnn, *WWHR* ii 36-7.)

1813-37 (VI): Mainly confined to south-west Wales and south-east Wales. Its maximum in those areas are: Narberth 0.42% and Talgarth 0.13% respectively.

Guppy: Bucks, 0.30%; Glos, 0.11%; Herts, 0.30%; Surrey, 0.30%.

NEVETT The W forename *Ednyfed* lost its initial syllable in colloquial speech and this form led to an uncommon patronymic surname, found also as Knevet, Nevet. (There is a separate English development in which Knevett/Nevett is an AN mispronunciation of OE *cniht* 'knight'.) Ednyfed averaged only small numbers (<0.25%) in Wales generally in 15C, but reached 1% in two areas of north Wales, Meirionydd and Rhos & Rhufoniog (Bartrum, 1981). Ednyfed was abbreviated to Eden, and *WS* raises the possibility that (ab) Ened may also have been a colloquial form of Ednyfed, leading to Bennet in some families. We found three isolated examples of Eden in the 1813-37 survey: Anglesey (Tyndaethwy), Carmarthenshire (Kidwelly) and Pembrokeshire (Dungleddy).

(*WG2* xii.)

1813-37 (VI): A minor incidence in Denbighshire (Chirk 0.03%).

NEWELL This English surname has two possible derivations: from (a) Nevill (found in DB); or (b) Nowell, Noel, given as a forename originally (as Christmas was). The Newells or Newills of Montgomeryshire were originally glovers in Frankwell, Shrewsbury, some of the family being Wardens of the Glover Company. Welshpool PR (1717) [Latin original] has: William Newell, son of William and Sara Newell of Pool was descended from Richard Newell of Worthen (alive in the reign of Henry VIII), hereditary burgess of Shrewsbury. Wm Newell or Newill was admitted Burgess of Shrewsbury 24 Feb 1721-2 (M.N. Owen, 1912).

1813-37 (VI): Found in several parts of Wales but mainly centred on Montgomeryshire (Llanidloes, 0.41%) and Radnorshire (Cefnllys, 0.24%).

Guppy: (Newall) Cheshire, 0.09%.

NICHOLAS The forename Nicholas became popular as a saint's name in England in the Middle Ages and gave rise to a large number of English surnames, mainly from diminutive forms, some of which took root in Wales (see COLE, but Nicholas as a surname is much later). Nicholas is found in modest numbers in most parts of Wales in 15C, but tended to be in the north (Bartrum, 1981). Presumably it dropped out of fashion, for in its strongest area later (as a surname of patronymic origin), north Pembrokeshire, only a small handful are found in 17C records (though it became more frequent by 18C, PemMarr). The surname was frequently written as Nicolas, and also as Nichol(l)s and survives as this to modern times.

(Dwnn i.)

1813-37 (V): Although chiefly confined to south Wales it is also to be found on the English border in Montgomeryshire and Denbighshire. It is particularly prominent in Pembrokeshire (Cemais 1.5%; Dewisland 1.3%).

Guppy: Monmouthshire, 0.80%.

NOCK English loc. name from *atten oc*, also found as Noke, 'one who lived by an oak-tree', though Hanks & Hodges (1988) have it also as Scots, Irish, etc, also top.; one Scots family traces its descent from a man granted lands at Knock near Greenock 13C. In Wales it can be compared with Nash, *atten asc*, found widely in Pembrokeshire and other counties over the centuries (see NASH).

1813-37 (VI): Found spasmodically along the English border with its main concentration in Montgomeryshire (Newtown, 0.69%).

Guppy: Shropshire, 0.12%.

NUTTALL This is ultimately from a place-name, either Nuttall in Lancashire or Nuthall in Nottinghamshire, but those Nuttalls who are concentrated in north-east Wales are believed to have migrated from Derbyshire. Parents of this name, who were baptising children in Ysceifiog from 1715, have been traced to Youlgreave in Derbyshire (Ellis, 1994).

1813-37 (VI): A name which is almost totally confined to Flintshire (Rhuddlan 0.36%).

Guppy: Derbyshire, 0.07%; Lancashire, 0.25%.

OLIVER (See also Fig. 4-16.) A patronymic surname, once more with a different pattern of development from the same name in England. Oliver was brought to England as a forename by the Normans, one of their favoured CG names (the name of one of Charlemagne's retainers, probably a version of *Olaf* rather than a botanical name, as has sometimes been suggested). It was the name of a landholder in DB, and became modestly popular, so that it developed into an English surname. The forename moved into Wales in due course: in 15C it is found in very small traces in Deheubarth and Powys Fadog, but reached 1% in Powys Wenwynwyn (Bartrum, 1981). The name is found in the Montgomeryshire Muster in 1574 (e.g. Oliver ap Morys, Newtown hundred; Oliver Lucas, Montgomery hundred; Oliver ap Oliver, Mathrafal hundred, etc). It appears too in mid 17C Cardiganshire as the name of adult men (e.g. Tregaron PR: 1653, Oliver Evan marries; 1654, Oliver David is father of a child). Therefore, there is no need to seek 17C origin, whether it be increased popularity at the time of the Commonwealth (which would undoubtedly have been cancelled out at the Restoration), or through incoming miners from Cornwall or elsewhere. A notable family is Oliver of Rhydoldog, Radnorshire, a descendant of which, Revd Thomas Oliver, founded the Grammar School in his native Lledrod, Cardiganshire. A large number of Cardiganshire Oliver descendants are listed in Porter (1993). *WS* quotes examples of Boliver, Bolver, etc (from ab Oliver), both in Shropshire and in Wales, and it is found in St Asaph Probate, e.g. 1725, Joan Bolliver, Llangyniew. However, we found only one occurrence of it in our survey (Denbighshire, Bromfield hundred, 0.01%).

1813-37 (V): The name is found in many parts of Wales but particularly along a diagonal line from Pembrokeshire to east Denbighshire. It is prominent in Cardiganshire (Ilar Upper 0.8%) and Montgomeryshire (Newtown 0.7%).

Guppy: Gloucestershire, 0.14%; Herefordshire, 0.31%; and in 14 other English counties.

OWEN *Owain* is a W forename of great antiquity, probably from Latin *Eugenius* (though in early PRs it is actually often latinised as *Audoenus*). It has always been popular as a forename, being the name of princes and leaders (see *DWB*), perhaps most influentially the names of Owain Gwynedd (*c.*1100-1170) and Owain Glyndwr (*c.*1354-1416). In 15C it is found throughout Wales, averaging at 2% (Bartrum, 1981). The surname is spelled Owen, from the anglicised, colloquial pronunciation. Owens is also common in Wales, as is Bowen, from ab Owen (see BOWEN).

(*WG1* xxv, *WG2* xii, Dwnn i, ii, Nicholas, Griffith.)

1813-37 (II): Very much a name of mid and north Wales, it is particularly prominent on Anglesey (Tyndaethwy 9.54%; Talybolion 9.52%). It is also found in significant numbers throughout Caernarfonshire (Nant Conwy 6.67%; Eifionydd 6.57%) and in one part of Montgomeryshire (Llanidloes 5.78%). It is, however, also to be found in Pembrokeshire (Cemais 2.36%), east Carmarthenshire (Iscennin 1.00%) and west Glamorgan (Gower 1.21%).

Guppy: North Wales, 3.80%; South Wales, 1.15%; (absent from Monmouthshire); found in some numbers in the border counties.

PARKER An English occ. surname meaning 'keeper of a (deer-) park', this was the 40th most common surname in England and Wales in 1853.

(*WG2* xii, Monmouthshire and Glamorgan.)

1813-37 (V): The name is found along the English border and intermittently across south Wales. It is at a maximum in west Glamorgan (Swansea 1.41%; Neath 0.81%).

Guppy: Monmouthshire, 0.50%.

PARRY Formed from ap Harry (see HARRIES, HARRIS, HARRY). (See also Fig. 6-3.)

(*WG2* xii, Dwnn i, ii, Griffith.)

1813-37 (II): Found generally throughout Wales, it is in the second rank of common surnames. It is strongest in north Wales (in the range 1% to 4%) and exceptionally strong in the Prestatyn hundred (6.67%). It also has something of a presence (0.8% to 2.8%) along the English border in Breconshire and Monmouthshire.

Guppy: North Wales, 0.66%; South Wales, 0.22%; Monmouthshire, 1.10%.

PASK This name came to Wales from the West Country of England and has its roots in Cornwall (Pascoe is the same name, as is Paish). It is from the personal name Pascall (the name of a 9C saint and pope), derived in turn from Latin *pascha*, Easter, often given to those born at Easter. There is also the surname Paskin, derived directly from the OW personal name *Paskent* (MW *Pascen*) – this appears to have left Wales early, but has re-entered in recent years (e.g. *WM* Deaths, 1 March 94).

1813-37 (VI): This name is only found in the south-east corner of Wales. It is at a maximum in Monmouthshire (Trelleck 0.71%) The variant Pascoe adds little to the incidence and is more widely spread.

PEATE An English surname believed to be derived from the ME for 'pet, darling' and to have a northern origin. Cottle (1978) says that it reached Montgomeryshire from Yorkshire 'in and before the 1600s', then moved to Breconshire, becoming Pate – though this is only a slight spelling change as Peat/e would have been pronounced Pate until modern times. The emigrant Peats of Llanbrynmair, Montgomeryshire, (whose descendants include Maurice Pate, Director of UNICEF), are described in an article (D. Peate, 1983).

1813-37 (VI): A surname which is local to a single hundred in Montgomeryshire (Cyfeiliog 0.29%) and has only a minimal and scattered incidence elsewhere.

Guppy: Peat: Derbyshire, 0.07%; Peet, Lancs, 0.08%; Notts, 0.12%.

PEREGRINE The Latin *peregrinus* 'pilgrim' would be known to learned families and may have given rise to a few Peregrines (given names and, therefore available as a patronymic surname). However, the majority of examples of this as a family name are due to the latinisation of Perkin (see PERKINS) in PRs and other documents. Peregrine is still used as a forename in this century in a few families.

1813-37 (VI): An incidental surname which is almost totally confined to south Wales where it is present in every county with the exception of Pembrokeshire. It has a maximum incidence in Carmarthenshire (Perfedd 0.17%).

PERKINS The forename Perkin is a double diminutive of Piers/Peter (see PIERCE). The surname Perkin/s is found widely in southern England and in south Wales. Perhaps the following examples taken from one area will suggest similar sources for its development elsewhere. In Pembrokeshire, always open to English influence, Perkyn was used as a forename in med. times: Perkyn Hode [Hood] 1392, Guillim ab Perkyn 1506 (Bronwydd MSS, NLW), Lewys Perkyn ab Perkyn Brown, p. Mathry (Dwnn i, 111) are north Pembrokeshire examples. (Perkin is in occasional use as a forename in the same area in modern times: *WM* Deaths, 17 Aug 1994, Eliot Jenkins of Llanrhian in his 98th year, father of Perkin, etc; *WT* Deaths, Sep 1995). David Perkins was churchwarden at Llanwnda in 1543 (LS). St David's Probate has a will of John William Perkin of p. St David's in 1606. In 1613 three examples of Perkin appear in the same area (Dewisland hundred) but nowhere else, two at least being probably settled surnames. HTPem 1670 has eight examples in the same area. Over the period of the earliest surviving register for the parish of St David's, 1720-1812, there are 56 marriages (2.76%) involving people of this name, the earlier entries being more often Perkin, the later ones more often Perkins; there is by this period a scattering of Perkins families in several Pembrokeshire parishes. In contrast, the Perkin family of Rhos-y-Gelli, Gower, claimed descent from Perkin Warbeck. (*WG2* xii, GTC 500.)

1813-37 (V): Found in pockets throughout mid and south Wales. The only pocket of significance (numerically) is in Pembrokeshire (Dewisland 1.33%).

Guppy: South Wales, 0.30%; Monmouthshire, 0.25%.

PETERS Peter, much more common than Piers (see PIERCE) as a forename now, was rare, with only small traces (<0.25%) in four areas in 15C (Bartrum, 1981). It grew in popularity later, so must have entered the patronymic pool of names relatively late. One modern Peters family (which arrived in south Wales in the early 19C) came from across the Bristol Channel – a salutary reminder that Welsh-sounding names may have other origins.

1813-37 (VI): This surname is found in most parts of Wales usually in small concentrations but occasionally having a modest presence as in Anglesey (Tyndaethwy 0.25%), Caernarfonshire (Nant Conwy 0.55%), Carmarthenshire (Caio 0.38%) and Pembrokeshire (Cilgerran 0.23%; Rhos 0.21%). It is, however, totally absent from Radnorshire.

Guppy: Peter: Cornwall 0.08%; Peter/s: North Wales, 0.09%; Cornwall, 0.10%; Somerset, 0.15%.

PHILLIPS Philip was a popular forename in med. England, probably because it was the name of several early saints; it was derived from Greek *Philippos* 'lover of horses'. It was imported into Wales quickly and is quite numerous in late 13C

Mer (LS) as Phelip, the spelling which led to *Phe:* being a standard abbreviation in early records. By 15C it is found in small numbers in several parts of Wales, but was concentrated in the southern areas, especially Gwent & Morgannwg, where it reached 3%. As it averaged 1% for all Wales (Bartrum, 1981), it was bound to form a significant modern surname by the patronymic route. The variant spellings of the surname/family name are a modern indexer's nightmare: one small area has in 17-18C marriages Philip, Philipp, Philipps, Philips, Phillip, Phillipp, Phillips (Cilgerran hundred, Pembrokeshire). Any argument for standardisation is complicated by the fact that a positive choice was made by some families. Philipps was the chosen spelling of the family of Picton Castle (Pembrokeshire), later Lords Milford, perhaps due to classical influence – however, they did not adopt this consistently until 18C, after which it was considered rather grand and sometimes copied by humbler families. Meanwhile, in the same county but paralleled in others, clergy and clerks frequently spelled the forename (by 18C very common) Phillip, leading to the predominance of Phillips in modern families. Philps and Philpin (*WG2* xii, Filpin) are other variants of Philip, chiefly found in Pembrokeshire, though some may be of south-west English origin.
(*WG2* xii, Dwnn i, ii, Nicholas.)
1813-37 (II): This surname is found across Wales but is far more common in the south than the north; and more common in the west than in the east. In south Wales its incidence is almost always greater than 0.7% and the greatest incidence is in Pembrokeshire (Narberth 5.39%). In north Wales its incidence is low (generally below 0.2%).
Guppy: North Wales, 0.30%; South Wales, 1.50%; Monmouthshire, 1.40%.

PICTON is a Pembrokeshire surname from the place in that county, site of Picton Castle. There are difficulties in interpreting the first element of the place-name (see Charles, 1992, 443). William de Picton, a follower of Arnulph de Montgomery, erected the castle (Fenton). William de Pyketon was a burgess of Haverford in the reign of Edward I, while there are numerous 14C references to the name (Picton Castle; Charles, 1960). The name was in Dungleddy, Rhos and Cemais hundreds in 17C (Pem Muster; HTPem). From this base it fanned out through (and latterly outside) the county. A famous son was Sir Thomas Picton (1758-1815), killed in action at Waterloo (*DWB*).
(*WG1* xxv, *WG2* xii, Dwnn, *WWHR* x.)
1813-37 (VI): Almost totally confined to Pembrokeshire and west Carmarthenshire. It has its maximum incidence in the former county (Rhos 0.37%).

PIERCE Piers (from OFr) was the usual form of the forename Peter in med. England. As such it led to the formation of several common surnames (Pearce, Pearson, etc) and Pierce was one of these. However, in Wales, Pirs/Pyrs (variant of Piers) was used as a forename, thus entering the patronymic system. Though never common, small traces of it are found throughout Wales in 15C, with a higher concentration in Tegeingl & Dyffryn Clwyd (Bartrum, 1981). See also PERKINS, PETERS.

(*WG2* xii, Dwnn ii, Nicholas.)

1813-37 (V): Prominent throughout north Wales (where it appears in almost every hundred) but found only intermittently in south Wales. It is most prominent in Denbighshire (Isaled 1.03%; Isdulas 0.90%) and Flintshire (Mold 0.94%; Rhuddlan 0.91%; Prestatyn 0.74%).

Guppy: North Wales, 0.30%.

POWELL From ap Howell (see HOWELLS). (See also Fig. 6-3.)

(*WG1* xxv, *WG2* xii, Dwnn i, ii, Nicholas.)

1813-37 (II): Although this surname is found throughout much of Wales it is particularly prominent in Breconshire (Defynnog 8.45%; Merthyr 6.09%). In Radnorshire and Monmouthshire its incidence always exceeds 0.7% and is above 3% in many hundreds.

Guppy: North Wales, 0.20%; South Wales, 0.95%; Monmouthshire, 1.60%; Herefordshire, 2.30%; Shropshire, 1.10%.

PRICE (See also Figs 4-10, 6-3.)) From ap Rice (see REES).

(*WG1* xxv, *WG2* xii, Dwnn i, ii, Nicholas.)

1813-37 (II): This surname has much the same distribution as POWELL. However, it has a much greater incidence in both Breconshire (Builth 11.7%) and Radnorshire (Colwyn 12.2%). Its incidence is generally much lower elsewhere – usually below 3%.

Guppy: North Wales, 0.70%; South Wales, 1.50%; Monmouthshire, 1.70%; Herefordshire, 2.60%; Shropshire, 1.32%.

PRITCHARD This is the most frequent spelling of the surname derived from ap Richard (see RICHARDS). Other variants include Prickett, Pritchett and Uprichard. (See also Fig. 6-3.)

(*WG2* xii, Dwnn i, Nicholas.)

1813-37 (III): Although it is found in Breconshire and Radnorshire, (as are many other surnames incorporating *ap*), it is mainly to be found in Anglesey and Caernarfonshire (in the range 2% to 4%). Elsewhere its incidence seldom rises above 0.25% and it is absent from a large part of Cardiganshire and Carmarthenshire.

Guppy: North Wales, 0.60%; South Wales, 1.00%; Monmouthshire, 1.32%; Herefordshire, 0.51%; Shropshire, 0.17%.

PROBERT From ap Robert (see ROBERTS), also found as Probart. The pronunciation now is usually Pro'-bert, though it cannot always have been. A variant is Propert, found in areas where Robert often appears in earlier documents as Roppert (this representing the colloquial pronunciation in many areas). (See also Fig. 6-3.)

(*WG2* xii, Dwnn i.)

1813-37 (V): Another name which is largely confined to south-east Wales. The main concentration of the name is found in Radnorshire (Radnor 1.83%; Painscastle 1.59%; etc) and Breconshire (Talgarth 1.14%). It is also found in Monmouthshire and Pembrokeshire in small numbers.

Guppy: South Wales, 0.22%; Monmouthshire, 0.45%; Herefordshire, 0.31%.

PROBYN From ap Robyn (Robin), a diminutive form of Robert. In med. Wales, Robin was far less popular than Robert as a forename, reaching its greatest popularity in Rhos & Rhufoniog (1%) but found only in very small traces (<0.25%) in other parts of north-west and south-east Wales (Bartrum, 1981). More formal versions of names would inevitably tend to be favoured in pedigrees and in documents generally and, similarly, this type of name produces a less common surname. Probyn is unusual in comparison with other *ap* names (e.g. Probert, Price) in that the simple root-name, Robin, does not seem to have contributed much to the stock of Welsh surnames (but see Dwnn ii). (See also Fig. 6-3.)

1813-37 (VI): Found mainly in Monmouthshire and east Glamorgan but in no great concentrations (maximum Monmouthshire, Trelleck 0.05%).

PROFIT The origin of the name seems to be OFr *prophète* 'prophet', probably a nickname derived from actors in med. mystery plays. As a surname, also spelt Prophet, it is found in med. London, 13C Buckinghamshire, 14C Essex (Reaney, 1961). Families called Prophet/t, Proffet/t, Profit/t have lived in the area round Llanasa, Gronant and Prestatyn, Flintshire, for three centuries (Young, 1985).

1813-37 (VI): Wholly confined to Flintshire and then only in the Prestatyn hundred (0.83%).

PROSSER From ap Rosser (see ROSSER). (See also Fig. 6-3.)

1813-37 (IV): This is totally a name of south Wales and is found in greatest strength along the English border, e.g. Radnorshire (Painscastle 2.88%), Breconshire (Talgarth 2.58%) and Monmouthshire (Skenfrith 1.29%). It is also fairly common in one part of Pembrokeshire (Dewisland 0.86%).

Guppy: South Wales, 0.22%; Monmouthshire, 0.42%; Gloucestershire, 0.14%; Herefordshire, 0.44%.

PROTHEROFrom ap Rhydderch (see RHYDDERCH). Like its root-name, it is often mis-spelt and has developed into a surname which can be found as Prydderch, Protheroe, Protherough, etc. The first syllable of Rhydderch rhymes with the first syllable of 'brother', leading to the tendency to use 'o' in anglicised spellings. (See also Fig. 6-3.)

(*WG2* xii; Griffith, Nicholas.)

1813-37 (IV): This name (including variant spellings) is found predominantly in south Wales. However, it is also found throughout Anglesey, due no doubt to a particularly strong presence in the Malltraeth hundred (1.09%). Although it is found right across south Wales the main concentration is in south Radnorshire (Colwyn 2.16%) and north Breconshire (Builth 1.17%; Talgarth 0.74%).

Guppy: South Wales, 0.10%; Monmouthshire, 0.10%; Herefordshire, 0.12%.

PUGH (See also Figs 4-14, 6-3.) From ap Hugh (see HUGHES).

(*WG1* xxv, *WG2* xii, Dwnn i, Nicholas.)

1813-37 (III): Mainly occurs along a diagonal line from Painscastle to Ardudwy with an incidence of between 1% and 3% but with a noticeable concentration in west Merionethshire (Talypont 5.43%; Estimaner 4.79%).

Guppy: North Wales, 1.60%; South Wales, 0.22%; Monmouthshire, 0.22%; Herefordshire, 0.17%; Shropshire, 0.48%; Worcestershire, 0.26%.

REES (See also Fig. 4-9.) *Rhys* was a common W forename in med. times, its popularity enhanced by many Welsh princes and leaders. In 15C, in no region is it less than 3% of names in pedigrees, whilst it reaches 9% in parts of north and mid Wales – the average throughout Wales was 5% (Bartrum, 1981). The surname Rees, though it has lost the rolled 'rh', retains a sibilant 's' at the end, sounding similar to the Welsh forename. English attempts to write the name led to Rice, on the wrong assumption that 'y' had this sound; inevitably pronunciation then followed the spelling in some areas. The forename appears in Latin documents as *Reseus, Rheseus* or *Riceus*, and is often abbreviated as *Rs*. As Rees and its variants, this became a very common surname. *Ap* + Rhys led to Preece and Price (see PRICE). Creese exists in Monmouthshire 1813-37, and in mid-Wales in modern times, but it is probably the English adj. name Crease rather than for *verch Rhys*.

1813-37 (II): Mainly to be found in south Wales, it has much less of a presence in mid Wales, and is seldom found in north Wales. The largest concentration of the name is in east Carmarthenshire (Iscennin 6.49%; Carnwallon 5.84%) and west Glamorgan (Llangyfelach 6.18%). The relative absence of the name in north Wales is inconsistent with the earlier use of the given name and the incidence recorded by Guppy.

Guppy: Reece: Monmouthshire, 0.60%; Herefordshire, 0.12%; Shropshire, 0.12%. Rees: North Wales, 0.50%; South Wales, 3.30%; Monmouthshire, 0.70%; Herefordshire, 0.12%.

REYNOLDS The forename Reynold is CG in origin, imported by the Normans and borrowed by the Welsh. Its W version is *Rheinallt.* This was found in very small numbers everywhere in Wales in 15C, rising to 1% in parts of north Wales and throughout Powys (Bartrum, 1981). Reynold/s is an example of a patronymic surname which is not exclusively Welsh (since it is found in 13C in England), but which followed the Welsh pattern. In 1574 (Mgy Muster) there are several examples, including Rynalt ap Edward and Rees ap Rynallt (Newtown hundred). Many examples of reduced forms of *ap* + Reynold/ Rheinallt are to be found in Shropshire PRs: there is one example of Prynallt in 1813-37 (Ystrad Marchell hundred).

(*WG1* xxv, *WG2* xii.)

1813-37 (VI): A name found extensively across south Wales occasionally in modest concentrations: Pembrokeshire (Dungleddy, 0.53%), Carmarthenshire (Derllys, 0.59%) and Glamorgan (Neath, 0.44%). It is also found in Montgomeryshire (Llanidloes, 0.43%).

Guppy: only noted in English counties, including Gloucestershire, 0.14%; Shropshire, 0.31%.

RHYDDERCH was a W forename of great antiquity, the name of a 6C leader Rhydderch Hael ('liberal') or Hen ('aged'). It was widely used in the Middle Ages – in 15C an average 1% throughout Wales, and 2% in Meirionnydd and Deheubarth (Bartrum, 1981) – and inevitably gave rise to a patronymic surname. As a name which was difficult for English speakers to say or write, it appears under many guises, especially when the *ap* forms are included (see PROTHERO). RODERICK is one approximation, and the name is found as Ruther, Rothero, Rotherough, Ruddock, Rutherch, etc. Rhydderch is frequently abbreviated in documents as *Ruddz*, the 'z' representing the *yogh* sound.

1813-37 (VI): A name almost totally confined to south Wales but never found in significant concentrations. At its maximum in Pembrokeshire (Dewisland 0.09%) and in Carmarthenshire (Elvet 0.09%).

RICHARDS Richard was a CG forename (from elements *ric* 'power' and *hard* 'strong, hardy'), imported via England, which became extremely popular in Wales. In England its diminutives have given rise to innumerable surnames (e.g. Hicks, Dickens, Dixon, etc.). In 15C the forename was common throughout Wales, every region having its quota, with an average of 3% overall (Bartrum, 1981). Naturally this base led to a widespread patronymic surname which has evolved chiefly in two ways: with possessive 's' as Richards, and with *ap* as

Prichard, Pritchard (see PRITCHARD) – their distribution around Wales is quite different. *WS* has examples of Crichett and Crichard, which may be from *verch* Richard.

(Nicholas.)

1813-37 (II): This name is found in significant numbers (in the range 1% to 3%) in all the areas in which the surname PRITCHARD is absent. Taken together these two surnames indicate the widespread popularity of the given name Richard over the whole of Wales.

Guppy: North Wales, 0.70%; South Wales, 0.93%; Monmouthshire, 1.00%; Herefordshire, 0.14%; Shropshire, 0.26%.

ROBERTS (See also Fig. 4-8.) Robert was one of the CG forenames brought by the Normans (from elements *hrod* 'fame' and *berht* 'bright'), as well as a similar OE name. It became very popular after its introduction to Wales: in 1292 four people of this name figure in Mer LS. By 15C it averaged 3% throughout Wales; the great majority of these were, however, in the north, in the areas of modern Gwynedd, Clwyd and northern Powys, raging from 5% to 8% (Bartrum, 1981). PROBERT is from ap Robert.

(*WG2* xii; Griffith, Nicholas.)

1813-37 (I): Although predominantly a surname of north Wales it is found in some measure through the whole country. In the north, with the exception of Anglesey, it is unusual to find it covering less than 10% of the population. The main concentration straddles the borders of Denbighshire (Isaled 14.87%), Caernarfonshire (Nant Conwy 14.55%; Isaf 14.56%) and Merionethshire (Edeyrnion 14.79%; Penllyn 14.10%).

Guppy: North Wales, 5.00%; South Wales, 1.10%; Monmouthshire, 1.00%; Cheshire, 0.32%; Gloucestershire, 0.50%; Herefordshire, 0.24%; Shropshire, 1.05%.

ROCH This name is one of the rare examples (in Wales generally) of the name of a Welsh place being represented by a surname. The parish of Roch, Pembrokeshire, (W *Y Garn*), takes its name from the Anglo-Norman castle built on a prominent rock, OFr *roche*. The name was taken to Ireland at the time of the Anglo-Norman invasion of that country in 12C, and has proliferated there, often as Roche. Meanwhile, offshoots, servants and tenants of the early bearers of Roch carried the name around the county and further afield, though in 1670 the preponderance of the name in Pembrokeshire was still in its original Rhos hundred. Roach is a common variant spelling, reflecting local pronunciation.

(*WG2* xii, Dwnn i, Nicholas.)

145

1813-37 (VI): Found throughout Pembrokeshire in reasonable concentrations (e.g. Dewisland 0.69%; Rhos 0.67%; Castlemartin 0.63%). Also found in small numbers in south-east Wales and north-east Wales.

RODERICK Roderick was not used in Wales as a forename, except that it was sometimes substituted for the W name *Rhodri*, *Rodericus* being used as the Latin version of the latter as well as of Rhydderch (see RHYDDERCH). In some areas Roderick sometimes replaced Rhydderch as a surname, though it is a CG name in origin, not Welsh, and is quite separate in origin. Meyrick (1808) refers to Penglais, Cardiganshire, 18C, as 'built by Roderic Richards. His father was Richard Rhydderch'.

1813-37 (V): Found throughout much of mid and south Wales, it is completely absent from the four northernmost counties of Wales (namely, Anglesey, Caernarfonshire, Denbighshire and Flintshire). It is also absent from a large part of Pembrokeshire, Radnorshire and Breconshire. The only concentration is in Carmarthenshire (Perfedd 0.80%).

ROGERS Roger was a CG forename (from elements *hrod* 'fame' and *gar* 'spear') imported by the Anglo-Normans. It became mildly popular as a forename in med. times: in 15C Roger comprised 1% of forenames in pedigrees throughout Wales (Bartrum, 1981). As Rogers, it became a patronymic surname, but we may also infer that, where the surname was settled early, as in places like Pembrokeshire, it was brought in from other parts of Britain. Rogers (1995) illustrates that in England the surname Rogers (and to some degree the variant Rodgers) was 'a name biased to the south and west'.The Welsh version of Roger was Rosier, Rhosier (medial 'sh' sound), which was later spelled and pronounced Rosser (see ROSSER, PROSSER). Prodger, Progers, are variants, from ap Roger. (*WG2* xii, Dwnn i, Nicholas.

1813-37 (IV): The name is found throughout Wales but seldom in significant numbers. It is most prominent on the English border: Denbighshire (Bromfield 1.4%), Montgomeryshire (Ystrad Marchell 0.99%), Radnorshire (Radnor 1.1%); and along parts of the south Wales coast: Monmouthshire (Usk 1.1%), Carmarthenshire (Carnwallon 0.92%), Pembrokeshire (Castlemartin 1.2%). It is, however, absent from the whole of the Llŷn peninsula (Caernarfonshire) and also from most of the coastal hundreds of Merioneth and Cardiganshire.

Guppy: North Wales, 0.18%; South Wales, 0.32%; Monmouthshire, 0.35%; Cheshire, 0.09%; Herefordshire, 0.65%; Shropshire, 0.65%.

ROSSER A patronymic surname from the W version of Roger (see ROGERS).

1813-37 (V): Totally confined to south Wales where is found in a rather disjointed pattern from Monmouthshire to Pembrokeshire. The main concentration is in Monmouthshire (Trelleck 0.8%; Usk 0.7%).

Guppy: Monmouthshire, 0.45%.

ROWLANDS (See also Fig. 4-15.) As Roland, yet another CG name imported by the Normans (from *hrod* 'fame' and *land* 'land') which was adopted in preference to native names. This was probably at a later date than, e.g. Robert or Roger, since there are only small traces (<0.25%) in most regions of Wales in 15C, apart from Caernarfonshire/Anglesey where it reached 1% (Bartrum, 1981). The preferred spelling became Rowland, evolving into a patronymic surname which is nearly always found now as Rowlands. People of English stock called Rowland may well take their names from the Derbyshire place-name.
(*WG2* xii, Dwnn ii, Griffith, Nicholas.)

1813-37 (III): It is found throughout Wales but chiefly in the western half of mid Wales (greatest Cyfeiliog, 3.3%) and on Anglesey (range 1% to 2.2%).

Guppy: North Wales, 0.40%; South Wales, 0.27%; Monmouthshire, 0.28%. It is worth noting that, though the spelling with added '-s' is only counted in Wales, Guppy finds Rowland only in England, in Cheshire, Derbyshire and Devon.

SALMON Solomon was a relatively modern – certainly post-Reformation – adoption in Wales, entering the patronymic system in a limited way, comparable with other OT names. Salmon is a variant of the same name, and perhaps the more common spelling as a surname. Either version may attract a final 's'. (See also Fig. 6-1.)
(Nicholas.)

1813-37 (VI): Found spasmodically around the periphery of Wales. The only place it is found in any numbers is in north Pembrokeshire (Cemais 0.29%).

SALUSBURY Few names could look more English than this, with its variants Salesbury, Salisbury, and most surname reference books relate it only to the Wiltshire place-name. D.H. Owen (1975) says of its origins as a surname in the Denbighshire Englishry, 'A district called Salusbury or Salebiri has been identified in Herefordshire, where Henry de Lacy held extensive estates, while de Lacey's lands in Lancashire included the manor of Salusbury'. The Salusbery family of Lleweni and their descendants are extensively documented – see *DWB*, with its comment 'in the course of time the Salusberies became entirely Welsh', and also Evans (1995), Smith (1954). William Salesbury (c.1520-1584) was the chief translator of the NT into Welsh. *DWB* tells us he was the second son of Ffwg ap Robert ap Thomas Salbri Hen.
(*WG1* xxv, *WG2* xii, Dwnn i, ii, Griffith, Nicholas.)

1813-37 (VI): A surname which is largely confined to north Wales and only occurs incidentally elsewhere. Its main concentrations are on Anglesey (Talybolion 0.42%) and in Denbighshire (Isaled 0.33%)

SAMBROOK This is an English loc. surname, from a Shropshire place-name (a few miles north-west of Newport) which has gradually worked its way across mid Wales. It is found in early 18C in south Cardiganshire and north Pembrokeshire, variant spellings including Sandbrook, Shambrook and Sambroth. So acclimatised did it become that the 'natural' order of things was reversed and this surname sometimes became a first name: 1721 Cilybebyll (Glamorgan) BT, Samrook fil. Ricardi Thomas bapt.

1813-37 (VI): Largely confined to the coastal area of south-west Wales from Pembrokeshire (Cilgerran, 0.23%) to west Glamorgan (Gower, 0.14%). It also occurs in a minor way in east Montgomeryshire.

SAMUEL (See Fig. 5-10 and also Fig. 6-1.) This is a biblical name, from the Hebrew judge and prophet, taken up chiefly by nonconformists as a forename and, therefore, as a patronymic surname. Examples are Christmas Samuel (1674-1764), Independent Minister born Llanegwad, Carmarthenshire (*DWB*). Samwell is a variant (see *DWB*, David Samwell).

1813-37 (V): The most common of all the Hebrew names to be found in Wales (see Chapter 6 for a general discussion of these names in Wales). Although found throughout Wales it is far stronger in the south than the north. It is particularly strong across Monmouthshire, Glamorgan, Carmarthenshire and into Cardiganshire. The main concentration is in west Glamorgan (Llangyfelach 0.9%) and east Carmarthenshire (Carnwallon 1.4%; Iscennin 0.8%).

SAVAGE The origin is a nickname and may be compared with GWILT and WILD – though they are unconnected except in meaning. William Sayvage is in 1574 Mgy Muster (Llanfyllin hundred). E.R. Morris (1982) says that a family of small landowners of this name went to Trefeglwys, Montgomeryshire, in 16C and that they were a cadet branch of the Rock Savage family of Cheshire. A different, 19C, origin is given for another Savage family in the county. However, both families used Rock as a forename. (*WG2* xii.)

1813-37 (VI): Found spasmodically along the English border mainly in Flint (Prestatyn, 0.37%) and Montgomeryshire (Caereinion, 0.33%).

SAYCE is one of the surnames formed from W adj. *sais* 'English', but it is generally accepted that in this context (i.e. attached as an epithet to a forename) it means 'English-speaking'. Like so many adj. names, Sayce and its variants (Saies, Sais, Says, Seys) have survived mainly in border areas – they are found in the English border counties (*WS* 189) and in Pembrokeshire: for the latter we may cite David Seys, 14C (Charles, 1960) and other med. examples in Haverfordwest; by 17C (HTPem) Sayce (the usual local spelling) and Sayse are in Castlemartin, Narberth and Rhos hundreds.

148

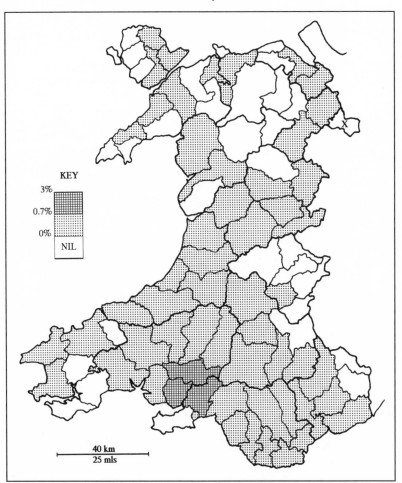

Fig. 5-10: Distribution and incidence of the surname SAMUEL
Maximum incidence – Carmarthenshire, Carnwallon 1.36%

149

(*WG2* xii, Nicholas.)

1813-37 (VI): Confined to Pembrokeshire and Monmouthshire/Breconshire, it has its maximum incidence in the former (Dewisland 0.23%). The incidence of the name in Wales found by Guppy is not reflected in our survey.

Guppy: Sayce: North Wales, 0.15%; Monmouthshire, 0.22%; Herefordshire, 0.14%; Shropshire, 0.08%. Seys: Monmouthshire, 0.17%.

SHEEN Although an alternative adj. origin has been suggested (Reaney, 1995) from OE for 'fair, handsome', this is also an English loc. surname, from places in Surrey or Staffordshire. The Surrey place gave its name to London immigrants 12-14C (Reaney, 1980). As Guppy found it peculiar to Cheshire, we may prefer the Staffordshire location (near the Derbyshire border) as the origin for the surname which found its way into Wales.

1813-37 (V): Almost totally confined to the area around the Colwyn hundred (1.5%) in south Radnorshire.

Guppy: Cheshire, 0.09%.

SHELDON This surname came to Wales from Derbyshire in the late 18C/early 19C. A Catholic family of this name are known to have lived in Rowland, Derbyshire, in 17C (Madge, 1995). In 1772 Job Sheldon of Staley in the parish of Bonsall, Derbyshire, yeoman and miner, took a lease of lead mines in the Llanfyrnach area of Pembrokeshire (Bronwydd MS 1983). At the beginning of the 19C another Job Sheldon (believed to be related to the one at Llanfyrnach) gained extensive lead mining interests in north Cardiganshire. However, he has been described as having come to the area from Scotland (Evans, 1902). He became mayor of Aberystwyth on upwards of nine occasions. The surname is part of a group of largely local names brought by Derbyshire lead-miners to various parts of Wales (see also BONSALL, HOOSON, NUTTALL).

1813-37 (VI): Found in the lead mining areas of Flintshire, Cardiganshire and Pembrokeshire as well as in Monmouthshire, but never in significant numbers (always less than 0.10%).

Guppy: Cheshire, 0.09%; Derbyshire, 0.21%; Oxfordshire, 0.15%; Staffs, 0.12%.

SMITH (See Fig. 5-11.) 'Easily the commonest surname in England and Wales, Scotland and the USA, and the fifth in Ireland in 1890' (Cottle). Its origin as an occ. surname is clear, and its widespread distribution reflects the ubiquity of the craft. Rogers (1995) has maps of the English distribution.

(*WG1* xxv, *WG2* xii, Dwnn i, ii, Nicholas.)

1813-37 (IV): Another name which is found in many parts of Wales but generally in very small numbers. Its greatest incidence coincides with those areas which have been subject to English influence such as Radnorshire (Radnor 2.01%), Monmouthshire (Skenfrith 1.34%), and Pembrokeshire (Narberth

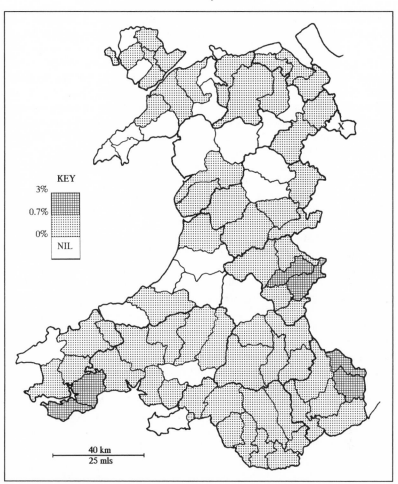

Fig. 5-11: Distribution and incidence of the surname SMITH
Maximum incidence – Radnorshire, Radnor 2.01%

0.78%). It is interesting to note that, although the incidence of this name in the Radnor hundred is unexceptional by Welsh standards, it is greater than its average incidence in England (1.37% in 1853).

Guppy: North Wales, 0.20%; South Wales, 0.32%; Monmouthshire, 0.90%; Cheshire, 0.56%; Gloucestershire, 2.70%; Herefordshire, 1.60%; Shropshire 0.50%.

SMOUT Rynolds Smout is listed in 1574 Mgy Muster (Cawres [Ystrad Marchell] hundred). The name probably came into Wales from Derbyshire and may be a variant of Smith – in the IGI Smout, Smoth, Smoot, Smuth are indexed together. (Smout is found often in Scotland in the IGI.)

1813-37 (VI): The name is almost totally confined to Montgomeryshire. It is found in significant numbers in the Kerry hundred (0.7%).

STEPHENS The forename from which this patronymic surname is derived had as its origin the Greek *stephanos* 'wreath', in the sense of 'garland or crown'. Stephen was the name of the first Christian martyr, it was used by early popes, and was brought to England by the Normans – it was already fairly popular on the Continent. Steven with 'v' represents the med. English pronunciation and spelling, and led to a common English surname Stevens (son of Steven). The forename is found as a very small trace in 15C in Deheubarth and Brycheiniog, but reached 1% in Rhwng Gwy a Hafren (Bartrum, 1981). The Welsh form of the forename is *Steffan*, so Welsh pronunciation reflects the root word more closely than its English version. Probably that led to Stephen/s being the preferred spelling in most areas of Wales as a late patronymic surname. Many Stephens who went to America became Stevens and, of course, there is no essential difference in the two versions, except that they may give a clue to origin.

1813-37 (IV): A name which is found throughout south and mid Wales but with a generally low level of incidence (usually below 0.3%). It has some prominence in Radnorshire (Knighton 1.1%; Rhaeadr 1.0%; Radnor 0.9%) as well as in parts of Glamorgan (Kibbor 0.7%) and Pembrokeshire (Castlemartin 1.1%). It is quite exceptional to find the alternative spelling of Stevens.

Guppy: North Wales, 0.20%; South Wales, 0.55%; Monmouthshire, 0.28%; Gloucestershire, 0.40%; Herefordshire, 0.50%; Shropshire, 0.12%. Guppy assesses the 'ph' and 'v' spellings together but says: 'Stephens is particularly characteristic of Cornwall and of the counties on and near the Welsh border and also South Wales itself'.

STRADLING A Tudor pedigree of this family (repeated by Nicholas) claimed that they had assisted Robert fitz Hamo in the conquest of Glamorgan, but their true origin is likely to lie in another continental direction than Normandy. John de Estratlinges is thought to have come from Strättligen in Switzerland in the reign of Edward I. His son, Peter de Stradelinges, custodian of Neath Castle in 1296-7, married an heiress and acquired the St Donat's estate in Glamorgan, thereby beginning the long and continuous connection with the county. The most up to date study of the Stradlings is to be found in Griffiths (1994), which has a summary of other recent writings on them.

(*DWB, WG1* xxv, *WG2* xii.)

1813-37 (VI): Confined to east Glamorgan and the western fringe of Monmouthshire. It has its only concentration in Glamorgan (Newcastle 0.27%).

SWANCOTT Phillip Swankott and Richard Swancock are listed in 1574 Mgy Muster (Llanidloes hundred); Richard Swancotte was in Trefeglwys in 1596/7, whilst the will of John Swancote of the same parish was proved in 1654 in PCC. The family has descendants around the world (Hancock, 1981; E.R. Morris, 1982). Their surname originated in the name of a place near Bridgnorth, Shropshire.

1813-37 (VI): Largely confined to Montgomeryshire (Llanidloes, 0.64%).

TANNATT This loc. surname is an example of a river-name (river Tanad or Tannat, Montgomeryshire) being taken by a gentry family, that of Neuadd-wen in the same county, in the sixteenth century. They became Tanat of Abertanat.

(Dwnn i, Griffith, Nicholas.)

1813-37 (VI): Found only in parts of Montgomeryshire and Denbighshire but never in any real concentrations. Its maximum incidence is in Montgomeryshire (Ystrad Marchell 0.17%).

TAYLOR An English occ. surname, the 4th commonest in England and Wales in 1853. Morys Taylo'r is listed in 1574 Mgy Muster (Montgomery hundred).

(*WG2* xii.)

1813-37 (V): This name is found in many parts of Wales but to a somewhat disjointed pattern. It occurs more consistently across Monmouthshire and Glamorgan and has its greatest concentration on Gower (1.45%).

Guppy: South Wales, 0.27%.; Monmouthshire, 0.40%; Cheshire, 0.80%; Gloucestershire, 0.80%; Herefordshire, 0.58%; Shropshire, 0.45%.

TEAGUE There are two possible explanations for the surname Teague in Wales, the first being adj. from W *teg* 'fair, beautiful' and probably the origin of most uses of the family name. The spelling has obviously been affected by the existence of the Irish surname (from a personal name), the amount of Irish presence and influence in (especially) west Wales being often underestimated. *WS* has numerous examples of Teague in its various manifestations (e.g. Deage, Degg, Teage, Tecka, Tegg, Tegue) on the eastern border, especially in Shropshire. Pembrokeshire Teagues may typify the greater survival of W adj. names in 'border' areas, though in this county there was much movement in from

Ireland over many centuries and a handful of Irish names have survived (e.g. in Pembrokeshire) – it is possible this is an example. By 17C it is found in Castlemartin hundred in a handful of parishes. Tegan is usually considered a derivative of *teg* (*WS* 196), though an alternative derivation is given from the place-name Tegeingl (Flintshire). Tegan is found in 15C Haverfordwest and 18C St David's, which may suggest the former origin in this area. The surname Tegan also exists in Ireland, again from a personal name.

(*WG2* xii, Tegin of Hope, and of Wrexham.)

1813-37 (VI): Chiefly found in some border hundreds of Radnorshire, Breconshire and Monmouthshire; it has a maximum incidence in Radnorshire (Painscastle 0.30%).

Guppy: Cornwall, 0.10%; Gloucestershire, 0.17%.

TEW is from the W adj. *tew* (mutated *dew*) 'fat'. Like many surnames of adj. origin, it tends to be found in numbers in English border counties. No regard should be paid to the statement in Reaney (1961) that it is from 'W *dhu* "swarthy" ', for *du/ddu* 'black, dark' are pron. (approximately) 'dee/thee' and not 'dew'.

1813-37 (VI): Found mainly in Pembrokeshire (Dewisland 0.11%), but occasionally found elsewhere with minor incidence.

Guppy: Hampshire, 0.08%; Northamptonshire, 0.20%.

THOMAS (See also Fig. 4-6.) The biblical name came from Greek *didymos* 'twin'. In England it was known before the Norman Conquest but only as a priest's name; after the Conquest it came into general use and became very popular as a result of the cult of St Thomas à Becket. This great prevalence led to many English surname variants such as Thoms, Tombs, Thom(p)son, Thom(p)kins, Tomlinson, etc. Its popularity in Wales came later, and the unadorned name became one of the predominant patronymic surnames. In 15C the forename averaged 8% throughout Wales, reaching 12% in Brycheiniog and also in Gwent & Morgannwg (Bartrum, 1981). Modern bearers of the surname sometimes adopt the Welsh version Tomos.

(*WG2* xii, Dwnn i, ii, Nicholas.)

1813-37 (I): This is amongst the first rank of common surnames in Wales. It is found everywhere and seldom with an incidence of less than 2%. The main concentration is in north Carmarthenshire (ranging from 10.4% to 12.6%), in adjacent parts of Cardiganshire (Troedyraur 11.39%) and Pembrokeshire (Cilgerran 11.07%), as well as in certain parts of the vale of Glamorgan (Newcastle 10.76%; Dinas Powis 10.19%).

Guppy: North Wales, 2.00%; South Wales, 7.00%; Monmouthshire, 2.80%; Cheshire, 0.24%; Gloucestershire, 0.53%; Herefordshire, 0.72%; Shropshire, 1.08%.

TIBBOT This is an English patronymic surname, Tibbot being probably from the personal name Theobald, originally pron. as Fr. *Thibaud.* An alternative origin is from a diminutive of Isabel. Either way, the surname came into Wales ready-made, being found in English midland counties from an early date. William Tybbotes of Llanbrynmair, Montgomeryshire, appears in a tax assessment of 1596 (E.R. Morris, 1982), and the name proliferated in the county. D. Peate (1994) stresses the nonconformist allegiance of many of the family.

1813-37 (VI): Found in a narrow band right across mid Wales but particularly in Montgomeryshire (Cyfeiliog, 0.66%). Also found on Anglesey (Malltraeth 0.11%).

Guppy: finds this (as Tibbett/s, Tibbitt/s) only in Cambridgeshire and Warwickshire.

TIMOTHY The Latin (from Greek) *Timotheus* means 'honouring God' and was the name of a companion of St Paul, to whom two Epistles were addressed. Timothy was not used in med. Wales but was a name typical of the post-Reformation revival of both classical and biblical names. Thus it entered the patronymic system late and formed a less common surname.

1813-37 (VI): Found in small numbers (usually less than 0.10%) throughout the upland areas of Monmouthshire, Glamorgan, Carmarthenshire and south Cardiganshire. There is a single area of minor concentration in Carmarthenshire (Perfedd 0.28%).

TREHARNE derives from the ancient W personal name *Trahaearn*, with the elements *tra* 'over, excessive' + *haearn* 'iron'. Trahaearn ap Caradog (d.1081) was a ruler of Gwynedd; Trahaearn Brydydd Mawr, an early 14C poet, was another prominent bearer of the name (*DWB*). The name had little popularity in 15C, being found almost exclusively in southern Wales – only in traces generally, but it reached 1% in Brycheiniog (Bartrum, 1981). Numerous examples of the surname are found in English border county registers (*WS*). Variants reflect the difficulty of pronouncing Trahaearn, including Traharn/e, Treharn/e, Trehearn/e, Trehern/e. (Nicholas.)

1813-37 (VI): Found right across the southern part of south Wales. It has areas of concentration in Glamorgan (Cowbridge 0.69%) and in Carmarthenshire (Iscennin 0.59%; Kidwelly 0.54%).

TREVOR This is an early example of a W loc. surname, in the category of estate names adopted by a few important families. *WS* quotes from Thomas, *A History*

155

of the Diocese of St Asaph, that 'John Trevor I = Ieuan ap Llewelyn o Drefawr', that is of Trefawr or Trefor (1346). *DWB* says that the surname in this line was settled in the time of John Trevor '*hên*' (d.1453). Key articles on the history of the Trevors are to be found in *DWB*: Trevor of Brynkynallt, Denbighshire, descended from Tudur Trevor (*fl.* 940) son-in-law of Hywel Dda; and Trevor of Trevalun, Denbighshire, Plas Têg, Flintshire, and Glynde, Sussex. (*WG1* xxv, *WG2* xii, Dwnn ii, Griffith, Nicholas.)

1813-37 (VI): Confined to the northernmost hundreds of north Wales and totally absent elsewhere, including Anglesey. Maximum incidence in Flintshire (Mold 0.10%).

TREWENT A surname in that less common category with origins in Welsh place-names: Trewent is in the p. of Stackpole Elidor, Pembrokeshire, and the surname is found in the general locality from med. times to 19C: Richard of Trewent, juror at Inquisition at Pembroke, 1331; Richard Trewent, juror at Pembroke in 1358; Richard Trovente tenant, Carew, 1541-2 (H. Owen, 1911-18); Thomas Trewent, a tenant of the manor of Penally died 29 Eliz and is mentioned in several contemporary documents (EP, co. Pem). The Trewent family were still in the Pembroke area in 1881. (Nicholas).

1813-37 (VI): Confined to one part of Pembrokeshire (Castlemartin, 0.16%).

TROW There are various possible derivations for this name: from the OE word for 'faithful, true'; or from one of the Devon place-names, Tree, Trew, True or Trow; or from Wiltshire place-names from OE *trog* 'trough'. Hanks & Hodges (1988) attribute it to the West Midlands, from where it could easily have come into Wales. Edward Trow was a flannel manufacturer in Newtown, Montgomeryshire, in 1838.

1813-37 (VI): Largely confined to Montgomeryshire, where it has its greatest concentration in the Kerry hundred (0.81%).

TUCKER An English occ. surname, meaning one who fulls cloth (so an alternative development to Fuller). This was a common surname in south-west England, especially in Devon. Pedigrees of the Pembrokeshire family, Tucker of Sealyham (and Halton, Cheshire), are in Dwnn i, 152, 192; see also *WWHR* viii. (*WG2* xii.)

1813-37 (V): A name which is confined to south Wales and mainly found in areas which have been subject to the greatest English influence – Monmouthshire, Glamorgan (Gower) and Pembrokeshire. Its main concentration is in Gower (1.21%).

Guppy: South Wales, 0.11%; Monmouthshire, 0.11%; Cornwall, 0.20%; Devon, 1.02%; Dorset, 0.26%; Hampshire, 0.25%; Somerset, 0.66%; Wiltshire, 0.35%.

TUDOR A patronymic name from the W forename *Tudur* (pron. approx. Tidder), used widely in north Wales. As Tudur it is found largely in that region in 15C, reaching 2% in Rhos & Rhufoniog and 1% in four other northern areas, including Powys Fadog (Bartrum, 1981). For the ancestry of the most famous inheritors of the name, the Tudor monarchs, see *DWB* (under Tudor family of Penmynydd, Anglesey, etc; Owain Tudor). We may reflect that Henry VII's grandfather's name was Owain ap Meredith ap Tudor, known as Owain Tudor – if he had chosen to use his father's name, we might have had a Meredith dynasty. Tudor was in widespread use as a forename so that modern families have many possible origins. Variant spellings are numerous, especially as Tudor is often confused with Tewdwr, a separate Welsh personal name derived from the Theodore group of names. Among variants are Tidder, Tither (see *WS* 199), and – in our survey – Tutor.

(*WG1* xxv, *WG2* xii, Nicholas.)

1813-37 (VI): Found at generally low incidence in Pembrokeshire, south-east Wales and across the northern part of mid Wales. It is at its highest incidence in Montgomeryshire (Cyfeiliog 0.58%; Newtown 0.44%).

Guppy: North Wales, 0.40%.

TURNER An English occ. surname, usually from one who turned objects (that is, worked with a lathe), especially in wood, though alternative occ. meanings are given by Reaney (1995). The spelling Turnor looks more distinctive, but is entirely the same name. In 1574 Mgy Muster, John ap John Turnor is listed (Llanfyllin hundred), George Tyrno'r (Llanidloes hundred).

(*WG2* xii, Nicholas.)

1813-37 (V): A name which is found right along the English border. There is a particular concentration of the name in Montgomeryshire (Newtown 0.87%).

Guppy: Monmouthshire, 0.22%; not listed elsewhere in Wales, but widespread in English counties, including Cheshire, 0.30%; Gloucestershire, 0.20%; Herefordshire, 0.37%; Shropshire, 0.26%.

VAUGHAN The W adj. *bychan*, mutated to *fychan*, 'younger', was a frequent epithet attached to personal names to distinguish father and son. In English orthography, *fychan* became *vychan*, while the first vowel sound (roughly as in Scottish 'Buchan') was modified in speech. Inevitably, the 'ch' sound caused problems, becoming guttural 'gh', then silent in Vaughan, the familiar form (pron. Vawn). In early lists the initial sound is often dropped, producing Ychan (e.g. Brecon Probate). Many slight spelling variants exist of which we might quote two extremes: the name appears as Vane in south Pembrokeshire 18C (perhaps cf. 'vase', pron. 'vawse' by older people locally); Baughan, Bawn (from the root word) on the eastern border of Wales. There are fifteen Vaughan families in *DWB*, including those of Golden Grove (Carmarthenshire), Trawsgoed (Cardiganshire), plus numerous individuals. Nowadays, bearers of the name sometimes choose to revert to Fychan.

(*WG1* xxv, *WG2* xii, Dwnn i, ii, Griffith, Nicholas.)

1813-37 (IV): Found in almost every area of Wales with the exception of Anglesey and west Caernarfonshire. Although its incidence is generally low, there are several areas of reasonable concentration, namely: east Caernarfonshire (Nant Conwy 0.87%); Denbighshire (Chirk 1.21%; Rhuddlan 0.91%; Isdulas 0.75%); Radnorshire (Painscastle 1.29%; Rhaeadr 0.72%; Cefnllys 0.83%) and Breconshire (Talgarth 1.44%; Penkelly 0.82%).

Guppy: North Wales, 0.55%; South Wales, 0.11%; Monmouthshire, 0.20%; Herefordshire, 0.17%; Shropshire, 0.34%.

VOYLE is a W adj. name, from *moel*, mutated as *foel*, 'bald'. Voyle represents the pronunciation of the mutated form; Moyle is rarer, though not unknown.

(*WG1* xxv, *WG2* xii, Dwnn i.)

1813-37 (VI): Mainly confined to Pembrokeshire (maximum Narberth 0.29%) but found occasionally elsewhere in south Wales.

WALBEOFF This has evolved from the name of an Anglo-Norman family, holders of land in Brycheiniog as followers of Bernard de Neufmarché, and thereafter spreading in the border counties. Waldebeuf is recorded in Breconshire from mid-12C (Siddons, 1991, 267). T. Jones (1898, i, 61), in remarking that the name was not extinct, has this story: 'In 1884 a woman named Walby asked relief at Crickhowell. She said the family name was Walbeof, but her husband had altered it because people laughed at it' – a sad commentary on a once eminent name in decline.

(*WG1* xxv, *WG2* xii, Dwnn ii, Nicholas.)

1813-37 (VI): Found only in the eastern part of Monmouthshire (Skenfrith, 0.10%).

WALTERS The forename Walter was of CG origin, introduced by the Normans; (The elements are *wald* 'rule' and *heri* 'warrior'). It was borrowed into Welsh as Gwallter (cf. William/Gwilym) and is found in this form in early records. Gwallter/Walter is not found in north Wales in 15C, but occurs throughout the southern regions, reaching 1% of names in Deheubarth and Gwent & Morgannwg, and 2% in Brycheiniog (Bartrum, 1981). The patronymic surname Walters was the natural outcome in these areas. Where the English Walter was the preferred pronunciation, the 'l' was silent (cf. palm), so the surname Waters is a variant of Walters, and the two were mostly interchangeable (though the spelling pronunciation eventually prevailed). Wattars is also found (e.g. Cardiganshire). This pronunciation of Walter led to the diminutive Wat or Watt,

also responsible for a surname in Watt/s (see WATTS). A double diminutive, Wat + kin, led to Watkin/s (see WATKINS). Occasionally, the surname Walters will be a corruption of Cadwaladr (see CADWALADER).
(*WG2* xii, Dwnn i, ii, Nicholas, *WWHR* v.)

1813-37 (IV): The spellings Walters and Waters taken together show the name to be largely confined to south Wales and only found very occasionally in north Wales, where Waters is totally absent. The ratio of the two spellings in south Wales shows Walters to be generally about three times more common than Waters, but the ratio is broadly equal in Monmouthshire. There are several areas of significant concentration such as in south Monmouthshire (Usk and Caldicott both 1.13%); west Glamorgan (Llangyfelach 1.03%); and east Carmarthenshire (Iscennin 1.88%; Perfedd 1.14%).

Guppy: South Wales, 0.60%; Monmouthshire, 0.60%. Waters: Monmouthshire, 0.50%.

WARLOW The earliest Pembrokeshire Warlow probably brought his surname with him and we can only guess why he, or an ancestor, had been given the nickname *warloc* (ME) 'warlock, wizard'. The name was still in an early form when we first encounter it in records: David Warlach, 1285; John Warlaz, reeve of Haverford, late 13C (Charles, 1967). There can be no mistaking it in this context for (e.g.) a variant of loc. Wardlow (Cottle). The forms evolved through Warlagh, Warla, quite numerous in med. Haverfordwest records, to Warlow, and by 17C was in Rhos and Dewisland hundreds (Pem Muster; HTPem).
(*WG2* xii.)

1813-37 (VI): Very much a Pembrokeshire name (Rhos 0.62%) with only a minor incidence in Carmarthenshire.

WARREN This patronymic surname derives from the CG personal name Warin, (OFr. *Guarin, Guérin*), which became W *Gwaren*. The family of Warren of Trewern, Pembrokeshire, has this origin. Warren is found in Castlemartin hundred in 1670 (HTPem); coincidentally there is Warren parish in this hundred, but this is not responsible for the surname.
(*WG1* xxv, *WG2* xii, Dwnn i, Griffith, Nicholas.)

1813-37 (VI): By this period almost totally absent from Pembrokeshire, but found fairly extensively (at low incidence) in Monmouthshire (Caldicott 0.14%).

WATKINS (See Fig. 5-12.) Watkin was commonly used as a forename in some parts of Wales. As explained under WALTERS, it is a double diminutive of Walter. In 15C it is used everywhere except in north-east Wales, being particularly common in Brycheiniog (3%) (Bartrum, 1981). It seems likely that Watkin was soon considered old-fashioned in England (perhaps it was comparable with some modern 'vogue' names), but it lasted well in Wales, where

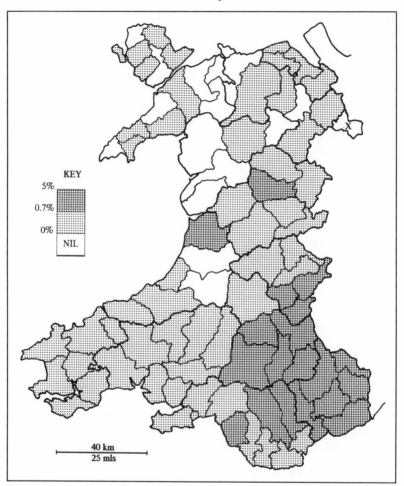

Fig. 5-12: Distribution and incidence of the surname WATKINS
Maximum incidence – Breconshire, Crickhowell 3.54%

names ending in '-kin' appealed. It was in general use in some areas in 17C and 18C (Glamorgan BT: 1672, Llangiwg, Watkin Rees Griffith buried; 1678, Llansamlet, Watkinus Francis buried). Watkiss and Watkeys are variants of Watkins; and just as Walter was borrowed in the form Gwallter, so Watkin became Gwatkin, frequently found in the English border counties.
(*WG2* xii, Nicholas.)

1813-37 (III): Although found throughout Wales, it is mainly a surname of south-east Wales being strongest in Breconshire (1.6% to 3.5%) and Monmouthshire (1.1% to 3.3%). There is an isolated concentration in Montgomeryshire (Caereinion 1.74%).

Guppy: North Wales; 0.18%; South Wales, 0.98%; Monmouthshire, 1.20%; Gloucestershire, 0.20%; Herefordshire, 1.93%; Shropshire, 0.12%.

WATTS Watt was a diminutive of Walter (see WALTERS) which formed a patronymic surname. Like many other borrowed names, it is not *only* W, being found for example in Scotland, but it becomes distinctively Welsh by its late adoption as a surname, and by its distribution in pockets in Wales.
(Nicholas.)

1813-37 (V): Almost totally a surname of south Wales, but only of low incidence, the only real concentration is in Pembrokeshire (Dewisland 1.15%).

Guppy: counts this in 14 English counties (including Gloucestershire, 0.46%) but not in Wales at all.

WEAL This must be a variant spelling of Wheal/e and Wheel/s, a loc. English surname, which is usually said to refer to someone who dwells at or by the (water-)wheel. However, the name, as Wheal, Whale and Whell, is also Cornish from *whel*, 'mine-working', an element in Cornish place-names such as Trenwheal (White, 1981).

1813-37 (V): A name which is confined to Radnorshire (Colwyn 1.08%; Rhaeadr 0.72%), Breconshire and Monmouthshire (these last two with very low incidence).

WEAVER This is generally thought to be an English occ. surname, from OE *wefan* 'to weave'; in Pembrokeshire, Webb, with the same occ. meaning as Weaver, is far from uncommon. However, Rogers (1995) illustrates an alternative loc. origin (from Cheshire) for the concentration he finds in post-med. western English counties. Shropshire and Herefordshire are the most dominant of these and could well account for the surname Weaver in Montgomeryshire. Roger Wever is listed in 1574 Mgy Muster (Llanfyllin hundred).
(*WG1* xxv, *WG2* xii, Wever of Presteign, Dwnn i.)

1813-37 (V): Found only along the English border it has a particular concentration in Montgomeryshire (Kerry 1.05%).

161

Guppy: Apart from Essex, 0.10%, all the English counties listed may be relevant to its existence in Wales: Gloucestershire, 0.20%; Herefordshire, 0.14%; Shropshire, 0.12%; Somerset, 0.30%; Worcestershire, 0.32%.

WHITTAL is a variant of Whittle, which has a loc. meaning, either from several English places meaning 'white hill', perhaps especially the one in Lancashire; or from Whitwell, in several counties. Whettall is also found. Vittle is a further variant, found particularly in Pembrokeshire.

1813-37 (V): This name (including its variants) is only found in two places. Although it is more widely spread in Pembrokeshire, it is at its greatest concentration in Radnorshire (Cefnllys 1.06%).

WIGLEY is a Derbyshire place-name which may well have moved as a surname into Wales, like several others (e.g. BAMFORD, HATFIELD, Thornhill – see *WFH*, 67). There is also a small place with the same name in Shropshire but the balance of probabilities, without more evidence, favours a Derbyshire origin.

1813-37 (VI): Found in as many as seven unconnected parts of Wales but never in significant numbers. It has a maximum incidence in Breconshire (Penkelly, 0.11%).

Guppy: Derbyshire, 0.11%.

WILD An English surname (often spelled with '-e') which may be either from 'wild' as a nickname or from a location: someone who dwelt in a wild place. Cottle describes it as a Midland name, which would help to explain its presence in Wales. The Wilde family was in Holt in 1292 (R.R. Davies, 1975).
(*WG1* xxv, *WG2* xii, de Wild.)

1813-37 (V): Largely confined to two distinct pockets; one centred on Radnorshire (Cefnllys 1.06%), the other taking in east Glamorgan and much of Monmouthshire, but the incidence is very low in this latter area.

Guppy: Cheshire, 0.12%; Derbyshire, 0.30%; Shropshire, 0.10%. (Of the latter, Guppy comments that the spelling Wilde is found also.)

WILDING derives from OE **Wilding,* either a personal name or a nickname.

1813-37 (V): Largely confined to Radnorshire (Knighton 0.75%) and adjacent parts of Montgomeryshire.

WILLIAMS (See also Fig. 4-4.) William is a CG forename, from elements meaning 'will' and 'helmet', appropriate concepts for a military race and used by the Normans at the highest level. Arriving in the forms Guilielm and Willhelm, William quickly became the leading male English name in the centuries immediately after the Norman Conquest. By 15C, William as a forename averaged 5% throughout Wales, with the largest occurrence (10%) in Anglesey & Caernarvon (Bartrum, 1981). Guilielm (cf. Guillaume) led to W *Gwilym* and is the ancestor of the occasional surname Gwilliam; this is pron. and often spelt

Gullam in Pembrokeshire. As a surname, Williams (as it nearly always became) is spread wider than Wales – the popularity of the forename in England was sufficiently early to provide it with a base in, particularly, southern counties and Cornwall. Nevertheless, because of its universality in Wales, it is often thought of as typically Welsh.

(*WG1* xxv, *WG2* xii, Dwnn i, ii, Griffith, Nicholas.)

1813-37 (I): The name is found throughout Wales and the incidence is never less than 2.82% (Radnorshire, Cefnllys). It is particularly strong in Caernarfonshire and on Anglesey (in the range 15.4% to 22.5%). Its incidence in south Wales is not much lower and it is found chiefly in south Breconshire/east Carmarthenshire (in the range 10.7% to 13.9%). It is also quite strong in Glamorgan (5.9% to 9.8%) and much of Monmouthshire (7.4% to 9.5%).

Guppy: Monmouthshire, 7.00%; North Wales, 7.00%; South Wales, 6.50%. The English counties in which it is numerous are Cheshire, 0.34%; Cornwall, 1.82%; Gloucestershire, 1.09%; Herefordshire, 2.72%; Shropshire, 1.58%; Worcestershire, 0.60%.

WOGAN This has the appearance of an Anglo-Norman name, not least because it has become a notable Irish surname (*WS* is inclined to attribute the presence of Wogan on the English border to Irish immigration). Nevertheless, it is Welsh and patronymic, from *Gwgan* (the initial letter habitually dropping in these circumstances) and the famous Pembrokeshire family is well-documented. It is not, however, always easy to connect modern bearers of the name to this distinguished line, for lack of continuous records. By 17C, Wogan is found in Castlemartin, Dewisland, Dungleddy and Rhos hundreds (Pem Muster; HTPem).

(*WG1* xxv, *WG2* xii, Dwnn ii, *WWHR* vi, vii; Griffith; Siddons i 277, Nicholas).

1813-37 (VI): Almost totally confined to south Pembrokeshire (Castlemartin 0.16%).

WOOSENCRAFT Though this surname has an exotic look and attracts legends, it has its origins in the Lancashire place-name Wolstencroft, from elements *Wulfstan* (pers name) + *croft* 'enclosure'.

1813-37 (VI): A Radnorshire name generally of low incidence (Knighton, 0.31%).

WOOSNAM As with Woosencraft, this name reflects the everyday pronunciation of an English place-name – in this case, Wolstenholme in Lancashire (from *Wulfstan* + *holm* 'dry land in fen'), from which direction it has moved towards and into Wales. It appears in Llanllwchaiarn, Montgomeryshire, in 1596 and became numerous in the area of Llandinam, Trefeglwys and Llanidloes in 17C (E.R. Morris, 1982). The golfer Ian Woosnam has brought worldwide modern fame to the name.

1813-37 (VI): Almost totally confined to Montgomeryshire (Llanidloes, 0.45%) and Radnorshire (Colwyn, 0.15%).

WORTHING An English loc. surname, possibly from Worthen in Shropshire rather than Worthing in Norfolk or Sussex. According to Cottle (1978), it may also be from the OE forename *Worth*, 'worthy'.

1813-37 (V): Another name which is confined to a small area centred on Radnorshire (Colwyn 1.70%; Cefnllys 1.06%).

WYNNE The origin of this name is covered under GWYNNE, of which it is the mutated form. There are ten main families outlined in *DWB* under Wynn (one Wynne); without exception these had their origin in north Wales.
(*WG2* xii, Dwnn i, ii, Griffith, Nicholas.)

1813-37 (V): A name which is chiefly found in north Wales, where it has greatest prominence in Denbighshire (Isdulas 1.87%; Isaled 0.86%) and Merionethshire (Edeyrnion 0.96%). It is rarely found south of Montgomeryshire.

Guppy: North Wales, 0.30%; Shropshire, 0.12%.

YORATH The W forename *Iorwerth* is a compound of the elements *ior* 'lord' and *berth* (mutated) 'handsome' and was once numerous in med. times (LS Mer). By the time of the 15C pedigrees, Iorwerth was found in only a very small trace (<0.25%) throughout Wales, the highest occurrence being in Anglesey & Caernarvon (1%) (Bartrum, 1981). It had, in the meantime, been overtaken by Edward, which was considered to be its equivalent (see EDWARDS). Iorwerth has itself led to the surnames Yorath, Yerward, etc.

1813-37 (VI): Confined to Monmouthshire, where it occurs in small numbers (Abergavenny, 0.07%). The variant Yerward occurs only in Pembrokeshire (Rhos, 0.02%).

YOUNG This is a fairly common English surname, originally a nickname, perhaps in the comparative sense of 'junior' (cf. W *fychan*, which Young may sometimes replace). It is found very early in Pembrokeshire: for Young/Yonge of Cemais, see also COLE. Hugh le Yonge was justice in eyre in the lordship of Haverford in 1380 (Owen, 1911-18, i 50). The name is found (as Yong, Yonge, Yongue and Young) in Cemais, Rhos and Castlemartin hundreds in 1613 (Pem Muster) and in most parts of the county by 1670.
(*WG1* xxv, Hanmer and Hope; *WG2* xii, families of Nevern, of Hanmer and Bryniorcyn, etc; Dwnn i, ii.)

1813-37 (V): A name which is found in pockets throughout Wales with the exception of north-west Wales. It is more extensive in Pembrokeshire (and adjacent hundreds), but has a greater incidence in Monmouthshire (Trelleck 1.05%).

Guppy: South Wales, 0.08%; Cheshire 0.10%; Gloucestershire, 0.46%.

CHAPTER 6

FURTHER USES OF THE SURVEY

The collection of surname information on the scale described in Chapter 4 allows further conclusions to be drawn on a number of fronts. For example, not only is it possible to establish the rate of occurrence by hundred of each individual surname, but it can also be used to identify (and comment on) differences in the annual rate of marriage in different parts of Wales. Then again it can be manipulated to show the distribution characteristics of different groups of surnames, such as the percentage of the population covered by the ten most common names, the distribution of all surnames derived from Old Testament names, or the proportion of surnames incorporating an *ap* prefix compared to that with the possessive 's'. Indeed, examples such as these are worth looking at in detail as they can give an insight into the cultural, social and religious background of different parts of Wales and, hence, the context in which one's ancestors would have lived.

Annual rate of marriages

The total number of marriages found over the whole of Wales gives a rate of 6.58 marriages/year/1000 population, which is well below the average of 7.50 which we had been led to expect (see Chapter 4). However, there is a variation about this figure at county level, with the following counties having marriage rates which are above the average for Wales as a whole: Carmarthenshire (7.53), Anglesey (7.41), Cardiganshire (7.15), Pembrokeshire (6.93), Caernarfonshire (6.91) and Glamorgan (6.63); the following are below the average: Merionethshire (6.36), Denbighshire (6.04), Monmouthshire (6.00), Montgomeryshire (5.99), Breconshire (5.59), Flintshire (allowing for the exclusion of the detached part) (5.58) and Radnorshire (5.54). As one might expect, a further variation was also found between hundreds within counties.

It is a matter for conjecture why the average for Wales should be so consistently in the lower half of the range for England found by other researchers. However, always assuming that that range is a realistic one, three possible explanations come to mind. First, there is the fact that during this period many of the parishes in Wales were very poor, the clergy were often poorly educated, and pluralism was common. As a result, standards of record-keeping might well have been low in some areas so that, whilst in theory Anglican parish registers should record all the population who had actually married, in practice this was not actually the case. Second, we had to rely on the bishops' transcripts for many areas and under-recording within these records is known to have existed. Third, the heavy migration of people of marriageable age into the rapidly developing areas of Glamorgan and Monmouthshire provided circumstances in which the controls on moral behaviour, which would have been present in more stable societies, were possibly much weaker. As a result, cohabitation rather than marriage could have existed on a significant scale.

The ten most common names

The percentage of the population covered by the ten most common names in each hundred is shown in the frontispiece to this book and also in Fig. 1-2. From the frontispiece it can be seen that more than 70% of the population is covered by this small number of surnames in two main areas of broadly equal size. In the north of Wales the area covers the whole of Anglesey, Caernarfonshire, Merionethshire and the larger part of Denbighshire. (Within this area it is worth noting that the figure exceeds 90% in the Uwchgwyrfai and Creuddyn areas of Caernarfonshire.) In the south of Wales the second area takes in much of Cardiganshire, the whole of north Carmarthenshire and also west Breconshire.

Closely associated (geographically) with these two areas there are a small number of hundreds in which Welsh traditions are also known to have been strong. In these areas the ten most common names generally cover between 60% and 70% of the population. In the remainder of Wales the range is between 30% and 60% and includes most of those areas known to have experienced longer-term influences from England. At the lower end of this range (30% to 40%) three specific areas – south Pembrokeshire, the Gower peninsula, and the eastern side of Monmouthshire – mirror where that influence has been at its strongest. The lowest percentage occurs in Pembrokeshire (Castlemartin, 33.08%).

Today the two areas in which we found common names to be most prominent are often described as the Welsh heartland, and these are certainly the areas within which the Welsh language is strongest and traditional customs have tended to prevail. In contrast to this, those areas in which common names are least prominent are ones which have been subject to the greatest outside influence over the longest period, a factor which has led to a much enhanced stock of surnames locally, both through in-migration and/or the early adoption of settled surnames.

Across Wales as a whole the ten most common names in the period 1813-37 (as found in our survey) are exactly the same – and in virtually the same order – as was reported in a Welsh newspaper in 1994 by a correspondent from Anglesey who had studied surnames listed in the four telephone directories which had covered Wales in 1959.[1] The only differences are that he found Evans more frequent than Thomas, and Lewis more frequent than Hughes.

These percentages for the ten most common names in Wales are in marked contrast to those for England, also given in Fig. 1-2, in which it can be seen that the most common name, Smith, is held by only 1.37% of the population and the top ten names cover only 5.15% of the population.

The incidence of Old Testament names

A casual observer of the surname scene in Wales could be forgiven for assuming that Wales had a high Jewish population, as surnames such as Samuel, Joseph, Isaac, Mordecai, and even Israel, may readily be found. The fact of the matter is, however, that the holders of these surnames are (usually) anything but Jewish.

We believe that our work has shown that the very high incidence of such names has come about as a result of their popularity as given names among certain nonconformist denominations just before the time when settled surnames were being taken. On the other hand, the authors of *WS* appear to consider that the taking of Old Testament names had a general appeal throughout Wales and, in their discussion of the surname Moses, they say: 'Like other O.T. names Moses was used as a christian name in the protestant period (i.e. not necessarily puritan and nonconformist) ...'.[2] However, the incidence of Old Testament names which we found in our survey (see Fig. 6-1) shows that, while these names can be found in most parts of Wales, they occur far more frequently in the south than in the north. It seems to us that the reason for this geographical emphasis towards south Wales is related more to differences in the denominational make-up of the two areas than to the level of nonconformity overall.

In north Wales by the middle of the nineteenth century the dominant nonconformist denomination was Calvinistic Methodism (see Fig. 6-2), which had its roots firmly within the Established Church. Indeed, it was not until 1811 that Calvinistic Methodism had become a separate denomination outside the Anglican Church. As the traditional names chosen for boys by Anglicans were usually taken from the New Testament, from the saints of the Christian church, or from those used by the monarchy, it is easy to see that the stock of given names from which settled surnames might develop would be heavily weighted towards such names as John, Thomas, William, Henry and Richard.

In south Wales on the other hand, it can be seen that the Independents and the Baptists had become the main denominations by the middle of the nineteenth

167

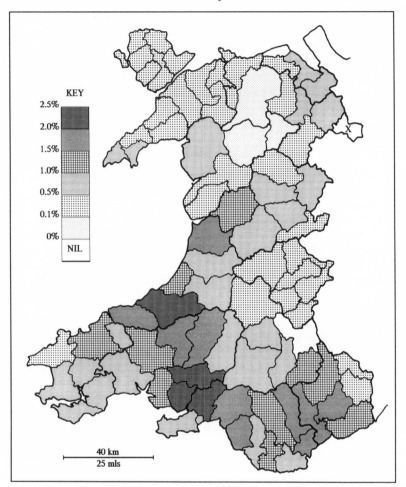

Fig. 6-1: Distribution and incidence of Old Testament names
  All such names combined (excluding the surnames ADAMS and
  DANIEL). Maximum incidence – Glamorgan, Llangyfelach 2.44%

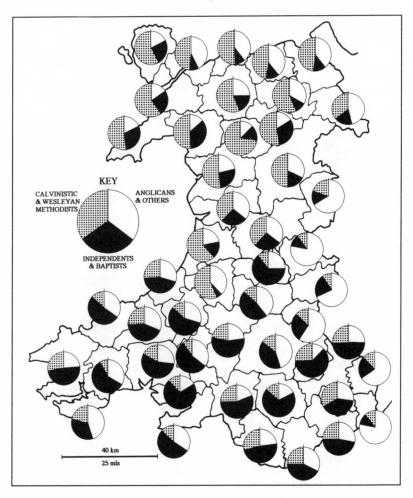

Fig. 6-2: Variations in religious affiliation

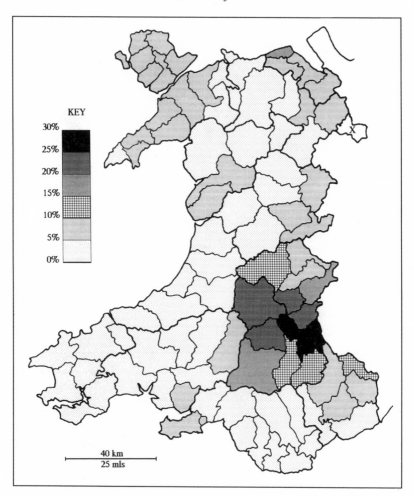

Fig. 6-3: Distribution and incidence of *Ap* names (combined)
Maximum incidence – Breconshire, Talgarth 25.20%
Minimum incidence – Carmarthenshire, Elvet 1.24%

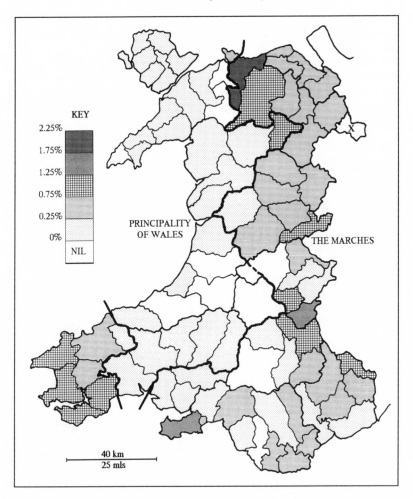

Fig. 6-4: Distribution and incidence of adjectival names
     All such names combined (excluding the surnames LLOYD and
     VAUGHAN). Maximum incidence – Denbighshire, Isdulas 1.87%

century (see again Fig. 6-2). As these two denominations had already been separated from the Established Church for well over a century by the time settled surnames were being taken in many areas, it is not surprising that their liking for Old Testament names should become reflected in the resultant stock of settled surnames. The similarities between the occurrence of Old Testament surnames and the preponderance of Independents and Baptists in the worshipping population would seem to explain this difference between north Wales and south Wales.

Ap surnames versus those with the possessive 's'

The process whereby patronymic names (involving the use of *ap* or *ab* to denote 'son of') were gradually transformed into settled surnames, first by the incorporation or dropping of this prefix, then later by the addition of the possessive 's', has been described in detail in Chapters 2 and 3. As this process of transformation usually took place over a significant period of time, the existence in an area of a large body of *ap* names (Powell, Parry, Pugh, etc) or those with the possessive 's' (Howells, Harris, Hughes, etc) can be used to infer the period when settled surnames were taken (early or late) within that area.

Work which we have done relating to north Cardiganshire (see Fig. 3-1), based on setting the rise over time in the incidence of the surnames Davies and Jones against the fall over the same period in the incidence of David and John, indicates that the transition to settled surnames took place in this particular area during the second half of the eighteenth century. This is supported by evidence from wills and other records relating to the area.

We have also done some preliminary work on other areas, but further detailed work is required before any real conclusions can be reached about the various periods when settled surnames were being taken across Wales as a whole. It has become immediately apparent, however, that the survival of the intermediate forms John and David in Glamorgan, Carmarthenshire and Pembrokeshire probably indicates that settled surnames were taken in these areas in the period after the dropping of the *ap* prefix but before the addition of the possessive 's' became fashionable. Unfortunately, this would have occurred during a period when the survival of parish registers is very poor, so it would be necessary to turn to other sources to confirm this.

It can be seen in Fig. 6-3 that the highest proportion of surnames incorporating the *ap* prefix occurs along the English border and in Breconshire (Talgarth 25.2%) and Radnorshire (Painscastle 22.42%) in particular.[3] This gives an indication of the areas in which surnames were taken early, but again more work needs to be done on other records to determine when this might have taken place.

172

Adjectival surnames

The incidence and distribution of surnames derived from Welsh adjectives are interesting. As Fig. 6-4 shows, this type of surname is largely confined to the hundreds along the English border and those which have been subject to long-standing English influence. In these areas they can be found (collectively) in significant concentrations – sometimes in excess of 1.5%. Elsewhere they are either totally absent or found in very small concentrations (generally less than 0.10%).

It would seem, therefore, that the English practice of taking adjectival surnames became fairly common in the Marcher areas, where it seems to have crossed the linguistic divide and become adopted in the Welsh-speaking areas. It is interesting to note (see again Fig. 6-4) how closely the boundary between the two areas follows the boundary which defined the Principality of Wales in the fourteenth century.[4]

Probabilities

On the face of it a knowledge of the percentage of the population which holds one of the particularly common surnames in each of the hundreds in Wales would seem unlikely to offer much help in identifying a particular individual holding that surname in the population as a whole.

For example, the fact that 30.71% of the population in the Bala area in Merionethshire (Penllyn hundred) hold the surname Jones – compared to only 1.06% doing so in the St David's area of Pembrokeshire (Dewisland hundred) – is certainly likely to arrest the attention, but it does not allow one to discount the St David's area completely when looking for a particular individual holding that surname. However, when seeking a particular marriage between two people with the surnames (say) of Jones and Rees, would one pay the same sort of attention to the Bala area? The answer is no. With an incidence of 0.18% the surname Rees is comparatively rare in the Bala area, while in the St David's area, at 2.61%, it is nearly 15 times more prominent.

What then can one do to determine which of these two areas is likely to be the better one to search in, and also to identify whether or not another area might be even better? Fortunately, a simple calculation can help us decide which of these two areas is the more likely to have resulted in this marriage, and we find that the relative probabilities are 5.53 (30.71 x 0.18) to 2.77 (1.06 x 2.61) in favour of it being in the Bala area. Equally, by doing this same calculation for all the other areas of Wales, it is possible to find out whether the Bala area is the most probable place overall. In fact, both the Bala area (as well as the area north of it) and the St David's area are amongst the last places to look for a marriage involving a couple named Jones and Rees. There is a whole area of mid and south Wales where, at 73.33, the probability is dramatically greater (Iscennin hundred, Carmarthenshire).

The hypothesis is then: **If a connected group of Welsh people (giving at least two surnames) move away from their place of origin, it should be possible to predict that place of origin using a knowledge of the incidence and distribution of all names across Wales.**

Our knowledge of the incidence and distribution of surnames across Wales is based on actual records for the period 1813-37 and there is a limit to the period both before and after those dates when our information can continue to reflect the situation which exists in the different areas. Inevitably this raises the question as to what that overall period might be. In order to identify this we need to consider two main factors. First, we must take into account the fact that the patronymic system gains in importance the earlier one goes back and the proportion of 'surnames' will decrease. Second, there was the continuing movement of people, both within Wales and into Wales, throughout the whole of the nineteenth century which modified the pool of surnames substantially in many areas. Bearing this in mind we are of the opinion that, using our survey data, the hypothesis is likely to remain valid over the period 1780-1880.

The first thing we needed to do, however, was to test the hypothesis thoroughly over this period. Although we had some events to enable us to carry out tests, they were too few in number to represent a rigorous enough test overall. We have been fortunate, therefore, to have been given information for additional tests by others who are involved with family history.[5] In all we have carried out 41 tests on the hypothesis and have found a high level of correlation between the predicted and actual places of origin. Very occasionally we were totally wrong. Indeed, it would be remarkable if this had not been the case as we have worked from only a sample of the population (albeit a significant one). A measure of the correlation between the actual origins of groups of people against that predicted by our method can be gauged from the following table:

	No.	%
Proportion correctly predicted (in one of three most likely hundreds)	23	56
Proportion closely predicted (in one of next seven most likely hundreds)	11	27
Proportion not predicted correctly (not in the ten most likely hundreds)	7	17

Fig. 6-5: Predicting origins using 1813-37 surname data

174

In effect, this shows that in 80% of the tests the place of origin had been successfully narrowed down from a total of 89 hundreds to as few as ten (11%). However, the figures do not reveal that, of the seven which were not correctly predicted, no fewer than three had been predicted to originate in a hundred immediately adjacent (geographically) to one of the three most likely locations in their particular test.

Needless to say, the many repetitive calculations involved in doing this are best carried out by computer and we were fortunate to be able to have a computer program specially developed for this.[6]

Even with assurances about the validity of such a hypothesis many family historians without a mathematical background might still feel uncomfortable about using such a method as the basis for beginning a search. However, if all that is known about an ancestor is that he, or she, 'came from Wales' – as might well be the case more often than not with emigrants from Britain – then any avenue which might provide help should not be ignored. To assure them, therefore, that the method is both simple and effective, it is worth looking at a case study which illustrates the principles involved. Further case studies are given in the next chapter.

In 1849 two families – Simon Davies, his wife Anne and their children, together with Isaac Oliver, his wife Rachel and their children – emigrated to the United States. In the Federal Census of 1850 for the Pomeroy area of Meigs County, Ohio, Simon Davis (sic) and his family are all shown as having been born in Wales. Where might descendants of one or both of these families start looking for evidence of their origins in Wales?

It would be reasonable to suppose that those descendants might well know from other family sources that the maiden names of the two wives had been Richards and Evans respectively, so in this particular case study we would have the luxury of knowing four surnames to help us in our search.

If we compute the probability of Davies/Richards/Oliver/Evans occurring together within Wales, we find that the ten most likely areas are those shown in Fig. 6-6. Within these areas, the Ilar Upper, Ilar Lower and Pennarth hundreds in Cardiganshire are the three most likely of all.

In fact the Davies and Oliver families emigrated to Ohio from the parish of Llanrhystud in the Ilar Lower hundred of Cardiganshire.[7]

This particular example has (purely as a test) been viewed *from* Cardiganshire, based on a recorded example of two families who are known to have emigrated from Llanrhystud. In this instance one of those families has been traced in the United States but the other has not, and it is entirely likely that the two families

175

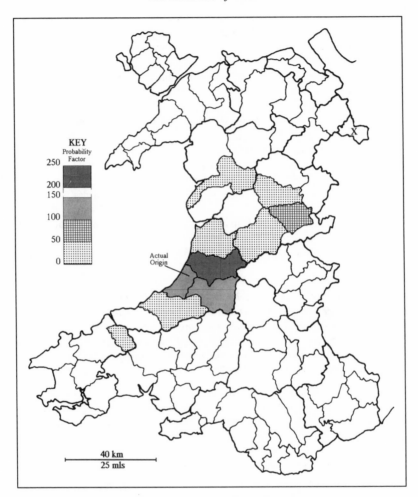

**Fig. 6-6: The main incidence of the surnames DAVIES/RICHARDS/
OLIVER/EVANS in combination.
The ten most likely locations.
Greatest probability – Cardiganshire, Ilar Upper Hundred.**

176

could have gone their separate ways soon after arrival in their new country. If this is the case, then there is a strong likelihood that the two families could have lost contact with one another and later generations would almost certainly have done so. In this event we could have two separate sets of descendants wishing to find their origins in Wales. What then is the picture for them?

If we compute the probability of Davies/Richards we find that the general picture shown in Fig. 6-6 remains substantially the same, with Ilar Lower, Pennarth and the Elvet hundred in Carmarthenshire being their most likely place of origin. For the combination Oliver/Evans, however, the picture does change somewhat, with areas of Montgomeryshire featuring as prominently as the actual place of origin and the other Cardiganshire hundreds which surround it. Nevertheless, we consider that, even as two separate families, their descendants could well have found their place of origin fairly readily by this method and using the many transcripts and indexes which have become available for these areas (and many other parts of Wales) in recent years. (See also Appendix B.)

CHAPTER 6: NOTES AND REFERENCES

[1] *Western Mail*, 29 October 1994, letter from J.Wynne Lewis of Moelfre, Anglesey.

[2] *WS*, 169.

[3] The *Ap* surnames which we have found in our survey – and hence on which Fig. 6-3 has been based – are: Badham, Bevan, Beynon, Bowen, Parry, Powell, Price, Pritchard, Probert, Prosser, Prothero and Pugh.

[4] See H. Carter (1989),*The National Atlas of Wales*, Map 2.1c.

[5] Both Mr David Peate of Little Neston, Cheshire, and Miss Helen Davies of Penrhyn-coch, Aberystwyth, have kindly provided a wide range of information for testing the hypothesis, including some of those used as case studies in the following chapter. The information they have provided has arisen out of their work as professional genealogists.

[6] We are deeply grateful to our daughter, Catherine Camfield, for developing a program for use with a conventional spreadsheet which enabled the many repetitive calculations to be carried out with the greatest of ease.

[7] One of the authors knows this to be true as Simon Davies was his great-grandfather's brother.

CHAPTER 7

MIGRATION, EMIGRATION AND PLACE OF ORIGIN

Prior to the extensive exploitation of its mineral wealth during the last century, Wales could only be considered to be a relatively poor country and, from the seventeenth century onwards, the land became increasingly incapable of supporting the expanding population despite improvements in agricultural methods. In addition, the move away from partible inheritance (whereby an inheritance was shared equally by all the sons) meant that younger sons in poorer families could be denied even a minimal stake in their communities. As a result, there has been a steady migration away from Wales – and its rural areas in particular – for several centuries, and this has continued until recent times.

Migration

Migration from Wales has been the subject of significant research over the years, and it is not proposed to go over it again here. Instead we are confining ourselves to providing a list of some of the more recent works to be published so that readers can pursue this specialist aspect more fully if they wish to.[1]

Much of the work we have listed has been based on research aimed at identifying why, when and *to where* people collectively (as distinct from individuals) have migrated. Family historians tend to approach migration from the opposite direction. While they may be interested in why people generally did things, they will be more interested in why their particular ancestors should have done so. They may also be interested in the reasons why they had gone to a particular place but this is, in all probability, the one piece of information they already have. They will be far more interested in the place they had come *from*. The greater the number of generations between the family historians of today and their migrant ancestor, the greater the likelihood that contact with the place of origin (or even knowledge of it) will have been lost. This is further exacerbated by the fact that, once a person has taken the decision – often a momentous one – to migrate, the greater is the likelihood that they will migrate (or even emigrate) a second or further time. The longer the chain of migration, the weaker the bonds and memories of the place of origin become. There must be many people in Britain today (outside Wales) who know that an ancestor must have come from Wales – perhaps by virtue of the surname they hold – without having any real knowledge of when this occurred or from where, precisely, they came.

Emigration

Those who have commented on the scale of emigration from Britain to the New World, either in their respective colonial periods or in the nineteenth/early twentieth centuries in particular, have usually failed to mention Welsh emigration at all, or have dismissed it as having been of little consequence compared with that from England, Ireland or Scotland. Nevertheless there is a great deal of direct and indirect evidence to suggest that it was anything but inconsequential and that, in percentage terms, emigration from Wales to the United States (in particular) might well have been at least on a par with that from Scotland and England in the last century. Furthermore, there are indications that it could well have been even greater during the colonial period. The direct evidence is to be found in published statistics, but it is also supported by indirect evidence from surname studies.

For example, details of British emigration to the United States, 1820-1950, taken from Berthoff are given in Fig 7-1.[2] These show that emigration from Wales was, on average, 2.49% of the total for Wales, Scotland and England combined. If we take this figure to be correct, then we can only conclude that emigration from Wales to the United States was indeed low, as the population of Wales averaged 4.79% of the total for the three countries during this period.

However, census information in the United States relating to those born in Wales (see Fig 7-2) shows increases during individual decades which are wildly different from those which can be inferred from Berthoff's figures. According to him, 4313 people emigrated from Wales during the period 1861-1870; yet the number of people recorded in the census as having been born in Wales increased by 28,770 over that same decade (nearly seven times Berthoff's figure). If we allow for the fact that some native-born Welsh people must have died and others may have returned to Wales, then the discrepancy between these two sets of figures becomes even greater. It has been suggested, however, that much of this discrepancy can be accounted for by the fact that, in many instances, immigrant statistics might have included only adults or those who were economically active. If this had been the case, one would expect a similar discrepancy in the figures for those with English or Scottish origins. In fact, although it is possible to reconcile the immigration figures from Scotland with the changes in the numbers

179

subsequently recorded (in US Censuses) as having been born in Scotland, no such reconciliation can be made with the figures relating to English immigrants. The published figures relating to them indicate consistently that throughout the nineteenth century there were many more immigrants recorded as English than subsequently gave England as their birth-place in the census.[3] The difference would account for the apparent under-recording of Welsh people several times over, which would suggest that many other European nationals who emigrated *via* England may also have been wrongly recorded.

	Wales	*England*	*Scotland*	*Ireland*	*Not specified*
1820-1830	170	15,837	3,180	54,338	8302
1831-1840	185	7,611	2,667	207,381	65,347
1841-1850	1,261	32,092	3,712	780,719	229,979
1851-1860	6,319	247,125	38,331	914,119	132,199
1861-1870	4,313	222,277	38,769	435,778	341,537
1871-1880	6,631	437,706	87,564	436,871	16,142
1881-1890	12,640	644,680	149,869	655,482	168
1891-1900	10,557	216,726	44,188	388,416	67
1901-1910	17,464	388,017	120,469	339,065	
1911-1920	13,107	249,944	78,357	146,181	
1921-1930	13,012	157,420	159,781	220,591	
1931-1940	735	21,756	6,887	13,167	
1941-1950	3,209	112,252	16,131	26,444	
Totals	89,603	2,753,443	749,905	4,618,552	793,741
% *	2.49	76.63	20.87	n/a	n/a

* excluding *Ireland* and *Not specified*

Fig. 7-1: British emigration to the United States, 1820-1950

The general underestimation of the involvement of Welsh people in everyday events is not a phenomenon which is confined to the nineteenth century. Even today Welsh people have to suffer the minor indignity of being called English in many contexts. In the latter part of the nineteenth century, when the major ports for embarkation to America for Welsh people were all English (Liverpool, Bristol and London), it would have been all too easy for an immigration official to place all new arrivals from these ports under a single national category.

Then again there appears to have been a lack of serious consideration of Welsh emigration to the New World in the seventeenth and eighteenth centuries, which can only lead to the conclusion that it was of little consequence numerically. Yet Professor David Thomas[4] has shown that, using the 25 most common surnames found today in south-west Wales, more than 7% of the landowners in North

180

Carolina in 1790 had surnames which featured in that list. Moreover, the figure rose to 10% if certain names commonly associated with Wales (but not in the list), such as Daniels, Gwynne and Humphreys, are taken into account.

Year	No. born in Wales	Decadal change
1850	29,868	
1860	45,763	+15,895
1870	74,533	+28,750
1880	83,302	+8,770
1890	100,079	+16,776
1900	93,586	-6,493
1910	82,488	-11,098
1920	67,066	-15,422
1930	60,205	-6,861
1940	35,360	-24,845
1950	30,060	-5,300
1960	23,469	-6,591
1970	17,014	-6,455

Fig. 7-2: Population of the United States born in Wales, 1850-1970[5]

This concentration of Welsh surnames may not have been confined to North Carolina, however. It has been maintained that, of the 56 representatives who signed the Declaration of Independence, no fewer than 18 (32%) had Welsh ancestry. While many of these could, in all probability, also claim ancestry in other countries as well, surnames such as Lloyd, Adams, Hopkins, Williams, Lewis, Morris and Gwinnett (see Fig 7-3) all suggest a strong connection with Wales and, indeed, Francis Lewis, the representative from New York, is known to have been born in Newport, Monmouthshire. It is also worth noting that Thomas Jefferson, whose surname hardly features at all in Wales, is known to have claimed Welsh ancestry and to have been particularly proud of it.[6]

On a more personal note, in 1990 one of the authors attended the 10th Anniversary Conference of the National Genealogical Society which was held in Washington, DC. There were nearly 2000 people listed as attending that conference and there was no reason to believe that they were in any way atypical of white, middle-class, American society today – a stratum of society likely to contain a fair share of immigrants with Welsh origins. Yet 120 of those attending (6%) had surnames commonly associated with Wales. This percentage is remarkably high when one takes into account the major components in the American population which have their roots (and with them their surnames) in the rest of Britain as well as in Ireland, Italy, Germany, Switzerland, the Scandinavian countries, etc.

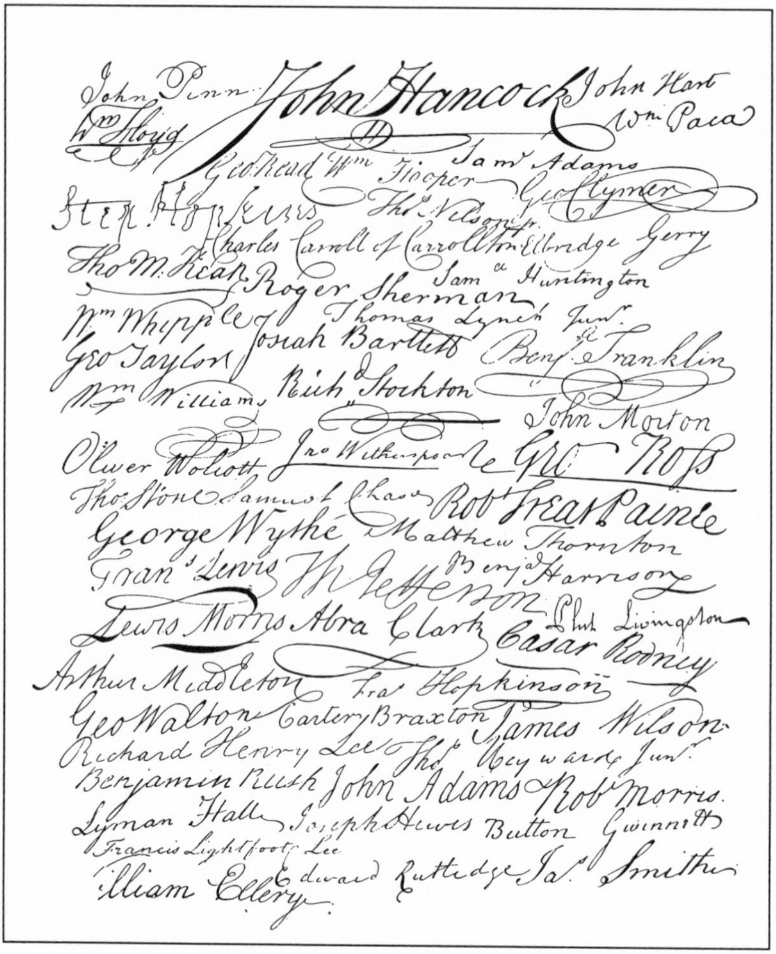

**Fig. 7-3: Facsimile of the Signatures to The Declaration of
Independence, 4 July 1776**

Rather harder to explain is the possession of distinctive Welsh surnames by a large number of black Americans, and in particular sportsmen, with the names of General Colin Powell and Carl Lewis springing most readily to mind. As Professor David Thomas says in his article, it has been found that, in the 1975-6 season, of the 432 black Americans playing in senior professional football, no fewer than 56 (13%) carried Welsh surnames. However, he attributes this to the fact that when (in the 1860s and 1870s) freed slaves took surnames they often took the names held by their former masters. This seems to be a very plausible explanation and, if true, would again suggest that Welsh surnames must have been fairly common in the southern States during this period. As the bulk of nineteenth century immigration from Wales is known to have been directed towards the northern States, this can only really be attributed to earlier waves of immigration.[7]

Place of origin

A method for predicting the likely place of origin of groups of people holding at least two surnames, who are known to have come from within the same community in Wales, has been described in Chapter 6. This could be of particular importance to descendants of Welsh migrants and emigrants, as perhaps can be illustrated by the following case studies:

Evans, Griffiths and Jones

The combination Evans/Griffiths/Jones was found to occur chiefly on the Llŷn peninsula but running down into Merionethshire and with significant (but isolated) outriders in Cardiganshire. However, both the level of occurrence and the concentration of possibilities on Llŷn would make this the obvious area to begin to find evidence of these people.

This particular combination of people actually came from the Dinllaen area of Caernarfonshire which is situated centrally on the Llŷn peninsula.

Davies and Owen

Applying our prediction method to this combination of names suggests that they could have come (with virtually the same likelihood) from three separate and widely separated hundreds, namely: Troedyraur (Cardiganshire), Llanidloes (Montgomeryshire) and Nant Conwy (Caernarfonshire).

By way of a subterfuge this test had been given to us by one researcher in relation to two quite separate couples who happened to have the same surnames. It was interesting (and encouraging) to find that one couple came from Troedyraur (Cardiganshire), which was one of the hundreds we had predicted, and that the second couple came from Newtown (Montgomeryshire), which is the hundred immediately adjacent to Llanidloes.

Coincidentally this same combination of surnames was also given for testing – totally independently – by another researcher. Once again it was encouraging to find that the couple in question were living in the Troedyraur (Cardiganshire) hundred in the early nineteenth century.

Clark, Jones and Stokes

It was found that this combination could well occur in the Chirk or Bromfield areas of Denbighshire, or alternatively (but with much less likelihood) in the Rhos hundred of Pembrokeshire, as well as in other isolated areas in south and south-east Wales.

This particular combination of names had, in fact, originated in the Bromfield area of Denbighshire.

Davies and Jones

Testing for the combined occurrence of the two most common names in Wales might seem to be a pointless exercise. However, the calculations show that an area of central Cardiganshire dominates as the most likely place in which these surnames might be found in combination.

In fact, David Davies and Anne his wife (née Jones) – to whom the search relates – lived at Derygoch in the parish of Silian (Cardiganshire) in the middle of the nineteenth century. The parish of Silian (Moyddin hundred) is at the focal point of the area suggested by our method.

The above case studies all involve a significant measure of success in using our predictive method. It might be useful, therefore, to consider a situation in which the application of the method might be seen as less than wholly successful.

Michael, Jenkins, Hoskin, Lloyd In the mid-nineteenth century a family with the surname Michael emigrated from Wales to Australia. Present day descendants of that family eventually traced their origin to the parish of Oystermouth (Glamorgan, Gower hundred) where Robert Michael and Sarah Jenkins were married on 20 May 1821. The marriage record gives John Hoskin and Mary Lloyd as witnesses to the marriage.

A calculation of the relative probabilities of the four surnames Michael/ Jenkins/Hoskin/Lloyd occurring in combination clearly illustrated what had already been found; namely that the Gower hundred was far and away (by a factor of x25) the most likely place of origin. However, while the use of these four surnames was perfectly valid for testing our hypothesis, it is unlikely that it would have helped the present day researcher who would, in all probability, not have known of the connection with John Hoskin and Mary Lloyd at the outset.

The most they are likely to have known is that Robert Michael had married Sarah Jenkins, with some idea of the likely date.

Clearly this poses the question: 'Would a calculation of the probabilities of Michael and Jenkins occurring together have led them to the right area?' The answer to this is: 'In time yes, but it would have involved a great deal more work'. This is because the Gower hundred drops to become the fifteenth (out of 89) most likely place of origin, although the immediately adjacent area of Swansea – which we have taken out of the Gower hundred for reasons which are set out in Appendix A – is the fifth most likely place. In fact a researcher who had followed our advice (see Appendix C) would have consulted one of the many marriage indexes which are now becoming available and when studying the Swansea area (as they probably would at a relatively early stage) they could not have failed to notice this marriage in the Glamorgan FHS Index. It is worth noting that this marriage is not in the IGI, albeit the baptism of Robert Michael, son of Robert and Sarah Michael, is recorded at Oystermouth on 20 June 1823.[8]

This case study illustrates how much greater the certainty within the predictive method becomes as the number of surnames increases, even with relatively common names.

CHAPTER 7: NOTES AND REFERENCES

[1] A large number of the books and articles given in References and Select Bibliography contain material directly relating to migration both from and to Wales. Significant works of recent date (which themselves contain further extensive references and bibliographies) are as follows: Hume & Pryce (1986), Lewis and Ward (1995), Pryce (1994) and *WFH* (1993).

[2] R.T. Berthoff (1953), 5.

[3] See *Historical Statistics of the United States, colonial times to 1957*, Dept. of State and Public Institutions, Bureau of Census, Washington, DC (1960).

[4] D. Thomas (1979).

[5] Based on Williams (1985), Vol. 1, 76.

[6] See D. Williams (1975), 49 and also the *Dictionary of American Biography*, New York, (1933) for further biographical references.

[7] This section has dealt with Welsh emigration in general; much has been written on individual Welsh emigrant communities and for these see the bibliography in *WFH* and Davies & Davies (1996).

[8] 1988 edition.

REFERENCES AND SELECT BIBLIOGRAPHY

A.D.M. Barrell & M.H. Brown (1995) 'A Settler community in post-Conquest rural Wales: the English of Dyffryn Clwyd, 1294-1399', *Welsh History Review, 17*, 3.

P.C. Bartrum (1965-6) 'Arthuriana from the genealogical manuscripts', *NLWJ, 14*, 2.

P.C. Bartrum (1966) *Early Welsh Genealogical Tracts* (Cardiff).

P.C. Bartrum (1980) *Welsh Genealogies, AD 300-1400* (microfiche; Aberystwyth).

P.C. Bartrum (1981-2) 'Personal names in Wales in the fifteenth century', *NLWJ, 22*, 4.

P.C. Bartrum (1983) *Welsh Genealogies, AD 1400-1500* (Aberystwyth).

R.E. Benbow (1983) 'Montgomeryshire Benbow Christian Names', *Cronicl* 7.

R.M. & G.A. Benwell (1973) 'Interpreting the census returns for rural Anglesey and Llŷn', *Trans. Anglesey Ant. Soc.*

R.M. & G.A. Benwell (1975) 'Interpreting the parish registers and bishops transcripts for Anglesey and Llŷn', *Trans. Anglesey Ant. Soc.*

R.M. & G.A. Benwell (1981) 'Naming patterns in Gwynedd', *Gwreiddiau/ Gwynedd Roots* (Gwynedd FHS).

R.T. Berthoff (1953) *British Immigrants in Industrial America, 1790-1850* (Cambridge, Mass).

L. Bradley (1978) *A Glossary for Local Population Studies* (LPS Supplt No. 1).

J.A Bradney (1904-33) *A History of Monmouthshire*, 4 vols (London).

Bureau of Census (1960) *Historical Statistics of the United States, colonial times to 1957* (Dept. of State and Public Institutions, Washington, DC).

P. Calvocoressi (1987) *Who's Who in the Bible* (Penguin Reference).

A.D. Carr (1977) 'The Mostyns of Mostyn, 1540-1642', *Flintshire Hist. Soc. Jnl, 28-30*.

A.D. Carr (1979) 'The making of the Mostyns: The genesis of a landed family', *THSC*.

H. Carter (ed.) (1989) *National Atlas of Wales* (Cardiff).

D.L. Chamberlain (1981) *Welsh Nicknames* (Caernarfon).

B.G. Charles (1960) *Schedule of Haverfordwest Records* (NLW; records now at Pembrokeshire Record Office and on film at NLW).

B.G. Charles (1967) *Calendar of the Records of the Borough of Haverfordwest, 1539-1660* (Board of Celtic Studies: History and Law Series, 24).

B.G. Charles (1973) *George Owen of Henllys: A Welsh Elizabethan* (Aberystwyth).

B.G. Charles (1982) *The English Dialect of South Pembrokeshire* (Haverfordwest).

B.G. Charles (1992) *The Place-Names of Pembrokeshire* (Aberystwyth).

G.T. Clark (1886) *Limbus Patrum Morganiae et Glamorganiae* (London).

B. Cottle (1978) *The Penguin Dictionary of Surnames* (Harmondsworth).

E. Davies (1975) *A Gazetteer of Welsh Place-Names* (Cardiff).

H.M. Davies (1995) *Transatlantic Brethren: Revd Samuel Jones (1735-1814) and His Friends: Baptists in Wales, Pennsylvania and Beyond* (Bethlehem & London).

J.B. Davies (1975) 'The Mathew Family of Llandaff, Radyr and Castell-y-Mynach', *Glamorgan Historian, 11* (Barry).

J.B. Davies (1980) 'Christian names in 16th-18th century Glamorgan', *South Wales FHS Journal, 4*.

P.G. & M. Davies (1996) 'A Selected Bibliography of Material on the Welsh in the United States', *Cardiganshire FHS Journal 1, 1*.

R.R. Davies (1975) 'Race relations in post-conquest Wales: confrontation and compromise', *THSC*.

Debrett's (1984) *Peerage, Baronetage and Knightage*.

Dictionary of American Biography (1933) (New York).

V.J. Doddrell (1993) *Land Holders of Somerset, 1235-1653* (microfiche; Windermere).

L. Dunkling (1993) *The Guinness Book of Names*, 6th edition (Enfield).

L. Dwnn (1846) (ed. S.R. Meyrick) *Heraldic Visitations of Wales and Part of the Marches* (Llandovery).

E. Ekwall (1960) *Concise Oxford Dictionary of Place-Names*, 4th edition (Oxford).

B. Ellis (1994) 'Lead mining on Halkyn Mountain – the Derbyshire connection', *Hel Achau, 44*.

H. Ellis (ed.) (1838) *The Record of Carnarvon* (London).

G.E. Evans (1902) *Aberystwyth and its Court Leet* (Aberystwyth).

W.A. Evans (1995) 'The Salusburies of Llewenni', *Denbs. Hist. Soc. Trans., 5.*

M.A. Faraday (ed.) (1973-4) 'Assessment for the Fifteenth of 1293 on Radnor and other Marcher lordships', *Radnorshire Society Transactions, 43, 44.* (Transcript of PRO E 179/242/57 and part of E 179/242/48).

R. Fenton (1811) *A Historical Tour of Pembrokeshire* (2nd ed. 1903; reprinted Dyfed County Council, 1994*).*

P. Franklin (1986) 'Normans, Saints and Politics: Forename-choice among fourteenth-century Gloucestershire peasants', *Local Population Studies, 36.*

F. Godwin and S. Toulson (1977) *The Drovers Roads of Wales* (London).

F. Green (1912-29) *West Wales Historical Records* (Trans. West Wales Hist. Soc.).

J.E. Griffith (1914) *Pedigrees of Anglesey and Carnarvonshire Families* (Horncastle, 1914; reprinted Wrexham, 1985).

R.A. Griffiths (1994) *Conquerors and Conquered in Medieval Wales* (New York & Stroud).

K.Ll. Gruffydd (1980) 'Localised distribution of a surname: Kendrick/Kenrick in north Flintshire', *Hel Achau, 2.*

H.B. Guppy (1890) *The Homes of Family Names in Great Britain* (London).

S. Hancock (1981) 'The Swancott family', *Cronicl, 2.*

P. Hanks & F. Hodges (1988) *A Dictionary of Surnames* (Oxford).

P. Hanks & F. Hodges (1990) *A Dictionary of First Names* (Oxford).

P.S. Harper & E. Sunderland (ed.) (1986) *Genetic & Population Studies in Wales* (Cardiff).

E.G. Hartmann (1967) *Americans from Wales* (The Christopher Publishing Co., Boston).

N. Henson (ed.) (1980) *Index of the Probate Records of the Bangor Consistory Court* Vol. I: Pre-1700 (NLW, Aberystwyth).

D. Hey (1993) *The Oxford Guide to Family History* (Oxford).

I. Hume & W.T.R. Pryce (eds.) (1986) *The Welsh and their country: Selected readings in the social sciences* (Llandysul).

D. Jenkins (1971) *The Agricultural Community in South-West Wales* (Cardiff).

R.T. Jenkins (ed.) (1959) *Dictionary of Welsh Biography down to 1940* (London).

C. Johnson and L. Sleigh (1973) *Names for Boys & Girls* (London).

F. Jones (1960) 'The old families of south-west Wales', *Ceredigion* iv, 1.

F. Jones (1984) 'Llechdwnni revisited', *Carmarthenshire Antiquary*, vol. x.

F. Jones (1987) *Historic Carmarthenshire Homes and their Families* (Carmarthen).

N.C. Jones (ed.) (1989) *Archdeaconry of Brecon Probate Records Vol. 1: Pre-1660* (NLW, Aberystwyth).

T. Jones (1898) *A History of the County of Brecknock* (Brecknock).

W.D. Jones (1993) *Wales in America: Scranton and the Welsh 1860-1920* (Cardiff).

A.K. Knowles (late 1996) *Calvinists Incorporated: Welsh Immigrants on Ohio's Industrial Frontier* (Chicago).

G.W. Lasker & C.G.N. Mascie-Taylor (1990) *Atlas of British Surnames* (Guild of One-Name Studies/Wayne State University, Detroit).

F. Leeson (1977) 'The distribution of Welsh surnames', *Genealogists' Magazine*, xix, 1.

R. Lewis & D. Ward (1995) 'Culture, Politics and Assimilation: The Welsh on Teesside, c.1850-1940', *Welsh History Review*, 17, 4.

R. Lucas (1986) *A Gower Family: The Lucases of Stouthall and Rhosili Rectory* (Lewes).

N. Madge (1995) *English Roots: A Family History* (Stroud).

G.W. Marshall (1967) *The Genealogist's Guide* 4th ed. (reprinted Baltimore).

M. McGarvie (1988) *The Meyricks of Bush* (privately published).

R.A. McKinley (1975) *Norfolk and Suffolk Surnames in the Middle Ages* (English Surname Series, Vol. 2).

R.A. McKinley (1977) *The Surnames of Oxfordshire* (English Surname Series, Vol. 3).

R.A. McKinley (1981) *The Surnames of Lancashire* (English Surname Series, Vol. 4).

R.A. McKinley (1986) 'Regional differences in the evolution of surnames', *English Genealogical Congress: Selected Papers Given at the Congresses of 1976 and 1984* (Society of Genealogists, London).

R.A. McKinley (1988) *The Surnames of Sussex* (English Surname Series, Vol. 5).

R.A. McKinley (1990) *A History of British Surnames* (Longman).

S.R. Meyrick (1808) *The History and Antiquities of the County of Cardigan* (London; reprinted Brecon, 1907).

P. Morgan (1990-1) 'Locative surnames in Wales: A preliminary list', *Nomina, XIV*, 7-24.

P. Morgan (1995) 'The Place-name as surname in Wales', *NLWJ*, xxix, 1.

T.J. Morgan & P. Morgan (1985) *Welsh Surnames* (Cardiff).

E.R. Morris (1982) 'Notes on some "Montgomeryshire" surnames', *Cronicl, 4.*.

T.E. Morris (1932) 'Welsh surnames in the border counties of Wales', *Y Cymmrodor*, xliii.

Lord Mostyn & T.A. Glenn (1925) *History of the Family of Mostyn of Mostyn* (London).

T. Nicholas (1872) *The Annals and Antiquities of the Counties and County Families of Wales* (reprinted Baltimore 1991).

D.H. Owen, (1975) 'The Englishry of Denbigh: an English colony in medieval Wales', *THSC,* 57-76.

H. Owen (1902) *Old Pembroke Families in the Ancient County Palatine of Pembroke* (London).

H. Owen (1911-18) *Calendar of the Public Records relating to Pembrokeshire* (Hon. Soc. of Cymmrodorion, London).

M.N. Owen (1912) [Notes on extracts from Welshpool PR], *MC 36,* 34.

T.M. Owen (1959) *Welsh Folk Customs* (Cardiff).

E. Parkinson (ed.) (1994) *The Glamorgan Hearth Tax Assessment of 1670* (South Wales Record Society, Cardiff).

D. Parry-Jones (1947) *Welsh Country Upbringing* (London).

D. Peate (1983) 'Emigrant Peates from Llanbrynmair', *Cronicl 5.*

D. Peate (1986) 'Hamer as a surname', *Cronicl 14.*

D. Peate (1994) 'What's in a name?' (various articles) *Ninnau.*

T. Pennant (1796) *History of the Parishes of Whiteford and Holywell* (London).

T. Pennant (1810) *Tours in Wales* (Caernarfon, 1883).

E.T. Porter (1993) *The Olivers of Cardiganshire 1778-1993: Their Descendants in Wales, England and North America and Some of Their Related Welsh Families* [USA].

W.T.R. Pryce (ed.) (1994) *From Family History to Community History* (Studying Family and Community History, Volume 2) (Cambridge/Open University).

P.H. Reaney (1961) *Dictionary of British Surnames* (London).

P.H. Reaney (1980) *The Origin of English Surnames* (London).

P.H. Reaney (ed. & revised by R.M. Wilson) (1995) *A Dictionary of English Surnames,* 3rd ed. (London and New York).

G. Redmonds (1973) *Yorkshire West Riding* (English Surname Series, Vol. 1).

M. Richards (1969) *Welsh Administrative and Territorial Units* (Cardiff).

T.R. Roberts (Asaph) (1908) *Eminent Welshmen: A Short Biographical Dictionary of Welshmen* (reprinted Baltimore, 1995).

A.J. Roderick (1968) 'Marriage and politics in Wales, 1066-1282', *Welsh History Review IV,* 1.

C.D. Rogers(1995) *The Surname Detective: Investigating surname distribution in England, 1086-present da*y (Manchester).

J. Rowlands and others (ed.) (1993) *Welsh Family History: A Guide to Research* (AFHSW/FFHS).

M.P. Siddons (1991-3*)* *The Development of Welsh Heraldry* (3 vols, Aberystwyth).

W.J. Smith (ed.) (1954) *Calendar of Salusbury Correspondence 1553-c.1700* (Cardiff).

D. Thomas (1979) 'Welsh emigration to the United States: a note on surname evidence', *Cambria 6*, 1.

S.P. Thomas (1976) 'Branches of the Blayney family in the XVI and XVII centuries', *MC, 64*, 9.

S.P. Thomas (1985) 'The Blayney Family of Maelienydd, Kinsham, and, ultimately, Evesham', *Trans. Radn. Soc., lv*, 27-38.

R.G. Thorne (1996) 'Patronymics or matronymics or what?', *Cardiganshire FHS Journal 1*, 1.

G.F. Tyler (1972) 'Bowdler, censor of Shakespeare', *Glamorgan Historian 8* (Barry).

G.P. White (1981) *A Handbook of Cornish Surnames* (Redruth).

D. Williams (1975) *Cymru ac America/Wales and America* (Cardiff).

D.E. Williams (1962) 'A short enquiry into the surnames of Glamorgan from the thirteenth to the eighteenth centuries', *THSC.*

J. Williams (Ysgafell) (introduction by Deirdre Beddoe) (1987) *An Autobiography of Elizabeth Davis – Betsy Cadwaladyr: A Balaclava Nurse* (Cardiff).

R.R. Williams (1994) 'John Jones Who?', *Gwreiddiau/Gwynedd Roots*, 27 (Gwynedd FHS).

K. Williams-Jones (ed.) (1976) *The Merioneth Lay Subsidy Roll 1292-3* (Cardiff).

J.W. Willis-Bund (ed.) (1902) *The Black Book of St David's* (Cymmrodorion Record Series, London).

E.G. Withycombe (1977) *The Oxford Dictionary of Christian Names,* 3rd ed. (Oxford).

D.P. Young (1985) 'The Family of Prophet [etc]', *Hel Achau*, 15.

APPENDIX A: PARISHES BY HUNDREDS WITHIN COUNTIES

This appendix lists all the parishes in Wales by hundred within each of the 13 historical counties which existed up to 1974. This is the basis on which the numerical results of our survey – described in detail in Chapter 4 – have been presented.

The basic information for defining the hundreds has been taken from the printed schedules for the 1851 Census. However, it has been necessary to rationalise the situation in those instances where, for example, parts of parishes are in different hundreds, parts of hundreds are in different counties, or where hundreds have detached parts. As a result, groupings of parishes may vary from those which readers may be familiar with in certain areas. In one instance – that of the Swansea Hundred – we have subdivided the hundred into two separate parts in order that the characteristics of the rapidly expanding town of Swansea would not mask the totally different (and very interesting) characteristics found on the sparsely populated area of Gower.

The names used for the hundreds are generally those given in the *National Atlas of Wales* (Map 2.1d).

Apart from listing all the parishes by name, this appendix also gives the number of surname occurrences (as found in our survey) after the name of each hundred. The total number of surname occurrences for each county is also given. Thus the hundreds within the county of Anglesey are headed:

ANGLESEY (15,964)

and the first hundred is headed:

A. Llifon (3540)

This indicates that 15,964 surnames occurred in the records for the county of Anglesey as a whole and to this the Llifon hundred contributed 3540. This will allow the reader to have some idea about the level of sensitivity of the percentages relating to the occurrence of surnames in the different hundreds. For example, a surname occurring four times in the Radnorshire hundred of Radnor (the least active hundred in Wales) would give an incidence of 0.73%; whereas that same level of occurrence in the Glamorgan hundred of Caerphilly (the most active hundred) would give an incidence of only 0.03%.

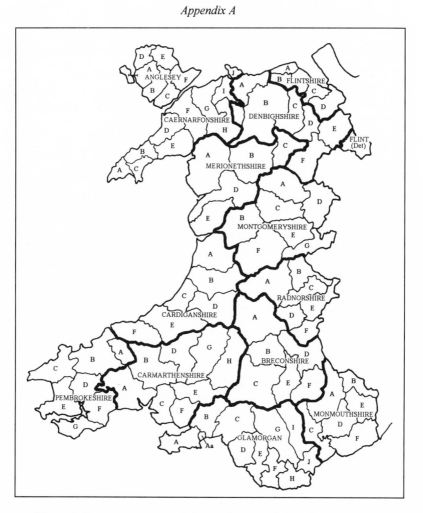

Fig. A-1: The Administrative Hundreds of Wales (a repeat of Fig. 4-1)

ANGLESEY (15,964)

A. Llifon (3540)
Bodedern
Bodwrog
Ceirchiog
Holyhead
Llanbeulan
Llandrygarn
Llanfaelog
Llanfair-yn-neubwll
Llanfihangel-yn-Nhywyn
Llanllibio
Llantrisant
Llanynghenedl
Llechgynfarwy
Llechylched
Rhoscolyn
Trewalchmai

B. Malltraeth (1658)
Aberffraw
Cerrigceinwen
Heneglwys
Llangadwaladr
Llangristiolus
Llangwyfan
Trefdraeth

C. Menai (2490)
Llanddaniel-Fab
Llanedwen
Llanfair-yn-y-cwmwd
Llanfihangel Ysgeifiog
Llanffinan
Llangaffo
Llangefni
Llangeinwen
Llangwyllog
Llanidan
Newborough
Rhodogeidio

D. Talybolion (1670)
Llanbabo
Llanbadrig
Llanddeusant

Llanfachreth
Llanfaethlu
Llanfair-yng-Nghornwy
Llanfechell
Llanfigael
Llanfwrog
Llanfflewin
Llanrhuddlad
Llanrhuddlad
Llanrhwydrys

E. Twrcelyn (3366)
Amlwch
Bodewryd
Coedana
Gwredog
Llanallgo
Llandyfrydog
Llaneilian
Llaneugrad
Llanfihangel Tre'r-beirdd
Llannerch-y-medd
Llanwenllwyfo
Penrhosllugwy
Rhosbeirio

F. Tyndaethwy (3240)
Beaumaris
Llanbedr-goch
Llandegfan
Llandysilio
Llanddona
Llanddyfnan
Llan-faes
Llanfair Mathafarn Eithaf
Llanfair Pwllgwyngyll
Llanfihangel Dinsylwy
Llangoed
Llaniestyn
Llansadwrn
Penmon
Penmynydd
Pentraeth
Tregaean

BRECONSHIRE (12,758)

A. Builth (2054)
Allt-mawr
Llanafan Fawr
Llanafan Fechan
Llanddewi Abergwesyn
Llanddewi'r-cwm
Llanfair (Builth)
Llanfihangel Abergwesyn
Llanfihangel Brynpabuan
Llangamarch
Llanganten
Llangynog
Llanlleonfel
Llanwrthwl
Llanwrtyd
Llanynys
Maemynys
Tirabad

B. Merthyr (2514)
Aberysgir
Battle
Brecon – St David
– St John
– St Mary
Garthbrengi
Llandyfaelog Fach
Llanfihangel Fechan
Llandeilo'r-fân
Llanfihangel Nant Brân
Llan-ddew
Merthyr Cynog
Trallong

C. Defynnog (1586)
Defynnog
Llan-faes
Llansbyddyd
Llywel
Penderyn
Ystradgynlais
Ystradfellte

D. Talgarth (2290)
Bronllys
Cathedin
Crickadarn
Gwenddwr
Hay
Llandyfalle
Llanelieu
Llanfihangel Tal-y-llyn
Llan-gors
Llanigon
Llys-wen
Talgarth

E. Penkelly (1828)
Cantref
Llandyfaelog Tre'r-graig
Llanfilo
Llanfrynach
Llangasty Tal-y-llyn
Llanhamlach
Llansanffraid
Llanthetty
Llan-y-wen
Talach-ddu
Vaynor

F. Crickhowell (2486)
Crickhowell
Llanbedr Ystrad Yw
Llanelly
Llanfihangel Cwm Du
Llangattock
Llangenny
Llangynidr
Partrishow

195

CAERNARFONSHIRE (22,122)

A. Cymydmaen (1320)
Aberdaron
Bodferin
Bryncroes
Llandygwnning
Llanfaelrhys
Llangwnnadl
Mellteyrn
Penllech
Rhiw

B. Dinllaen (2408)
Aber-erch
Bodfean
Ceidio
Edern
Llandudwen
Llaniestyn
Llannor
Nefyn
Pistyll
Tudweiliog

C. Cafflogion (1878)
Botwnnog
Carnguwch
Deneio
Llanbedrog
Llanengan
Llanfihangel Bachellaeth
Llangïan
Penrhos

D. Uwchgwyrfai (2326)
Clynnog Fawr
Llandwrog
Llanaelhaearn
Llanllyfni
Llanwnda

E. Eifionydd (2586)
Beddgelert
Criccieth
Dolbenmaen
Llanarmon
Llanfihangel-y-Pennant

Llangybi
Llanystumdwy
Penmorfa
Ynyscynhaearn
Treflys

F. Isgwyrfai (6322)
Bangor
Betws Garmon
Llanbeblig
Llanberis
Llanddeiniolen
Llanfaglan
Llanfair-is-gaer
Llanrug
Pentir

G. Uchaf (2640)
Aber(gwyngregin)
Capel Curig
Dwygyfylchi
Llandegái
Llanfairfechan
Llanllechid

H. Nant Conwy (914)
Betws-y-coed
Capel Garmon
Dolwyddelan
Llanrhychwyn
Penmachno
Trefriw

I. Isaf (1236)
Caerhun
Conwy
Gyffin
Llanbedrycennin
Llangelynnin

J. Creuddyn (492)
Llandudno
Llangystennin
Llandrillo-yn-Rhos

196

Appendix A

CARDIGANSHIRE (20,338)

A. Genau'r Glyn (4574)
Eglwys Fach
Llanbadarn Fawr
Llangynfelin
Llanfihangel Geneu'r Glyn
Ysbyty Cynfyn

B. Ilar Upper (1896)
Eglwys Newydd
Gwnnws
Llanafan
Llanfihangel-y-Creuddyn
Llanilar
Lledrod
Rhostïe
Ysbyty Ystwyth
Ystrad Meurig

C. Ilar Lower (2538)
Cilcennin
Henfynyw
Llanbadarn Trefeglwys
Llanddeiniol
Llanddewi Aberarth
Llangwyryfon
Llanrhystud
Llansantffraid
Llanychaearn
Trefilan

D. Pennarth (1970)
Betws Leucu
Blaenpennal
Gartheli
Llanbadarn Odwyn
Llanddewi Brefi
Llangeitho
Nantcwnlle
Strata Florida
Tregaron

E. Moyddin (4246)
Betws Bledrws
Capel Cynon
Cellan
Ciliau Aeron
Dihewyd
Llannarth
Lampeter
Llandisiliogogo
Llanfair Clydogau
Llanfihangel Ystrad
Llangrannog
Llangybi
Llanina
Llanllwchaearn
Llannerch Aeron
Llanwenog
Llanwnnen
Silian

F. Troedyraur (5114)
Aberporth
Bangor Teifi
Betws Ifan
Blaenporth
Brongwyn
Cardigan St Mary
Ferwig
Henllan
Llandyfrïog
Llandygwydd
Llandysul
Llanfair Orllwyn
Llangoedmor
Llangynllo
Llechryd
Mwnt
Penbryn
Tremain
Troed-yr-Aur

CARMARTHENSHIRE (33,890)

A. Derllys (5090)
Castell Dwyran
Cilymaenllwyd
Cyffig
Eglwys Cymyn
Eglwys Fair a Churig
Egremont
Henllan Amgoed
Laugharne
Llanboidy
Llandawke
Llandeilo Abercywyn
Llanddowror
Llanfallteg
Llanfihangel Abercywyn
Llangain
Llangan
Llanglydwen
Llangynin
Llangynog
Llansadwrnen
Llanstephan
Llanwinio
Marros
Meidrim
Pendine
St Clears
Whitland

B. Elvet (4594)
Abergwili
Abernant
Cenarth
Cynwyl Elfed
Llangeler
Llanllawddog
Llanpumsaint
Merthyr
Newchurch
Pen-Boyr
Trelech a'r Betws

C. Kidwelly (6292)
Carmarthen St Peter
Kidwelly
Llandyfaelog

Llangyndeyrn
Llangunnor
Llanllwch
St Ishmaels

D. Cathinog (3590)
Brechfa
Llanegwad
Llanfihangel-ar-Arth
Llanfihangel Cilfargen
Llanfihangel Rhos-y-Corn
Llanfynydd
Llangathen
Llanllwni
Llanybydder
Pencarreg

E. Iscennin (2388)
Betws
Llanarthney
Llandybïe
Llanddarog
Llanfihangel Aberbythych

F. Carnwallon (4472)
Llanedi
Llanelli
Llangennech
Llannon
Pembrey

G. Caio (4208)
Cilycwm
Cynwyl Gaio
Llandeilo Fawr
Llandyfeisant
Llansawel
Llanwrda
Llanycrwys
Talley

H. Perfedd (3256)
Llandingad
Llanddeusant
Llanfair-ar-y-Bryn
Llangadog
Llansadwrn
Myddfai

198

Appendix A

DENBIGHSHIRE (22,618)

A. Isdulas (1340)
Abergele
Betws-yn-Rhos
Eglwys-bach
Llanddoged
Llandrillo-yn-Rhos
Llandulas
Llaneilian-yn-Rhos
Llanfair Talhaearn
Llangernyw
Llanrwst
Llansanffraid Glan Conwy
St George

B. Isaled(5220)
Betws Gwerful Goch
Cerrigydrudion
Denbigh
Gwytherin
Henllan
Llanfair Talhaiarn
Llanfihangel Glyn Myfyr
Llangwm
Llanrhaeadr-yn-Nghinmeirch
Llansannan
Llanefydd
Nantglyn
Pentrefoelas
Ysbyty Ifan

C. Rhuthun (2970)
Clocaenog
Cyffylliog
Derwen
Efenechtyd
Llanbedr Dyffryn Clwyd

Llandyrnog
Llaneliden
Llanfair Dyffryn Clwyd
Llanfwrog
Llangwyfan
Llangynhafal
Llanrhydd
Llanychan
Llanynys
Ruthin

D. Iâl (1090)
Bryneglwys
Llanarmon-yn-Iâl
Llandegla
Llanferres
Llandysilio

E. Maelor Bromfield (8644)
Erbistock
Gresford
Marchwiel
Ruabon
Wrexham

F. Chirk (3354)
Chirk
Llanarmon Dyffryn Ceiriog
Llanarmon Mynydd Mawr
Llangadwaladr
Llangedwyn
Llangollen
Llanrhaeadr-ym-Mochnant
Llansanffraid Glynceiriog
Llansilin

FLINTSHIRE (13,016)

A. Prestatyn (1080)
Dyserth
Gwaenysgor
Llanasa
Meliden
Newmarket

B. Rhuddlan (2754)
Bodfari
Caerwys
Cwm
Tremeirchion
Nannerch
Rhuddlan
St Asaph
Ysceifiog

C. Coleshill (6190)
Cilcain
Flint
Halkyn
Holywell
Northop
Whitford

D. Mold (2992)
Broughton
Buckley
Hawarden
Hope
Mold
Nercwys
Treuddyn

E. Maelor (Nil)
The Maelor Hundred is the detached part of Flintshire. As both its parish registers and bishops' transcripts are held outside Wales, it has been excluded from consideration in the survey of surnames (from marriage records) for the period 1813-37.

GLAMORGAN (41,627)

A. Gower (2070)
Bishopston
Cheriton
Ilston
Llanddewi
Llangennith
Llanmadog
Llanrhidian
Loughor
Nicholaston
Oxwich
Oystermouth
Penmaen
Pennard
Penrice
Port Eynon
Reynoldston
Rhosili

Aa. Swansea (5258)
Swansea
— St John
— St Mary

B. Llangyfelach (4558)
Llandeilo
    Talybont
Llangyfelach
Llangiwg
Llansamlet

C. Neath (4066)
Aberavon
Baglan
Briton Ferry
Cadoxton-
    juxta-Neath
Cilybebyll
Glyncorrwg
Llantwit-
    juxta-Neath

Michaelston-
    super-avon
Neath

D. Newcastle (3622)
Betws
Coity
Coychurch
Laleston
Llandyfodwg
Llangeinor
Llangynwyd
Margam
Newcastle
Newton
    Nottage
Peterston super
    Montem
Pyle and
    Kenfig
St Bride's
Tythegston

E. Ogmore (1008)
Colwinston
Ewenny
Llandow
Llangan
Marcross
Merthyr Mawr
Monknash
Penllyn
St Bride's
    Major
St Donat's
St Mary Hill
Wick

F. Cowbridge (1876)
Cowbridge
Eglwys Brewis
Flemingston

Gileston
Llanblethian
Llandough jux.
    Cowbridge
Llanharan
Llanharry
Llanilid
Llanmaes
Llanmihangel
Llansannor
Llantwit Major
Llysworney
St Athan
St Hilary
St Mary
    Church
Ystradowen

G. Miskin(3296)
Aberdare
Llantrisant
Llantwit Fardre
Llanwonno
Pentyrch
Radyr
Ystradyfodwg

H. Dinas Powis (1698)
Barry
Bonvilston
Cadoxton-
    juxta-Barry
Cogan
Lavernock
Leckwith
Llancarvan
Llandough-
    juxta-Barry
Llanilltern
Llantrithyd
Merthyr Dyfan
Michaelston-
    le-Pit

Michaelston-
    super-Ely
Penarth
Penmark
Peterston-
    super-Ely
Porthkerry
St Andrew
St Brides-
    super-Ely
St Fagans
St George-
    super-Ely
St Lythan's
St Nicholas
Sully
Wenvoe

I. Caerphilly (11,539)
Caerphilly
Eglwysilan
Gelligaer
Llanfabon
Merthyr Tydfil
Rudry
Whitchurch

J. Kibbor (2634)
Caerau
Cardiff
— St John
— St Mary
Lisvane
Llandaff
Llanedern
Llanishen
Roath

MERIONETHSHIRE (10,942)

A. Ardudwy (3388)
Ffestiniog
Llanaber
Llanbedr
Llandecwyn
Llandanwg
Llanddwywe
Llanelltyd
Llanenddwyn
Llanfair
Llanfihangel-y-Traethau
Llanfrothen
Maentwrog
Trawsfynydd
B. Penllyn (2198)
Llandderfel
Llanfor
Llangower
Llanuwchllyn
Llanycil

C. Edeyrnion (1460)
Corwen
Gwyddelwern
Llandrillo
Llangar
Llansantffraid Glyndyfrdwy
D. Talpont/Mawddwy (2560)
Dolgellau
Llanfachreth
Llangelynnin
Llanymawddwy
Mallwyd
E. Estimaner (1336)
Llanegryn
Llanfihangel-y-Pennant
Pennal
Tal-y-llyn
Towyn

Appendix A

MONMOUTHSHIRE (29282)

A. Abergavenny (10516)
Abergavenny
Aberystruth
Cwmyoy
Goetre
Llan-arth
Llanddewi
  Rhydderch
Llanddewi
  Skirrid
Llanelen
Llanfair
  Cilgedin
Llanfihangel
  Crucorney
Llanfihangel-
  nigh-Usk
Llanfoist
Llangattock
  Lingoed
Llangattock-
  nigh-Usk
Llanhilleth
Llanover
Llansantffraed
Llanthony
Llantilio
  Pertholey
Llanvapley
Llanvetherine
Llanwenarth
Mamhilad
Oldcastle
Trevethin

B. Skenfrith (2016)
Dixton Newton
Grosmont
Llangattock
  Vibon Avel
Llangua

Llantilio
  Crossenny
Monmouth
Rockfield
St Maughans
Skenfrith

C. Wentloog (7216)
Bassaleg
Bedwas
Bedwellty
Betws
Coedkernew
Machen
Marshfield
Mynyddislwyn
Michaelston-y-
  Vedw
Peterstone
Rumney
St Brides
  Wentloog
St Mellons

D. Usk (3002)
Betws Newydd
Gwernesney
Henllys
Kemeys
  Commander
Kemeys
  Inferior
Llanbadog
Llandegfedd
Llanfihangel
  Llantarnam
Llanfihangel
  Pont-y-Moel
Llanfrechfa
Llangattock
  (Caerleon)
Llangeview
Llangibby

Llangwn
Llanhennock
  Llanllowell
Llanddewi Fach
Llantrisant
Monkswood
Panteg
Risca
Tredunnock
Trostrey
Usk

E. Raglan/ Trelleck (2102)
Bryngwyn
Chapel Hill
Cwmcarvan
Dingestow
Kilgwrrwg
Llandenny
Llandogo
Llangovan
Llanishen
Llansoy
Llanfihangel
  Torymynydd
Llanfihangel
  Ystern Llewern
Mitchel Troy
Pen-allt
Pen-rhos
Penyclawdd
Raglan
Tintern
Tregare
Trelleck
Wolves
  Newton
Wonastow

F. Caldicott (4436)
Bishton
Caerwent
Caldicot
Chepstow
Christchurch
Goldcliff
Howick
Ifton
Itton
Langstone
Llanfair
  Discoed
Llanfihangel
  juxta Roggiett
Llanmartin
Llanvaches
Llanwern
Magor
Malpas
Mathern
Mounton
Nash
Newchurch
Penhow
Penterry
Portscuett
Redwick
Roggiett
St Arvans
St Brides
  Netherwent
St Pierre
St Woolos
Shire Newton
Undy
Whitson
Wilcrick

MONTGOMERYSHIRE (17,870)

A. Llanfyllin (1846)
Hirnant
Llanfihangel-yng-Ngwynfa
Llanfyllin
Llangynog
Llanwddyn
Meifod
Pennant

B. Cyfeiliog (2736)
Cemais
Darowen
Llanbrynmair
Llanwrin
Machynlleth
Penegoes

C. Caereinion (2128)
Castell Caereinion
Garthbeibio
Llanerfyl
Llanfair Caereinion
Llangadfan
Llangyniyw

D. Ystrad Marchell (3024)
Buttington
Forden
Guilsfield
Llandysilio
Llandrinio
Llanfechain
Llansanffraid-ym-Mechain
Llanymynech
Welshpool

E. Newtown (4334)
Aberhafesp
Betws Cedewain
Berriew
Llandysul
Llanllwchaearn
Llanllugan
Llanmerewig
Llanwyddelan
Manafon
Newtown
Tregynon

F. Llanidloes (2664)
Carno
Llandinam
Llangurig
Llanidloes
Llanwnnog
Penstrowed
Trefeglwys

G. Kerry/Montgomery (1138)
Churchstoke
Hyssington
Kerry
Mochdre
Montgomery
Snead

PEMBROKESHIRE (25,242)

A. Cilgerran (2186)
Bridell
Capel Colman
Cilgerran
Cilrhedyn
Clydau
Llanfair
Nant-gwyn
Llanfihangel
Penbedw
Llanfyrnach
Maenordeifi
Penrhydd

B. Cemais (4500)
Bayvil
Castlebythe
Dinas
Eglwyswrw
Fishguard
Henry's Moat
Little Newcastle
Llandeilo
Llangolman
Llanllawer
Llantwyd
Llanychaer
Llanychlwydog
Maenclochog
Meline
Monington
Morfil
Moylgrove
Mynachlogddu
Nevern
Newport
Pontfaen
Puncheston
St Dogmaels
Whitechurch

C. Dewisland (3486)
Brawdy
Granston
Hayscastle
Jordanston
Letterston
Llandeloy
Llanfair
Nant-y-gof
Llanhowel
Llanrheithan
Llanrhian
Llanstinan
Llanwnda
Manorowen
Mathry
St Davids
St Dogwells
St Edrens
St Elvis
St Lawrence
St Nicholas
Trefgarn
Whitchurch

D. Dungleddy (2814)
Ambleston
Bletherston
Boulston
Clarbeston
Llandysilio
Llanycefn
Llawhaden
Llys-y-Fran
New Moat
Prendergast
Rudbaxton
Slebech
Spittal
Uzmaston
Walton East

Wiston

E. Rhos (5966)
Burton
Camrose
Dale
Freystrop
Haroldston St
Issells
Haroldston
West
Haverfordwest
– St Martin
– St Mary
– St Thomas
Herbrandston
Hubberston
Johnston
Lambston
Llangwm
Llanstadwell
Marloes
Nolton
Robeston West
Roch
Rosemarket
St Brides
St Ishmaels
Steynton
Talbenny
Walton West
Walwyn's
Castle

F. Narberth (4490)
Amroth
Begelly
Carew
Crinow
Crunwear
Gumfreston
Jeffreyston

Lampeter
Velfrey
Lawrenny
Llanddewi
Velfrey
Loveston
Ludchurch
Martletwy
Minwear
Narberth
Newton North
Redberth
Reynalton
Robeston
Wathen
St Issells
Tenby
Yerbeston

G. Castlemartin (3200)
Angle
Bosherston
Castlemartin
Cosheston
Hodgeston
Lamphey
Manorbeir
Monkton
Nash with
Upton
Pembroke
– St Mary
– St Michael
Penally
Pwllcrochan
Rhoscrowther
St Florence
St Petrox
St Twynells
Stackpole
Elidor
Warren

RADNORSHIRE (6236)

A. Rhaeadr (1258)
Llanfihangel Helygen
Llanyre
Llansanffraid Cwmteuddwr
Nantmel
Rhayader
St Harmon

B. Knighton (1614)
Beguildy
Heyope
Knighton
Llananno
Llanbadarn Fynydd
Llanbister
Llanddewi Ystradenny

C. Cefnllys (850)
Bleddfa
Cefnllys
Llanbadarn Fawr
Llandegley
Llandrindod
Llanfihangel Rhydithon
Llangynllo
Pilleth
Whitton

D. Colwyn (648)
Aberedw
Betws Disserth
Cregrina
Diserth
Llanbadarn-y-Garreg
Llanelwedd
Llansanffraid-yn-Elfael
Llanfaredd
Rhulen

E. Radnor (546)
Casgob
Colfa
Gladestry
Llanfihangel Nant Melan
New Radnor
Norton
Radnor

F. Painscastle (1320)
Boughrood
Bryngwyn
Clyro
Glasbury
Llanbedr Painscastle
Llanddewi Fach
Llandeilo Graban
Llanstephan
Llowes
Michaelchurch
Newchurch

APPENDIX B

SURNAMES DERIVED FROM OLD TESTAMENT GIVEN NAMES
The surnames derived from Old Testament given names which we found in our survey (a total of 55 names), and which form the basis for the map shown in Fig. 6-1, are:

Aaron, Abednego, Abel, Abraham, Absalom, Amos, Benjamin, Caleb, Elias, Elisha, Emmanuel, Enoch, Enos, Ephraim, Esaias, Esau, Ezekiel, Gabriel, Habakkuk, Hoseah, Isaac, Ishmael, Israel, Jacob, Japheth, Jehu, Jehosophat, Jeremiah, Jesse, Job, Joel, Jonah, Jonathan, Joseph, Joshua, Josiah, Levi, Lot, Meshach, Methusalem, Micah, Mordecai, Moses, Nathan, Nathaniel, Rachel, Salathiel, Samuel, Samson, Shadrach, Sim(e)on, Solomon, Tobias, Zacharias, Zacchaeus.

Note: The surname **Daniel** has not been included in this list. This particular surname had become common in every part of Wales and its inclusion would only have masked the more local incidence of these less common names.

SURNAMES INCORPORATING THE *AP* PREFIX
The surnames incorporating the a*p* prefix which we found in our survey (a total of 13 names), and which form the basis for the map shown in Fig. 6-3, are:

Badham, Bevan, Beynon, Bowen, Parry, Powell, Price, Pritchard, Probert, Probyn, Prosser, Prothero, Pugh.

ADJECTIVAL SURNAMES
The surnames of adjectival origin which we found in our survey (a total of 21 names), and which form the basis for the map shown in Fig. 6-4, are:

Annwyl, Baugh, Bengough, Brace, Crunn, Cull, Dee, Games, Gethin, Glace, Gough, Gwilt, Hier, Landeg, Mabe, Mayn, Melling, Sayce, Teague, Tew, Voyle

Note: The surnames **Lloyd** and **Vaughan** have not been included in this list. As with the surname Daniel, they became so common in Wales that their inclusion would only have masked the more local incidence of less common names.

APPENDIX C

In Chapters 6 and 7 we have shown how the results of our survey of surnames in Wales in the period 1813-37 can be used to suggest a place of origin within Wales of groups of people (a minimum of two) about whom all that is known is that 'they came from Wales'. For many people whose ancestors left Wales for other parts of Britain or the New World this predictive method could offer the first real opportunity for making progress in tracing those elusive (and often seemingly anonymous) Welsh ancestors by narrowing down the potential search area.

Because of this, we have decided to offer a limited service to enquirers at a relatively nominal cost. In addition, we are able to provide larger-scale maps for individual surnames which have not been illustrated in this book for those engaged in one-name research. Please note, however, that the maps will only give the percentage incidence of the surname by area, and will not give any details of the persons creating that incidence.

If you wish to avail yourself of this service please write to: **PO Box 37, Aberystwyth SY23 2WL, UK,** for an application form, enclosing an SAE or 2 IRCs, stating whether you are interested in the origins of groups of individuals or in the general distribution of a specific surname. We must emphasise, however, that this service can only be used to suggest a possible area of search for those ancestors in line with the principles set out in Chapters 6 and 7. The search itself will have to be carried out using original documents or one of the many transcripts/indexes which now exist for many parts of Wales, either by direct research or by using the services of a paid researcher. We ourselves do not carry out such work.

Readers may find it useful to know that:
1: A comprehensive list of accessible indexes may be found in *Marriage, Census, and other Indexes for Family Historians* by Jeremy Gibson and Elizabeth Hampson, Federation of Family History Societies, 6th ed., 1996.
2: Indexes to parish registers may also be listed in *The Phillimore Atlas and Index to Parish Registers*, Cecil Humphery-Smith (ed.), Phillimore, 2nd ed., 1995.

3: Local Family History Societies should also be able to assist with detailed information about different localities but they may provide this sort of service to members only. The addresses of all Welsh societies may be obtained from The Federation of Family History Societies, The Benson Room, Birmingham and Midland Institute, Margaret Street, Birmingham B3 3BS (SAE or IRCs please).

4: Local searches in different areas may also be carried any one of the many professional researchers who regularly advertise in the journals of local societies as well as in *Family Tree Magazine,* and in the *Genealogists' Magazine*, the journal of the Society of Genealogists.

SUBJECT INDEX

Page numbers in bold refer to maps.

210

SURNAME INDEX

Page numbers in bold refer to maps.

217